Steeler Nation
A Pittsburgh Team, An American Phenomenon

Pittsburgh Sports Publishing
709 Short Street
Irwin, PA, 15642

Book Design by Derek Bishop.

Manufactured in the United States of America

ISBN 978-0-9820225-0-4

Library of Congress Control Number: 2008934944

Steeler Nation

A Pittsburgh Team,
An American Phenomenon

Jim Wexell

Pittsburgh Sports Publishing, Irwin, Pa.

To Karen and Ken McDonough,
The world's greatest parents

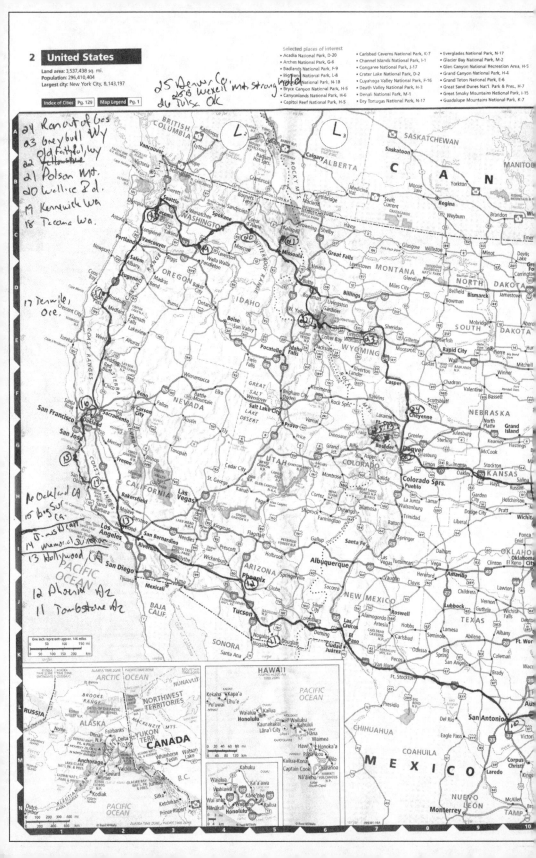

Land area: 3,537,438 sq. mi.
Population: 296,410,404
Largest city: New York City, 8,143,197

Index of Cities Pg. 129   Map Legend Pg. 1

Selected places of interest
- Acadia National Park, D-20
- Arches National Park, G-6
- Badlands National Park, F-9
- Big Bend National Park, L-8
- Biscayne National Park, N-18
- Bryce Canyon National Park, H-5
- Canyonlands National Park, H-6
- Capitol Reef National Park, H-5
- Carlsbad Caverns National Park, K-7
- Channel Islands National Park, I-1
- Congaree National Park, J-17
- Crater Lake National Park, D-2
- Cuyahoga Valley National Park, F-16
- Death Valley National Park, H-3
- Denali National Park, M-1
- Dry Tortugas National Park, N-17
- Everglades National Park, N-17
- Glacier Bay National Park, M-2
- Glen Canyon National Recreation Area, H-5
- Grand Canyon National Park, H-4
- Grand Teton National Park, E-6
- Great Sand Dunes Nat'l. Park & Pres., H-7
- Great Smoky Mountains National Park, I-15
- Guadalupe Mountains National Park, K-7

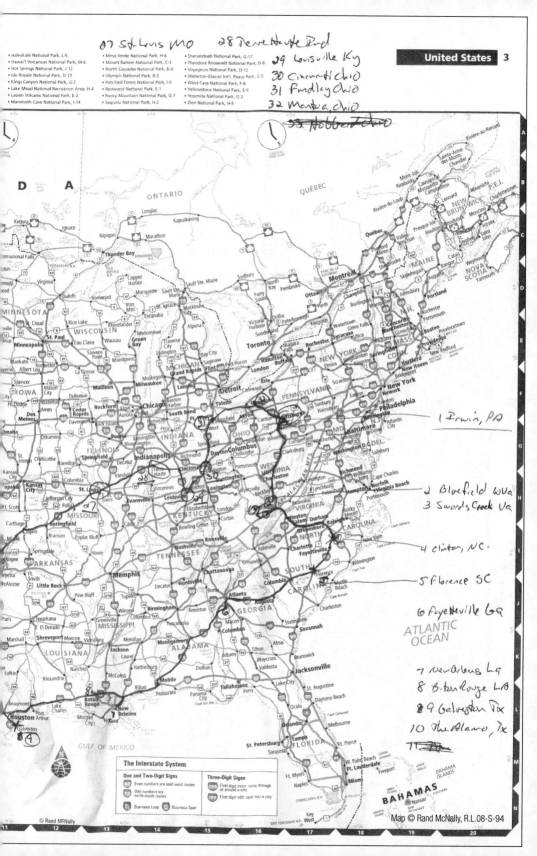

Contents

Introduction

Shock waves ripped through the most passionate fan base in all of American sports in the summer of 2008 when members of the Rooney family considered selling their shares of the Pittsburgh Steelers. Losing the team became a real possibility for Dan Rooney.

Couldn't happen, you say?

Well, time marches on, they say.

Yes, change is inevitable, even in the most stable of all sports organizations. Steelers fans love their team for many reasons, and stability is a big one. The dignity the Rooney family brings to the NFL is another. This book examines all of the reasons, but I want to make this clear right here: This book is not just about the fans. Let me explain.

I've covered the Steelers since 1995 and have seen their fans' great passion play repeated at least eight times a year on the road. For 12 years my perspective was formed from the inside out, so in 2007 I changed gears. I went on the road, a real, concrete road, to cover the Steelers from the outside in. For 44 days that season I traveled around the country. During the week I visited with the families and friends and rivals of the players; on weekends I visited with the fans, either at the stadium or in the bars. The result is this version of the 2007 season, a landmark season in that it was Mike Tomlin's first, the organization's 75th, and perhaps the Rooneys' last.

The idea for the book struck me while reading Kevin Chong's road trip book *Neil Young Nation*. Chong made no point or broke no new ground. He just drove around North America and talked to people about rock and roll. The journey was the thing, and it was a fun read. I decided to do the same with Steelers Nation, the only true sports nation.

I realize it's become trendy for every other team to use the suffix "Nation" these days, but John Facenda, the "Voice of God" himself, bestowed the moniker upon Steelers fans first in his 1978 season wrap for NFL Films. He called it "Steeler Nation." Grammarians call it "Steelers Nation." I use both to suit my needs.

So, yes, I'd traverse The Nation and talk about what I normally talk about: Steelers football. It couldn't miss. The plan required only a map and a vehicle and a football schedule. My friend Jan Jones liked the plan so much he volunteered to drive me in his RV. Then the Steelers' 2007 schedule came out, and it fit.

Of course, I'd have made anything fit, but this schedule allowed visits to the big cities such as Phoenix, Seattle, Denver and Cincinnati on weekends, and small towns like Swords Creek, Clinton, Tenmile, Greybull and Findlay during the week.

It was a dream trip, but the hope was that it would also prove educational. The great historian David McCullough, in his book *Brave Companions*, wrote that "at times I've not known for certain whether I wanted to go ahead with a story until I have been where it happened." McCullough believes that to gain a better understanding of subject matter, a writer must understand the subject's terrain.

So if Chong got me thinking, McCullough kicked me in the rear end and the plan came to life. In the fall of 2007 I spent two weeks in an RV and four weeks in my car on a Steelers-driven road trip that wound around the country. I think I uncovered enough fresh football information to satisfy the hardcore fans, and experienced enough passion from the fans to properly explain a phenomenon that awed so many outsiders along the way.

There was another benefit. My partner Jan put it best as he tried to explain our harebrained scheme to his wife:

"Because it's fun," he told her. "That's all. It's an adventure, and it's fun."

Chapter One
PRACTICE RUN

THE MAP to Akron was easy to find, and cheap. The hotel room was not. A standard room here cost $215 per night.

"You have to understand," the clerk at the front desk said. "The NFL and the PGA are in town this weekend."

That meant Tiger Woods was in town. It also meant James Harrison was back in town.

Harrison and the Pittsburgh Steelers would play the New Orleans Saints in the 2007 Hall of Fame game in nearby Canton, and the Akron-born Harrison was getting his first shot at a full-time job. The Steelers had released Joey Porter and Harrison was stepping in as the important blind-side pass-rusher. No one close to the team expected a fall off. *Sports Illustrated* once posed Porter on its cover next to the words: Most feared player in the NFL. But even then, Harrison was the most feared man in Porter's locker room.

✦ ✦ ✦

AT THE HOME of Mildred and James Harrison, the signs set the tone.

Warning: Pit Bull dog on premises.

Beware of Dog.

No Trespassing.

They framed the door that Mildred Harrison opened. She's the mother of 14 children. She has 28 grandchildren, 10 great-grandchildren and loves to hear people say she looks too young to have put up such numbers.

Her husband, James Harrison Sr., is a tall man, easygoing, a latter-day George Foreman — strong and confident and warm. It quickly becomes apparent that James Harrison Jr., the 14th of the 14 kids, has his dad's face and his mother's disposition.

"You be nice to people and they take kindness as a weakness," said Mildred.

She raised her son with that philosophy, which might explain the foreboding signs. James grew up in this three-story house in West Akron. There are a few shuttered houses on the street, but even those have been well kept – shuttered but neat. James attended the elementary school down the block, and when he graduated high school, mom and dad put a sign in the yard that read: We batted a thousand!

"James was my last baby to walk the stage," Mildred said. "All my kids have diplomas."

What was James like as a child?

"All my children, I have to say, were so well-mannered because I believed in discipline." Pointing to her husband, Mildred said, "Not him."

"Yeah, she believed in strict discipline," nodded James Sr. "And James had seen the beatings that the other kids …"

"Don't say beatings," interrupted mom.

"I've got to say beatings because that's what it was. It was a *beat* down," dad said. "You did something wrong here, you got a *beat* down."

"You just want everyone to know I beat my children," said mom.

Dad said he only had to discipline James once. "We had two pistols," he said. "We had them in our bedroom. I don't know, but some kind of way he got up there, him and his little nephew, and was playing with them. So I sort of whupped him that day real good. My grandson is 30 and he will not touch a gun to this day."

But James did. And he got into trouble with a BB gun. His high school football team fooled around with them in the locker room, and in his senior year James was accused of shooting one player in the keister.

"They pressed the issue," dad said. "James wouldn't say anything. He didn't shoot the boy that pressed the charges. The coach shot him, but James didn't want to tell on his coach."

The coach?

"He cried," said mom. "He didn't want to tell on his coach. He has this thing for football and everything that's connected with football. It's so holy to him and he just didn't want to tell on the coach."

The *coach*?!

"The assistant coach," dad said. "But they wanted to press all kinds of charges on James. They were going to charge him with a felony. I told him, 'Son, you got to let this go. You got to tell it like it is.'"

James eventually told authorities who shot the boy in the locker room. The coach was fired by the school and pled out to a misdemeanor.

JAMES HARRISON was attending Coventry High at the time only because he'd transferred from Archbishop Hoban to follow his coach – Ohio prep coaching legend Mo Tipton. Harrison broke the color line at Coventry and the players at the mostly white schools surrounding Coventry let him know what they thought of it.

"The N-word was coming at him from the left and the right," said James Sr. "It got rough, especially as good as they were after he got there."

The racial tension bubbled over the week before the end-of-season rivalry game against Manchester High. James walked off the field saluting his tormentors and got himself suspended for the big game, a game that could've put Coventry into the playoffs for the first time in school history. Coventry lost to Manchester and a few months later the BB gun case exploded. It cost James scholarship offers from Ohio State, Michigan, Michigan State and Nebraska, among others.

"He was the best player in the state at the time," said James Sr. "James even got shot with that BB gun."

After the big schools stopped recruiting Harrison, he enrolled at nearby Kent State as a Prop 48 student. He was about to follow the same path blazed by another linebacker from Northeast Ohio, but James Harrison knew nothing of Jack Lambert.

"James has never seen a pro any-kind-of-sport, never wanted to go, never watched them on TV," dad said. "I offered to take him to Browns games, to the Indians. It just wasn't one of his things. If he wasn't playing it, he wasn't interested. He had heard of Jack Lambert, but as far as what Lambert had done, he didn't know anything. He didn't care. And I think that's one thing that really helped him when he got to the pros. He was never in awe of anybody."

In Harrison's first three seasons, Kent won 3 games and lost 30. Of course, losing wasn't new to the Kent program. The school last played in a bowl game in 1972 – Lambert's junior season. After Lambert left, Kent wouldn't crack .500 until 1987, and then it took another 14 years.

With Harrison a senior in 2001, Kent entered its finale at Miami (Ohio) with a 5-5 record. Harrison sacked quarterback Ben Roethlisberger five times and Kent won, 24-20, to finish 6-5.

"Lit Drew Brees' ass up three times, too," said James Sr. "And he hit Byron Leftwich so hard it was a shame."

Harrison led the MAC with 15 sacks his senior season, but every team – including the Steelers – passed on him in the NFL draft. The Steelers signed him after the draft, and then cut him – twice.

THE WEEK before camp opened in 2004, the Baltimore Ravens cut James Harrison, so he began lining himself up for a truck-driving job. Then Clark Haggans broke his hand and the desperate Steelers called Harrison.

"The rest is history," said James Sr.

Harrison made his first start thanks to Joey Porter and William Green. The Steelers were in Cleveland on Nov. 14, 2004 and Porter and Green were ejected for a pre-game fight. Harrison got the call.

"I was in the kitchen getting food together for some people coming over," said Mildred. "My one son screamed, 'Mama, James is playing football.' I thought he was lying, but I came in and James was playing. We all started screaming then. And when James made a play and he tackled the quarterback, everybody on the street knew it."

On the same field 13 months later, Harrison became a cult hero to Steelers fans. It was on Christmas Eve 2005 when he body-slammed a Browns fan who'd run onto the field.

"He laid him down gently," corrected Mildred.

"He held him until the police came," said James Sr.

The Harrisons attended the Super Bowl later that season. Dad was offered $3,500 for his ticket, and he thought about selling but didn't. Mom, meanwhile, was caught in an uncomfortable pre-game elevator ride with Coach Bill Cowher. She said hello; Cowher said nothing. "He's so full of himself," Mildred said. "I don't care for that man."

"The only person I knew that James didn't like was Cowher," said James Sr. "But he said, 'I don't have to like him to play for him.'"

Mike Tomlin replaced Cowher and his first draft pick was linebacker Lawrence Timmons, who at the time was behind James on the depth chart.

"James will get his shot there," James Sr. said. "But to be honest, I thought he should've got his shot two years ago. Haggans does nothing. I know you've seen it. A tight end will have him five yards in his backfield! Ain't no damn tight end supposed to be blocking no linebacker."

"Mmm-hmm," said Mildred. "Now you see where James gets his attitude."

✦ ✦ ✦

ZAC JACKSON covers the NFL for ClevelandBrowns.com, but once upon a time he played high school football against James "Silverback" Harrison.

"He was the scariest dude around," said Jackson. "He was known in communities for miles around as somebody you didn't mess with – on the field or off.

"There was an incident with smashing mailboxes. A bunch of Coventry players got suspended. There was some talk about whether James was involved or not, and it turned out he wasn't, but you were much more worried about him smashing your face than you were a mailbox."

And on the field?

"Coventry beat Manchester one time in 20 years in football and it was James' junior year and it was because he did it by himself. On one play he caught a middle screen and threw the first guy off him and literally jumped over the second guy and took it 50 yards for a touchdown. That was the play that won it. It's funny, because in that Monday night game in San Diego, when James picked the ball up and jumped over Antonio Gates, my phone line started buzzing with all the Manchester guys saying, 'We've seen that!' The guy he'd jumped over in high school was about 5-4, but Gates is 6-6.

"I was over at Steelers camp in '05. He was sitting over by the locker room by himself. I introduced myself, said hello, told him I'm from Manchester, that I know all his friends, blah, blah, blah, and he just glared at me. Didn't say a word, just glared, so I left.

"I root for him, certainly. Even though he didn't want to talk to me that day, I root for him."

Chapter Two

SATURDAY NIGHT IN CLEVELAND

STEELERS-BROWNS just might be the greatest rivalry in NFL history, but I'm not the guy who can tell that story. In the days when Jack Lambert was throwing Brian Sipe into his own bench, I was more concerned with my hometown Chicago Bears.

My family settled in Pittsburgh in 1974, when I, a mere eighth-grader, was alone defending my hapless Bears. By the time I matured enough to appreciate the local club, the Browns were gone.

The Browns have returned, but to this point the so-called rivalry only seems cli-chéd and forced. I thought about this as I prepared to cover the Steelers' 2007 season opener against the Phase II Brownies, and wondered if veteran football fans in Cleveland felt the same way. I headed out before kickoff to a tailgate in Cleveland's Warehouse District to find out, and as soon as I walked in the door I could smell a party.

"Must've been Cheech and Chong," cracked Joe, the building's owner.

Joe's a big man who could probably pass for the notorious "Big Dawg" of "Dawg Pound" fame, but at 52 he doesn't care all that much to be disagreeable; neither, it seemed, did his brother Kenny, nor his good friend Tim, the gang's old quarterback at Holy Name High School.

"From our standpoint, the rivalry's always been friendly," Joe said. "We just enjoy the party."

"When the rivalry was intense there was a lot of jawing," said Tim. "It still goes on with some people. But, really, you get a little gun-shy. It's hard to be cocky when you get your ass kicked a few times — unless you're hardcore."

"We call the hardcore guys the 'Section 1 Boys,'" Joe said.

"Yeah, the guys who used to sit in Section 1 at the old stadium, they were intense," said Tim. "We had season tickets there for years. That's when you could actually carry a keg in. But the rules, they're different now."

"Section 1, up in the corner, man," Joe said. "On a cold day the lake's coming right in your face. You're the closest section to Lake Erie. But we're in club seats today and our backs are to the lake."

"If we get too cold we go inside," said Tim.

These 50-somethings have seen the greats, gone through the wars, done their share of heckling, brawling, and now they've mellowed. In fact, they're a bit giddy today about one player in particular.

"I have three daughters and a son and they are in love with Brady Quinn," Tim said. "The young people are more excited about him coming to play than who they're playing and I kind of feel the same way. My opinion is he's going to take them to the top of this division, and maybe some day – and I don't want to sound stupid – he'll get them to the Super Bowl and they can win the damn thing."

"I like the way the guy handles himself," said Joe. "He doesn't tip off defenders. He throws hard. He's got good motion and fluidness. And he's from Ohio."

"So is Charlie Frye," said Tim.

"So is Ben Roethlisberger," I blurted out.

The Browns, of course, passed on the big junior from Findlay, Ohio, in the 2004 draft. How did Browns fans take that decision?

"Don't quote me on this," said Tim.

"I won't," I said.

"But I know a guy at Miami, Ohio. Another guy told him that, without a doubt, Ben wanted to come to Cleveland, that he had talked to Cleveland and thought he was coming to Cleveland. That's where he wanted to go."

OK ... so?

"He wanted to come to Cleveland," Tim said.

But did it bother the Section 1 Boys that one of their own went to Pittsburgh?

"Ben would've gotten killed just like Tim Couch and everybody else," Joe said. "Ben's career would've been totally different had the Browns drafted him instead of the Steelers. He walked into a better situation with them."

So that's where we stood at the time, a better situation. The Steelers had won 20 of the last 23 meetings with the Browns, and that's the main reason these old Section 1 Boys had mellowed.

"Let me put it this way," Joe said. "If the Browns win today, it'll be right back to where it was, this rivalry, because all of a sudden we're now all competing on the same level.

"All it takes is one and we're back, baby."

✦ ✦ ✦

STEEELERS FANS have been storming Cleveland for years. It's called the Turnpike Rivalry, and that's how the road show known as Steelers Nation got its start. At least that's what Vic Ketchman believes.

"Cleveland did this," said Ketchman, and he ought to know. Ketchman covered the Steelers for 23 years before becoming the editor of Jaguars.com in 1995.

"It's the truth," he said. "The idea of traveling to a professional football game to see your team play did not exist when I was a kid. It didn't exist in the '50s and it didn't exist in the '60s, except for one game."

Steelers-Browns.

Ketchman grew up a Steelers fan in the Pittsburgh suburb of Natrona Heights. He attended Kent State a couple of years before Jack Lambert and a couple of decades before James Harrison. His first paid professional assignment was a feature on Steelers guard Bruce Van Dyke in 1972.

"I was a kid. I still had acne," Ketchman said. "But he treated me as though I were

Grantland Rice. He was wonderful and I did the story and knew right then and there that this is what I wanted to do."

Ketchman relayed the story to his readers in his fabulously free Internet column "Ask Vic." A couple of days later he received an e-mail from Van Dyke.

"I felt a connection. I felt like I had come full circle," Ketchman said.

He felt the same way in 2004 as he sat in the press box at Alltel Stadium before the Jaguars' game against the visiting Steelers. Ketchman, buried in his laptop, looked up as he heard a thunderous ovation. He expected to see the Jaguars taking the field, but it was the Steelers.

"I was stunned," he said. "When I looked up I saw a sea of yellow. My mouth dropped open. I couldn't believe what I was seeing."

Ketchman said that particular game, and that particular throng of visiting fans, led the Jaguars to cover 10,000 seats in the upper decks and reduce the capacity at Alltel Stadium.

"It was the Cleveland thing," Ketchman said. "There were a lot of tickets available and Steelers fans bought them up."

Steelers fans began doing this in Cleveland in the 1960s thanks to a marketing gimmick — Saturday Night in Cleveland – by the Browns.

"It was Art Modell's idea," said Steelers chairman Dan Rooney. "We had developed the rivalry at the time and he said it would really be something and it turned out to be really great. We played those games and they were very successful. We always had big crowds."

"Saturday Night in Cleveland" debuted in 1963 and ran through 1970. It ended because the league agreed with Congress not to play on Friday or Saturday nights until the end of the high school and college seasons.

"It was just wildly popular," Ketchman said. "The notion that you could take Saturday off and not Sunday – and you didn't have to worry about church and all that stuff – and go up to Cleveland, watch a game, come back, and have all of Sunday to recover, which is usually what it took because it was a drunken brawl."

Both teams were undefeated that first Saturday night in Cleveland in 1963. Two goal-line stands by the Browns' defense and 175 yards rushing by Jim Brown led the Browns to a 35-23 win. The game set a Browns attendance record with 84,684 fans.

The same teams drew 80,530 to the 1964 Saturday night game. It was the only Saturday game in the series won by the Steelers. They beat the Browns, the team that would win the NFL championship that year, 23-7, behind John Henry Johnson, a 35-year-old fullback who rushed for what then was a Steelers record 200 yards.

The Steelers floundered throughout the rest of the decade, but the game remained popular. The 1962 game between the teams in Cleveland drew 53,601, but the average attendance for the next eight games there – all played on Saturday nights – was 82,666. It laid the foundation for a phenomenon.

"It's the defining game for fans traveling," Ketchman said. "It's the game, as far as I'm concerned, that started the mania."

THE MANIA. It often starts without warning, but before long the room is thumping:

"Here we go, Steelers, here we go!"

Are the Steelers America's real team?

"That one makes me puke," said Ketchman. "When the Cowboys did that America's Team shit, and they painted those red and blue lines on either side of the 20-yard lines — as if their 20-yard line was America's line — that's when I was sure I hated cutesy tags."

Hmmm. Is "Steeler Nation" OK?

"Every team uses it now: Jaguar Nation," Ketchman said as he wrinkled his nose. "I don't know that I've ever used 'Steeler Nation' and I don't think I ever would use 'Steeler Nation.' I don't like that kind of stuff. And I think it's almost offensive. These people are so genuine and so real in their passion for this team, they speak with their actions. They don't need cute little phrases and labels. This is for real. These people really care about this. They don't travel because they want to go someplace and get drunk, and they don't travel because they have nothing else to do. They travel because they can't imagine being anywhere else, and I'm kind of stealing Joe Greene's words there."

Joe Greene, in his Hall of Fame induction ceremony in 1987, said: "If you weren't in the stadium on a Sunday in the fall, you were in the wrong place."

"I really do believe that's the feeling and that it's a purely genuine thing," Ketchman said. "People travel because that's where they want to be. There's no other fan base like them. It really is a phenomenon and it doesn't appear to be ending anytime real soon."

Steelers fans found their way to Cincinnati in the mid 1970s. Ketchman said that's when travel agents got involved. "And then it just snowballed," he said.

"Cincinnati actually promoted it," said Dan Rooney. "They don't anymore, but then they promoted us playing the games there. We used to take 5,000 people to Cincinnati."

Art Modell used to give the Steelers 5,000 tickets back then, but the Steelers, for the games in Pittsburgh, would give Modell only 500.

"But of course," Rooney said, "it was a situation where they had the big stadium and were doing everything they could to fill it. To my knowledge they never really traveled like Steelers fans did. Pitt Stadium would be full for that game, but I think we did it ourselves."

The Mania didn't show up much in the 1980s, but, when the winning resumed in the 1990s, displaced steel workers popped up all over the map. Rooney first noticed the nationwide popularity in 1994.

"It was at Phoenix," he said. "When we played the Super Bowl there it was like that, but this was not a Super Bowl. This was a game we played in Phoenix after they had moved. I was really surprised by the number of people."

Of course, the Super Bowl in Phoenix, in January 1996, surprised Rooney, as it did most Steelers, their fans, and the reporters covering the game. Phoenix was supposed to be Dallas Cowboys country, but Steelers fans far outnumbered Cowboys fans on the streets and in the stands. Since then, The Mania has only grown.

"I think it's tremendous for Pittsburgh," Rooney said. "It's a tremendous thing for the city because these people are showing A) loyalty to the city and, B) that they want to do something, that they want to continue their relationship with the city. So I think that's a real plus."

Much of it, according to many fans, comes out of respect for the way Rooney and his family run the team.

"I've been told that," Rooney said. "And I've read letters about how we represent a team that's trying to play by the rules, a team that does things in the community, things like that. With the New England situation (Spygate), I had a lot of letters saying this was something the Steelers would never do. Things like that."

That's part of the reason, but there has to be a deeper reason for The Mania.

"I don't know," Ketchman said. "I don't want to get long-winded about this, and I'd be bullshitty if I tried to answer that. I don't know. It's a phenomenon. It's real and I'm not going to try to play sociologist and psychologist and start reciting a bunch of socio-economic babble about displaced steelworkers and all that. This has nothing to do with displaced steelworkers. This has to do with honest-to-God football fans, and for whatever reason this team has touched them and they have never been the same since."

Then it came into focus for Ketchman.

"Why? Because of four Super Bowls, that's why. Those guys in the '70s, that's the reason. They're the reason: Bradshaw and Harris and Lambert and Greene and all of them. Give the credit where the credit is deserved. None of this existed until they came along. None of this existed until '72, until the Immaculate Reception. Forget about the displaced steelworkers. Forget about Milltown and all that crap. It all started with them. Those guys did it. They were the greatest football team that ever lived and it's not just because of what they did on the field, it's also because of what they caused off the field. They caused a mania that's growing to this day."

✦ ✦ ✦

DRUNKEN BRAWLS. That's what Vic Ketchman called these games in Cleveland, and that was pretty much the extent of today's entertainment. The Browns came out and lost three yards on their first series and punted 15 yards. Four plays later the Steelers were in the end zone. By the end of the quarter the Steelers led 17-0 on their way to a 34-7 rout.

Heading to the locker room after the game, reporters heard one security guard ask another if he saw "those two Browns fans kick that Steeler fan's ass?"

"That's all they beat up today," deadpanned the elevator operator.

The talk-show callers were incensed. One retort to an on-air defense of Browns coach Romeo Crennel went like this:

"And when I see you I'll *kill* you," the caller told the host.

Another fan sounded as if he were weeping. "Why?" he said. "Why did it have to be the dang Steelers?"

The only positive for the Browns that day was the play of their new quarterback, and he wasn't Brady Quinn. Derek Anderson replaced Charlie Frye with 6:34 left in the second quarter. He led the Browns to a touchdown on their first drive of the second half to ruin the shutout.

"I ruined the shutout," said Steelers defensive captain James Farrior. "It's all my fault. Blame me."

Farrior dropped an interception on the first play of the Browns' scoring drive. It was only a big deal to those who had scrawled this message on the locker-room chalkboard:

Happy Birthday Coach Dad. The next 70 will be even better.

It was defensive coordinator Dick LeBeau's 70th birthday. The night before, in an emotional defensive meeting, Farrior presented gifts to LeBeau: a gold Rolex watch and an autographed poster of *Twas The Night Before Christmas*, which LeBeau performs for the players every Christmas.

LeBeau flashed the Rolex in the locker room after the game. "Do you want to know what time it is?" he asked. The most humble man in the locker room was radiant. His defense had honored him on and off the field. The shutout? It didn't matter.

"No, I just told them a victory is all we really want and I think they pretty much guaranteed that. They played pretty well," LeBeau said.

The Steelers notched six sacks against a rebuilt Browns offensive line that was playing together for the first time. James Harrison had one of the sacks and led the Steelers with seven tackles. He also played on all special teams and was exhausted. Someone asked him if he'd tangled with any fans on this particular day.

"No," he said. "Not yet."

Of course, fighting and getting drunk in Cleveland is part of the road trip. Dan

Rooney remembers taping directions to the jacket of a drunken Steelers fan and sending him home before one game.

"We put him in a cab and told the driver to send us the bill. We figured he'd get arrested if we didn't," Rooney said. "The cops were regular guys. They said, 'Look, we don't mind when your fans get off the bus drunk, but when the bus driver gets off the bus drunk that's too much.'"

"There were always fights," said Ketchman. "We'd be covering a game and all of the sudden we'd look down from the press box and we'd see three or four sections standing and you'd wonder where it was. Then you'd see the arm go up and the arm go down; the hand go up, the hand come down. 'Right there, the fourth row, the fifth guy in,' and we'd put the binoculars on the fight like it was a sideshow. You don't see that much anymore – thank God. We've found a new way to embarrass ourselves. We've found a new way to lose our dignity. It's called trash-talking, or talking smack. And nowadays we do a very, very courageous thing: We go onto message boards and use a fictitious name and we curse people. I think I almost like the fighting in the stands better."

Chapter Three

COAL COUNTRY

WE FILED into the Applebees in Lebanon, Virginia, the three of us, and were seated for dinner in the corner underneath a bunch of posters and photos of the local football hero, Heath Miller.

Lebanon is the county seat of Russell County here in westernmost Virginia. Denise and Earl Miller and I had driven over from Swords Creek, a town of 2,626 that's about 40 miles from the Kentucky border. It's where the Millers – four generations of them – grew up.

The hostess did right by seating us in this particular corner. With all the frills, it should've been dubbed Heath Miller Corner. Funny thing though: The hostess didn't pay any respect to Mr. and Mrs. Miller. There was no extra effort, no realization that these two people had just classed up the joint.

"They don't know who we are," said Denise Miller. "We don't tell people things like that."

Heath wouldn't have, either. In fact, Heath Miller just might be the most reserved player in the Steelers' locker room, but it has nothing to do with a lack of intelligence. Some guys are quiet because they have nothing to say. Heath is quiet because he has nothing to say to me. And he processes information quickly.

"She's not going to like this," Heath said of my interview request. He was right.

"Coal, poor, small town," Mrs. Miller explained. "One of the Pittsburgh TV stations came down here to do a story on us and that was it: coal, poor, small town. You get tired of the stereotype."

The TV reporter told Mrs. Miller that wouldn't have anything to worry about, that he wasn't chasing that particular angle. "But then I looked back," she said, "and they stopped to shoot the only coal tipple in town."

✦ ✦ ✦

THE ROAD TRIP had started much earlier in the day, when Jan Jones and I left Pittsburgh. Jan is a sixty-something in the physical shape of someone half his age. He's not only healthy, he's wealthy and wise, so he, in theory, had the time and resources to drive me across the country as part of this adventure. But he also has a wife.

"I don't know, man, she kinda funny," went George Thorogood's legendary line, and Jan said something similar as the departure date drew near.

Of course, Jan's wife had every reason to be wary. The Dutch Star is a 35-foot RV that's been kept in near-mint condition for five years, and I'm just another messy sportswriter. Working in my favor was the fact that Jan loves the road. He also likes to help people when he can. And, third, he has a cousin in Arizona he hasn't seen in years. It added up because Arizona is where I needed to be in two weeks for the Steelers-Cardinals game, so Jan agreed to the plan: He'd drive for two weeks with my Grand Am in tow before unleashing me on the West Coast.

We left Pittsburgh in separate vehicles the morning after the Steelers played the Buffalo Bills in Week 2. Jan cruised to a Flying J's rest stop in Wytheville, Va., while I made side trips to Bluefield and Swords Creek. I told Jan my story idea was something like this: coal, poor, small town. He told me to get a shot of the coal tipple.

✦ ✦ ✦

THE STEELERS' 26-3 win over the Bills gave Mike Tomlin a 2-0 record to start his career and fans in Pittsburgh were already talking about the playoffs. My interest was more serious: Linebacker James Harrison had been injured by Casey Hampton's butt.

Harrison was taken from the field on a stretcher right before halftime after slamming into Casey's rear end. Harrison went down and experienced numbness in his extremities, so the training staff wouldn't let him move. They held him out the rest of the game, but it didn't matter to the Steelers. Rookie LaMarr Woodley stepped in and recorded his first career sack as the Steelers ground the Bills down. Willie Parker rushed for 126 rushing and the offensive line allowed only one sack – a coverage sack.

Harrison returned to the sideline in full uniform at one point in the second half. A source mentioned that the medical staff had failed to properly sedate the linebacker, and that Harrison had ripped off his neck halo and trashed an ambulance.

"I saw him. He was upset," Clark Haggans said.

Was it true? Had Harrison trashed an ambulance?

"He might have slashed the tires so they couldn't get him to the hospital," Haggans joked. "What's important is he's OK. Whatever's mangled in the ambulance, I'm sure they can fix."

✦ ✦ ✦

AND WITH THAT, the road trip was on. The first stop was the town of Bluefield in southwestern Virginia. It's where the Steelers' last rushing champion, Bill Dudley, was born (on Christmas Eve 1921) and raised before moving on to the University of Virginia.

"He was one of Doc Whitten's boys," said my first tour guide, Bill Archer. "He's the one who recommended Dudley to UVA."

Jack "Doc" Whitten was a local Virginia state legislator who stood up in front of a committee that had been debating a financial package for the University of Virginia and said: "I'm not going to give them a damned dime unless they come out to our part of the state and give some boys some scholarships."

So Whitten arranged for five of "his boys" to meet with Virginia Coach Frank Murray in the summer of 1938. Only Dudley accepted the $500 grant, and off he went to kick extra-points for the Cavaliers.

Of course, Dudley became the starting tailback in 1940 and won the Maxwell

Award his senior season, after which he was chosen first in the 1942 NFL draft by the Steelers. Dudley led the NFL in rushing as a rookie and again in 1946, before a tiff with Coach Jock Sutherland preceded his trade to the Detroit Lions.

The "Bluefield Bullet" is still honored at Graham High School. New York Giants running back Ahmad Bradshaw is one of many Graham students who've walked under Dudley's photo upon entering the building over the years. Archer wrote that the oil portrait of Dudley "looks like the Colossus of Rhodes."

Archer is a newsman for the *Bluefield Daily Telegraph* and a fan of the Pittsburgh Steelers. "When my wife first asked me if I liked football, I told her I could take it or leave it," he wrote in an e-mail. "I didn't tell her that Brady Keys was the first grown man I'd ever heard cuss in public back in the days when they drug cheap bleachers onto the grass at Forbes Field, and that my heroes were Ernie Stautner and Bobby Layne. Of course, my wife knew how much it meant to me when Mel Blount visited my sister at my family's home in Claysville, Pa., in the summer of 1990 about two weeks before she lost her battle with cancer."

Archer also wrote that, "as a proud WVU grad, I forgave Heath Miller in my heart for following Bill Dudley's footsteps to UVA when he signed with the Steelers."

BILL ARCHER is a guy you're going to meet in heaven. In fact, he'll probably show you around. He showed me Bluefield – both of them. Bluefield, Virginia, is adjoined to the north, on the other side of Interstate 77, by Bluefield, West Virginia. Archer called the area the epicenter of the coal industry.

"I work with troubled youth down here," he said. "I tried to co-mingle some of Mel Blount's kids with the kids I was working with, but mine were already a little bit older than the ones he worked with, maybe in their late teens. I was just hoping to get them out of this setting because there's a lot of poverty here in addition to drug abuse, and there's really no opportunities for black kids to pursue careers in much of anything."

Bill said that the Steelers creep into his daily work.

"I'm working on a book right now about a bank collapse in Keystone, West Virginia," he said. "The bank president was a guy from McKeesport named Knox McConnell. It was the seventh-largest bank collapse in the history of the FDIC, so it was a pretty major story for a number of years. I got to know the bank president personally because he has a southwestern Pennsylvania accent – 'dahntahn' and 'upair' – and we became friends. But he got his start in banking because of his relationship with Art Rooney. So as a result he knew those people; he was in the mix of the Steelers. Knox was a good friend of Billy Conn. Through Conn, he got to know Art Rooney and Rooney helped him with different banking projects that he had. So as I'm working on the history of this bank and the collapse, the relationship between McConnell and Pittsburgh and the Steelers keeps cropping up.

"Really, there's no level of what I do that doesn't somehow interact with a connection to Pittsburgh and a connection to the Steelers. In one way or another, if it happened in the modern era, the Steelers had something to do with it. In fact, the town that keeps coming up is the next town over from where the Beasleys live. We better get rolling."

TOM BEASLEY, of tiny Elkhorn, West Virginia, played basketball and football at powerful Northfork High School. The school closed in 1985, just four years after winning its eighth consecutive state AA basketball championship. That's a national record, but greatness had been expected – said Archer – when the school was formed by a merger of black and white schools.

"The schools were slow to de-segregate in southern West Virginia because it's a little more isolated, and also because the black schools had such great traditions of state championships," Archer said. "Beasley benefited from the combined power of two great schools – a great white school and a great black school – and together they became an exceptional school."

Beasley went to college at nearby Virginia Tech and in 1977 became the first Tech player drafted by the Steelers. The defensive tackle won two Super Bowl rings with the team. Archer said that Beasley, by experience of the high school merger, was the right fit at the right time.

"The Steelers under Rooney were experimenting with a real integrated society, working together for common goals and common purposes," Archer said. "And there were characters inside that, the Frenchy Fuquas and Fats Holmeses, and all those guys had their personalities and it was a real homogenous society that was being created, and that's the imprint that was put on it. Of course, that imprint existed on the Steelers long before that. John Henry Johnson was really something special, someone everybody could root for. Maybe it wasn't as big as Jackie Robinson and those barriers, but these guys were really finding new ground when our society was still troubled with busing and trying to achieve racial equality and other issues that were tending to polarize us. These guys found a way to co-exist, and they did it inside the paternalistic management of a conservative guy in Art Rooney.

"I think it's just great that Mike Tomlin is there now because of the Rooney Rule and it continues through a family. Pittsburgh needs that kind of thing. But even more, small pockets throughout this country need to get over those problems that are in the past and don't need to bristle up and display hatred constantly. We can work together. That's what I like about the Steelers more than anything else, that they're able to achieve that, that you're able to find heroes and not look at them as being a white hero or a black hero. You just look at them as being your hero."

✦ ✦ ✦

THE ROLLER COASTER ride through the southernmost tip of West Virginia came to a halt at a road-side stand run by a young man in a Steelers No. 83 jersey. He was selling coal-mining equipment and pointed the way to his favorite player's hometown. I arrived a bit early in Sword's Creek, Virginia, and watched the end of Honaker High's football practice with four guys wearing Castlewood Football T-shirts. I asked them if they knew anything about Heath Miller.

"The hardest I was ever hit was by Heath Miller," said the first Castlewood coach.

His buddy chimed in rhythmically. "The hardest baseball I ever seen hit was by Heath Miller," he said.

"He was a heck of a baseball player," said the first.

"He was a heck of a safety," said the second.

"Heath Miller was a heck of a quarterback," Doug Hubbard said after practice.

Hubbard was Miller's high school coach. He's been the coach at Honaker for 26 seasons, all of them spent as a diehard fan of the Pittsburgh Steelers.

"In 2005," he said slowly and with a smile, "my favorite team drafted one of my players and they won the Super Bowl. I call that a pretty good year."

Hubbard played defensive tackle at East Tennessee State and likes to think he took after Joe Greene. Hubbard has some size, but looks – and sounds – more like Tennessee coach Phil Fulmer than a Hall of Fame defensive tackle. Today, Hubbard is putting together "Heath Miller Day," a day when the stadium road would be renamed Heath Miller Circle.

"Heath was a joy to coach," Hubbard said. "He worked hard. He did the same thing at UVA and I imagine he's doing the same thing in Pittsburgh. But he's a quiet person and that probably hurts him a little bit in the public eye because he doesn't require much attention."

Miller is quiet, but he's no dummy. He scored a 39 on his Wonderlic, the test scouts use to gauge intelligence. Miller's test score was third of all the pro prospects in 2005. He was also third in his high school class of about 100 when he graduated from Honaker in 2001.

"He's very intelligent, very artistic. He can draw. He can do a lot of things," Hubbard said. "His parents have a low-key type nature, so therefore that's what you get from him and that's the way he was here. In the NFL, when you watch him, he's probably more excited when one of the other guys scores than when he scores."

Miller led Honaker to the state 2-A title game in 2000, but was limited by a sore knee and Honaker lost for the first time that season, 25-15, to King William. Miller completed only 8 of 24 passes with an interception in the game, but he made 18 tackles on defense. He was named Virginia's Player of the Year by the Associated Press and finished his career at Honaker with 6,182 yards passing and 77 touchdowns.

"I've known Heath since he was in diapers. I played ball with his dad and was in the same first-grade class as his mom," Hubbard said. "Probably one of the best football stories I could tell you is from our opener one year. We had our cross-town rivalry game with Lebanon, and Heath throws an out route to a kid. It was a great ball. The kid's got coverage on him and the receiver makes a super catch, but he gets mud in his helmet and throws some mud down at the kid who covered him and gets a 15-yard penalty. Needless to say I was a little upset, but when he got back to the huddle Heath looked at him and said, 'If you do that again, I'll never throw you another ball. We're not going to play like that.' And that was before I ever got a chance. He very seldom will say anything, but he wanted that kid to know that he made a great catch, but hurt the team with his actions.

"I've seen Heath make superior athletic plays. One time he sprinted to his left, set up outside the numbers and threw a backside post and hit a receiver, from the 40, at the 2-yard line, and it thumped when it hit him. That was against Powell Valley, where the Jones boys came from – Thomas and Julius. We were playing them in the playoffs and Heath threw the backside post. The coach looked at me after the game and said, 'Coach, in high school, you shouldn't even have to defend that.'

"He was a heck of a baseball player and a heck of a basketball player. I mean, the kid was talented. We were playing Patrick Henry one night and they had a good running back. He turned the corner and had 10, 15 extra yards, and he sees Heath coming from safety and he just turned and stepped out of bounds 10 yards before Heath even got there."

THE MILLER'S home in Swords Creek sits on a winding two-lane road that could be any two-lane road in rural Western Pennsylvania. The home's elegance crushed the coal-poor-small town angle, and where was the damn coal tipple anyway?

"It's more farming than coal," Doug Hubbard said of Swords Creek. "Call it a coal-type farming community."

Denise Miller, a striking blond, introduced her husband Earl, which is also Heath's given name.

"I grew up next door," said Denise. "Earl's parents live in Honaker. I have seven sisters and one brother and he has a twin brother and another brother and sister who all live around here. So the kids grew up with their grandparents next door and their family nearby."

Denise is a counselor at the local community college, and Earl builds houses with one of his brothers. Denise's father worked in a coal mine for a while, but spent more time as a mechanic and welder. Earl's father was a farmer. We talked about Heath's quiet nature.

"If you watch him on the sideline, you'll notice he's always to himself," said Earl. "I think it comes from playing quarterback. He wants to stay focused."

"He was almost like a little Howard Cosell when he was young," said Denise. "He would do commentary on every ball game on TV. But when he goes out he's different. He's very private. He doesn't enjoy a lot of the attention." She paused a moment and said, "I've been so proud of who he is over what he does."

Heath grew up in this house with his sister Amanda. She, a senior at the University of Virginia, made better grades than Heath in high school.

"She was valedictorian of her class and Heath was third in his class," Denise said. "Everybody said he did that deliberately so he wouldn't have to give a speech."

Earl took me into the garage where he showed off his peaceful corner of the universe. A quiet guy as well, Earl talked about his proudest moment with his son.

"It really gets to me when he's in the tunnel ready to come out onto the field," he said. "That's when your eyes well up. That's when it hits you, again, that he's made it to the league."

Chapter Four

TOBACCO ROAD

GREG GRIFFIN said to stop by at noon. He's Willie Parker's hometown confidant – a lawyer who's a generation older than the Steelers' running back.

Griffin has an office on Main Street in downtown Clinton, North Carolina, a sleepy town of 8,386 right out of Mayberry R.F.D. My vision of the visit had Griffin turning on his speakerphone and the two of us peppering someone – (I had a name and a number) – from the University of North Carolina football program over Willie's role as benchwarmer there. On that day, Parker was second in the NFL in rushing.

"You've got to understand," Griffin said, "coaches come and go ..."

Wait. This guy sounds like a local sympathizer.

"... my son graduated a couple years ahead of Willie," Griffin said. "He went to Carolina as a quarterback ..."

This was not part of my vision.

"... because at Carolina, you don't earn a letter just for being on the team, you earn a letter because you've been involved in over 100 snaps in a year, so he lettered a couple years and ..."

I wanted to interrupt and remind him that his friend, Willie Parker, had been disrespected.

"... unfortunately, things didn't work out at Carolina as well as they could have.

He had different assistants and then you had head coaches from Mack Brown to Carl Torbush and then to John Bunting and the styles of the offenses changed. They had differences in halfback coaches. They had differences in offensive coordinators ..."

I'd heard it all before. This time I did interrupt Mr. Griffin to remind him that Willie Parker runs a 4.2 40.

"You're absolutely right," Griffin said. "Willie was used to, in high school, taking the ball and looking for the hole and then bouncing and going wherever he felt like he needed to go. I think he outran his blocking coverage and schemes and everything else, and he could do that in high school. In college, guys are a little bit faster and they knew how to play the angles better. Sometimes he'd break one and go 70 yards for a touchdown, and other times when he was out there bouncing, the coaches said, 'Well, you need to stick with the block, you need to be patient.'"

"Was this," I asked Griffin, "another instance of coaches feeling the need to coach?"

"That's right. That's right," he said.

We both smiled. This guy might be all right after all.

"One other thing that did occur," Griffin said, "Bunting wasn't having the success overall that people expected and the rumblings were coming down the pike. I think he sat down some upperclassmen he should've played – Willie included – so he could stand up in front of the media and other people and say, 'We have a young team. I've got my recruits here. It's going to take time. You have to be patient.'

"He was a man who cared a great deal about the university. He really did, but I don't know that he had all the right people in the right places, staff-wise, and a head coach has to have some good people and he's got to be able to delegate. And I think that's where things were missing and it was easier to say, 'We're going to have a young team; be patient with us.' But it never came to fruition and finally the university said, 'enough's enough.' So I think Willie got caught up in that."

GREG GRIFFIN was coaching his son's local rec team when he came to know Willie Parker. Griffin and Parker's dad, Willie Sr., went to high school together in 1972, and Griffin's son Bryan played basketball with Willie's older brothers. Willie Jr. eventually came to Griffin to ask why his beloved Tar Heels weren't recruiting him. Griffin found a problem with the paperwork and contacted UNC. He asked the staff to take another look at Parker and the rest became benchwarmer history.

"He came to me one time," Griffin said, "and he felt like quitting, and I said, 'I'll tell you what, come on home and I'll see if I can get a job for you at the local plant. And I know a farmer who could use some people. Come on home.' I reminded Willie he was getting a free ride and to use it and to keep on working, that he might catch a break. He sat right where you are and we talked about that, and lo and behold he made the most of the opportunity."

Parker, of course, made the Steelers as an undrafted rookie in 2004. He rushed for 1,202 yards in 2005 and ripped off a record 75-yard run that broke open Super Bowl XL.

What does Clinton, N.C., think of Willie Parker now?

"The kids, oh, my God, they follow him around," said Griffin's secretary, Rebecca Bixler. "He draws quite a crowd when he's in town."

A lifelong Steelers fan from Steubenville, Ohio, Bixler was surprised the day she met Fast Willie Parker. "He's much smaller than I had envisioned," she said. "He came in one day and started walking back to the offices and I told him, 'Sir, you'll have to wait up front.' And I called Mr. Griffin, 'Mr. Griffin, there's a man here who says he's Willie Parker.' I didn't think it was *that* Willie Parker. I was expecting this great big player, but he's built like my husband."

Willie Parker obviously wore his shirt that day.

✦ ✦ ✦

WILLIE PARKER'S PARENTS still live in the same house in which they raised their four kids. The field where their youngest, Willie Jr., played rec ball takes up most of the block across the street. The Parker house was in need of some work, at least on the roof where some sort of stoppage had occurred. I didn't ask Willie Parker Sr. about it. For some reason we started talking about Joey Porter instead.

"We saw him and his family at the Outback," said Willie Sr. "He paid for our meal. Great guy, man. He worked in that hot son at Willie's football camp here in town and the kids enjoyed every minute of it. Then he wanted to come and see the dogs. We have a couple of Pit Bulls out back and he wanted to see them, but he had to get back."

Are those the same Pit Bulls that Willie used to race against?

"No, that dog's gone on now," said Willie Sr. "His name was Tyson. My nephew Earl, he had Tyson trained real well. He could make him sit and walk way across the field. Then he'd whistle and the dog would come full gallop. My son saw this and he asked if the dog could do that all the time. Earl said yeah, so they got right in front of the yard, out on the street. Earl would whistle and the dog would come flying. Willie would start out good with him, but you can't outrun that dog. He tried so hard. You could see the veins popping, the muscles. He was digging, trying. He knew he couldn't beat the dog, but it couldn't do nothing but increase his speed."

So, it helped him become "Fast Willie Parker"?

"He's always been fast," Willie Sr. said, "but they never just said 'Fast Willie Parker.' We always called him Junior."

As Mr. Parker talked in the kitchen, his wife Lorraine popped in and out. She gave Willie Jr. his good looks. Dad gave him his name after naming his other sons Jamaul and Juwayne.

"My wife let the sisters and cousins name them,'" Willie Sr. said. "The last baby, his grandmother said, 'Name that boy Willie Parker Jr.' So he got lucky and got a great name."

Did Senior give Junior his speed, too?

"I wasn't that slow," Senior said. "I played a little football."

Willie Sr. was raised by his grandparents. They, too, grew up in Clinton.

"I was a receiver. I could catch the ball," Willie Sr. said. "But when you're raised by a couple of old people who could barely read and write their name, sports wasn't the priority. They didn't know anything about sports, really. Their main thing, as I could remember it, was 'You've got a home, food, so stay out of trouble.' There'd be people saying, 'Did you see your grandson laying a mean streak?' They'd say, 'No. What did he do? Get in trouble?' I'd just scored 20 or 30 points with 10 or 15 rebounds, that kind of mean streak, but they didn't care. I didn't get the chance to go to college. Right after high school I had to go to work. Had a baby on the way. Wished I had gone to college, but it didn't happen so I can't reflect on that."

WILLIE JR.'S college and pro dreams began in front of a TV. Both parents remember that's the spot from where he boldly predicted his future.

"In my house, you watched [North] Carolina and the Dallas Cowboys," Willie Sr. said. "I became a Carolina fan when they picked up a kid named Charlie Scott. That goes back about 40 years. He was the first black to play at Carolina, so I rode with them ever since. Willie started watching as a kid and one day he said he's going to play for them. He was only five, but you almost believed him just by the way he said it."

Because of his aggressiveness, Willie Jr. began his rec career as a defensive player. "They called him 'Wild Willie,'" said Willie Sr. "He was crazy."

After Wild Willie grew up a bit, his coach gave him the ball and got out of his way. "Whew, that baby boy got speed," he told Mr. Parker. And one day even Mr. Parker was surprised by his son's speed.

"I just watched practice," he said. "Some old guy was standing over there and I said, 'Hey, who's that running the ball?' He said, 'That's that Parker boy.' I thought, damn, Junior, you're looking good."

Junior only got better. After leading Clinton High to the state championship, he was the MVP of a postseason all-star game and drew heavy interest from college coaches.

"But what got me," said Willie Sr., "was he was so intent on going to Carolina. It was kind of frightening at first, him turning down all these other schools. I told my pastor about it and we prayed. He had to pass his SAT. If he missed that, he would've had to sit out and go to an academy school. I came in on Friday and Willie was standing at the back of my old car and he had a smile on his face and he said, 'I passed the SATs.' It was the last signing day, so he went and sent the letter to Carolina. They were recruiting him as a corner, but he didn't care. He said as long as he gets to play."

Of course, Parker didn't play much. He flirted with the starting job as a freshman, but lost it early as a sophomore.

"One time he was about to quit," said Willie Sr. "His good friend got killed and they were real tight. Whoa, I think that hurt that boy. That did something to him. He gave up for a while. He even lost his starting position. Wouldn't go to practice; wouldn't do nothing. When he came back, the coach said, 'We can't believe in you. Something happens in the family, you shut down and we've got games to prepare for.' He didn't get his starting job back until the Peach Bowl. That's when he got his chance, and he went in and cut up in the Peach Bowl. Then he was on the bench again."

Parker gained 131 yards on 10 carries in North Carolina's win over Auburn in the 2001 Peach Bowl. But Parker remained on the Carolina bench, where he rode out his scholarship.

"I'll never forget his last game," his dad said. "We had gotten used to the idea that he wasn't going to play, and Willie told us we didn't really have to come. 'I'm not going to play anyway,' he said. It was sad. It was sad to see his momma. And I looked out there and said, 'Don't say that.' We get a chance to see our baby. We'll still go out and tailgate. He's not the happiest, but I could tell that it delighted him that he had support still with him. Duke was the last home game. That's the game they honor the seniors; they come out on to the field with the parents. And so my daughter, she felt so sad for him that she had called Bunting and the offensive coordinator and said, 'Look, we're aware of what's going on. We're aware he's not going to play. But can you at least let him get one more play? Could you let him hit the field one last time? Please, just let him hit the field one more time.' He didn't hit the field. Not one play. Not one play. But we had got there before the game and walked out there with him. I was on one side; his mom on the other side. I put my arm around him and he said, 'I would've been mad if y'all hadn't been here.' And then he said, 'Read this here.' He had a white wrist band on. He said, 'Read it.' It said, 'We are going to make it.' I said, 'OK, go get it.' I got kind of sad. I was about to cry."

We are going to make it?

"We are going to make it. In other words, 'It doesn't stop here. I'm going to do what I'm supposed to do.' So I said, 'Son, go get it.' We had our tailgate thing and had a good time that day. After that he went to work. He just went to work and people were starting to watch him. They went to see him at the pro timing day at Carolina and he stole the show again, and when I got home about six pro teams had called me and gave me their numbers of where they'll be on draft day. They said he had a phenomenal day, that he was outrunning corners and everything, that he'd been clocked with the fastest speed. The scouts, they were amazed."

But, they didn't draft him.

"I can't understand it. I guessed they looked back and said he hadn't really done something. I really thought we were going to Florida to play for the Jaguars, but Pittsburgh gave him another deal."

And now, he's Fast Willie Superstar. Has it sunk in yet?

"It happened so fast," Willie Sr. said. "Every time I see him it reflects what he told me: 'We're going to make it.' Every time I see him set a record, or make a long run, or after he'd score a touchdown, go over 3,000 yards, it always reflects back: 'We're going to make it.' As a matter of fact, I made this little chain here and I wear it. It says 'We're going to make it.'

"I've seen him do great things and I thank God. I know God is in there. You can't put it no other way. I'm a church person and sometimes scripture comes back to my mind like, first will be last and last will be first. From sitting on the bench to where he is now — he was just never given the chance. I don't know why, but I look at it now that it was good. He didn't really go into the camp all beat up because he never really played a lot.

"After he made the roster, finally made it, he called me a couple times late at night. I asked him what's wrong. He said, 'I just want to thank you all. I just thought about where I'm at now and I want to thank you.' He'd be crying, saying he loved us all, 'Thank you, thank you, thank you.' I said: 'Thank God.' I can't pronounce it no other way.

"When he was a little kid, he prophesied he was going to play. He saw the Cowboys play and he said he was going to play in the NFL one day. I said, 'Move, we're trying to watch the game. Pittsburgh's killing us and you're saying you want to play. Move.' But here he is today. Thank God for it."

ACCORDING TO Willie Parker Sr., if you "keep yourself prayed up," you just might find yourself in a heaven one day sitting next to famous people watching your boy run to daylight. Or domelight.

"That was just a perfect play," Mr. Parker said of his son's Super Bowl record run. "Every block was perfect. Everything I saw was perfect. The key, to me, was he and Bettis were on the sideline; Jerome said, 'They're looking for you to take it outside. Fake it like you're going to the outside and take it back inside.' Hines Ward might've been the key block downfield and that Seattle safety, No. 35 (Etric Pruitt), all he could do was grab. He was gone.

"I was there. Went crazy. I started praying because that first half was crazy. By the time I finished with my little prayer, I looked up, heard the crowd, and I said, 'Oh, Lord, he's gone.' After I calmed down, this guy tapped me on the back of my shoulder and he congratulated me. I said, 'Who are you?' He was Isaiah Thomas. We took pictures and everything. And then another guy came in and said, 'Hey, I'm proud of that boy of y'all. He can run that ball.' He had on platinum gold diamonds and everything. He said, 'You don't even know who I am, do you?' I said, 'No.' And he said, 'Are you ready for some football?' It was Hank Williams Jr. and he said, 'I'm proud of that boy of yours.'

"I met so many celebrities. They were all around me. It was crazy, man. It was incredible to go down on the field with all that glitter. I was just so outdone. I didn't have anything left. I was walking in the back of the pack thanking the Lord, 'Thank you. Thank you. Thank you.' Everybody else was going wild and Willie grabs my arm and said, 'You don't have to worry about nothing. I'm going to make sure you get everything you need.' And so they were celebrating and calling me to hurry up, but I'm just so thankful. God blessed me. I never thought I'd be at an NFL game watching my son play, let alone a Super Bowl."

✦ ✦ ✦

THE CITY of Florence, South Carolina, sits off Interstate 95 halfway between New York City and Miami. It's a town of 30,248 that in 2006 was ranked the fifth most dangerous metropolitan area in the country behind Detroit, Memphis, Los Angeles and Las Vegas.

The list of athletes who've made it out includes Harry Carson, Reggie Sanders, Darien Durant, Justin Durant, and the Steelers' No. 1 draft pick in 2007, linebacker Lawrence Timmons. All of them went to Wilson High School. I asked a man on a sidewalk in Florence for directions to the school.

"Go TIGERS!" the man shouted. He appeared to be under the influence of a powerful narcotic.

"Are you a fan of the TIGERS?" he bellowed.

I told him no, that I was doing a story on Lawrence Timmons.

"Ohhhhh, he done moved to the RIGHT side of town," the man said. "He done got a B-I-I-I-G contract."

I agreed, but was looking for Wilson High. The man gave me lousy directions, but I eventually found my way to the school that had been founded for African-Americans. Apparently, exceptions have since been made for white punters and kickers. In the midst of videotaping this phenomenon, my camera picked up a burly man dressed in purple coming my way at a pretty good clip.

"Can I help you, sir?" he asked as he continued walking.

I put my camera down and told him that Bill Belichick had sent me. The man laughed. He introduced himself as the Wilson head coach and told me he'd have time to talk about Timmons at the end of practice.

"You know, I had two pro linebackers on that team." he said.

Justin Durant was drafted in the second round the same year Timmons was picked in the first and plays for the Jacksonville Jaguars. I wanted to ask the coach what it was like coaching that kind of talent, and, as I saw the words "2002 State Champions" painted on the back of the nearby baseball dugout, I figured he'd say he liked it a lot. But 5 p.m. turned to 6 p.m. and my appointment with the Timmons family was drawing close. I left the football field at 6:45 with no sign of practice ending anytime soon.

Was this team going to practice into the night?

"Maybe. That coach is something else," said Lindsey Timmons. "Did he talk to you at all?"

I told Lawrence Timmons' father about my Belichick moment and mentioned that he must be a good coach, considering the state championship and all.

"What state championship?" Mr. Timmons said. "That was baseball. The football team didn't even come close."

Well, that would explain the dugout.

LINDSEY TIMMONS played basketball at Duquesne University and looks like it. He was listed in the day at 6-foot-8, 205, but is probably closer to 6-foot-6. He's thin and could probably still play today. His son isn't so tall, but he can run and hit. Lawrence Timmons is named after his grandfather and uncle.

"My daddy's name was Lawrence Timmons and I had a brother named Lawrence Timmons Jr.," Lindsey Timmons said. "Both of them died, so I told my wife I wanted to spend some time myself, personally, with Lawrence Timmons, so I wanted to name him that. She didn't want to do that at first."

Audrey Timmons wanted to name their son Hakeem Olajuwon, after the Houston Rockets' great basketball player. But Lindsey, the former basketball player, overruled mom and her suggestion took the consolation prize.

"My daddy didn't have a middle name," Lindsey said. "So she told me, 'The only way you're going to name him Lawrence is if I choose the middle name.' I said okay, so she chose Olajuwon. His middle name is Olajuwon. That's how I got my way."

Lawrence Olajuwon Timmons, or "Juan," as his parents call him, was born to play basketball.

Both parents laughed.

"He's not any good at basketball," said his mom. "Noooo, sir."

"We never forced anything on him," said dad. "I used to play in the leagues around here and the guys used to say, 'Man, your son will be a *good* basketball player if you spend time with him.' But he was never interested in it and I didn't force it on him. Then when he came up he dabbled in baseball but baseball wasn't it. Then when he got to football, he found out certain things he could do that he didn't know he could do. You would've enjoyed him on the field as a little kid. You would've enjoyed him because he would do amazing things as a little kid on the field."

"He hit," said mom.

Dad smiled at mom's enthusiasm. "He could hit hard," he said, and he repeated it. "He could hit hard. He could hit so hard. Little, but he could hit hard. Fast. He had an unorthodox run. He looked like a chicken running, but he was just so fast. And Justin Durant taught him how to play linebacker when he got to high school, and he could pick them holes a lot quicker than Justin could, because Justin was really reading and Juan was reacting to whatever they gave him. Those two, they were tough together."

LINDSEY TIMMONS was determined to see that his son fulfilled his potential, probably because he hadn't done so himself. Lindsey went to Duquesne to play basketball in 1975. John Cinicola was in his second year as coach and Norm

Nixon was the junior point guard. At the same time Tony Dorsett was playing football at Pitt and Keith Starr was the Panthers' best basketball player.

"We used to all roam together," said Timmons. "We'd all meet up in groups and play basketball at Duquesne. Sometimes we'd go to Pitt and play, or to a park in Aliquippa. Sometimes we'd go by Dorsett's house. I don't remember too much. I only stayed one year."

Timmons played in only one game at Duquesne and didn't record any statistics. He had averaged 18 points, 18 rebounds and 8 blocks as an All-Dade County player at Carroll Senior High School in Miami, Florida. That's where he went, back to Miami, after his year on the Bluff.

"My parents were dead," Lindsey said. "So I was kind of living by myself in Miami, and I got to the point where I was kind of tired of just being hemmed up at school and being told what to do all the time. I wanted to get married, too, so I got out of school and got married."

Lindsey was born in Florence, but his brother, Lawrence Jr., came for him after their parents died. Lindsey was close with his brother, who died a year later.

"That was all into what messed my head up," Lindsey said. "My brother was the only one who came and paid attention to me. When he died I lived in Miami Beach at a $45-a-week apartment until I went to Duquesne. So all of that was all in the mix."

Lindsey and Audrey raised three children – Juan and his older sister Valerie and younger sister Lakendra. Only two days before my visit, the family moved into a big, beautiful home on the RIGHT side of Florence. It's a family that likes to do everything together. Like bowling

"I don't try to compete," said Lindsey. "I'm just looking for the unity of the family."

It shows. Juan Timmons doesn't possess the rough edges one might expect in a young man – a young run-and-hit linebacker — from some of the meanest streets in the country. The kid's a jock, raised by a jock who'd been through the wringer. Lindsey knew what he was doing as he steered his son around the obstacles, but he gives his son the credit.

"He's got a lot of character in him, and he's learning a lot more," Lindsey said. "He's learning how to handle his situations. He doesn't do stupid things. Florida State is one of the biggest party houses in America and he went through there with a pretty level head. People around there all talked good about him. Now that he's in the NFL he hasn't changed his personality at all. He's the same as he's always been. He's a great son."

FLORIDA STATE won the recruiting war, but not before a couple of other big programs made a run.

"John Bunting at North Carolina was his biggest recruiter coming out of high school," Lindsey said. "He was a very convincing guy, and after we talked to him, it was all go – until I thought about my son's dream. I just couldn't see his dream there."

Lindsey Timmons decided that only three schools could make his son's dream come true: Miami, Florida and Florida State. Just after Lawrence indicated he'd go to Florida State, Phil Fulmer of Tennessee showed up. And since Fulmer was the only head coach to visit Florence, Lawrence reciprocated. The week he visited, the campus was hit by an ice storm and Lawrence had to stay.

"The NCAA gives you three days and he stayed five days," Lindsey said. "He stayed so long he ran out of clothes. It was an emergency type thing, and he called me from the airport and said, 'Dad, I'm getting ready to come home, but I have something to tell you. You're going to have to sit down.' I asked him if he was all right and he said, 'Yeah. But I don't think I'm going to Florida State. I'm going to Tennessee.' And I said, 'The hell you are. You can't do that to us. We talked to Bobby (Bowden). You gave that man your word. You're going to Florida State.' But he didn't want to hear that, so he came home and said, 'Dad we have to talk about this again.' I told him there was nobody to talk to about it."

Lawrence, of course, went to Florida State. Three years later he was drafted 15th in the first round by the Steelers.

Was Lindsey happy to see his son head off to his old stomping grounds?

"I was real glad Pittsburgh took him," he said. "I was glad anybody took him, if you want to know the truth. But considering the little bit of roots I had in Pittsburgh, it was kind of weird that after all these years everything went back to Pittsburgh. I never would've imagined anything like that."

Chapter Five
HOT, SMOLDERING ATLANTA

HINES WARD read me like I was a rookie cornerback. I needed a different kind of interview and Hines gave me the contact info of his best friend in Atlanta.

"We were rivals in high school," Ward said.

"Delicious," I said.

Corey Allen was a friend, then a rival, and then Ward's college roommate at Georgia. He grew up with Ward in the south Atlanta suburb of Forest Park. They played sports together until middle school, when Allen entered the North Clayton school district and Ward entered the Forest Park district.

"I hated playing against him," Allen said. "One time, as a ninth-grader in JV ball, I told my teammates, 'Look, he played quarterback the year before. They're going to throw the halfback pass.' He was playing tailback in this game. He had probably 150 yards rushing. He was killing us. I was at safety on one side of the field. Fourth quarter, we're up three points and of course 40 yards in they throw the halfback pass. We all bite on the fake. He's laughing. And you could see him smiling the whole time. That still bothers me to this day, that when you played against him he's laughing the entire time. You can literally hear him laughing and joking. He never liked a mouthpiece so you can always see that Cheshire-cat smile, and that just used to irk me whenever I played against him. I hate to see that smile. It's a nasty little smirk."

In the Steelers' opener in Cleveland, Ward's "nasty little smirk" appeared in the middle of a play. He hadn't even caught the pass yet; it was in mid-air when the cameras picked up that big smile behind the facemask. Ward settled under the pass and torched the Browns for a 24-yard touchdown, laughing all the way to the back of the end zone.

Didn't like that one, Corey?

"As a fan I can relax now," Allen said. "But going against him, you don't like that. You don't want to see him smile. Nothing good is coming out of the situation as long as he's smiling."

WARD IS the son of an African-American father and an Asian mother and he was born in Seoul, South Korea. He came to Atlanta as an infant, went with his dad by divorce decree to Monroe, Louisiana. His grandmother raised him, but gave him back to Ward's mother – Kim Young He – in Forest Park when he was seven. Ward has told the story of how he came to be embarrassed by his Korean mother, but Corey Allen saw it differently.

"I think that story is taking on a lot more weight than what the truth really is," he said. "I think he was more ashamed of the culture. He wasn't ashamed of his mom."

Kim Young He worked one job till 3 a.m., when she came home to check on Hines, and then went back out at 4 a.m. to her next job. Through it all, Hines graduated with a perfect attendance record.

"She had a very firm hand," Allen said. "Even though she wasn't there, there was a list of things for him to do and they had to be done. The grass was always cut. He still had those responsibilities; he just didn't have her there to monitor him. I think it gave him a lot of focus. He's always had a very high individual focus. That's one thing I've always noticed about him and one thing I've always admired, but I think it's something he got from his mom.

"When we were younger, he was the one who picked everyone up and took us to practice. His mom worked hard enough to get him a car, which was always funny to me: She worked two jobs and was never home but she had enough money to get him a car. So he was one of the first kids in our neighborhood to have a car, but he wouldn't go out and hang out with us; he was taking us to practice. He was making sure we were all where we were supposed to be. He's always been a real good ringleader. He's always been very focused and driven, especially in sports

"Growing up the way he did I think manifested itself in a lot of different ways, on and off the field. He loves the fans of Pittsburgh because they're dedicated to him. He's committed to them and the organization, but he's driven by all the naysayers. He may highlight them more than he should, but that's what keeps him focused."

The two met on a baseball field at the age of 12. "He had an afro that could barely fit under his cap," Allen said. "He became one of the best center fielders I ever played with: fast, could cover the field, and he could hit like gangbusters. He had an open stance in the front of the box, so he was basically facing the pitcher. He hit a lot of home runs, but he had great speed, too. Anytime he got on base, consider him on third."

Ward was drafted by the Florida Marlins in 1994 but didn't sign. The Marlins stayed after Ward until the middle of his college football career, when a coaching change at Georgia put an end to his baseball days.

Ray Goff, the outgoing Georgia coach, had recruited Ward to play quarterback, and Allen loved those early college days.

"I was a receiver on the other side," he said. "I was the roommate, so I got most of his passes. Peach Bowl '95 he almost broke the record when he threw for maybe 400 yards. I had a great game that day. I just LOVED when he was at quarterback. We had that bond where he knew I would do anything to catch a ball for him. He was a very good quarterback."

As Allen put it, Georgia developed "a running back situation" their sophomore year, so Ward moved to running back. He then chose to become a receiver because, as Allen said, "it was better for the team." Ward caught 52 passes as a junior and 55 as a senior and expected to be drafted at the end of the first round because of his 4.5 40 time. But he wasn't drafted until the end of the third round. Ward took it hard and remembers it as one of many slights, which amuses his old buddy.

"He's a crybaby," Allen said with a chuckle.

Allen told a story of their sophomore season at Georgia. Ward was second team at every position: quarterback, running back, receiver, and return man, and in a game at Clemson, Ward didn't play a snap. He took it so hard he considered transferring.

"I encouraged him," Allen said. "That's my best friend and he thought he was being shortchanged, and he was. He was going to go out to Notre Dame or to

Florida State. He definitely had the options. He talked to his mom. He talked about it with the Georgia people. He decided to stay, but he was so upset. I think we won the game, but it was so close that he never had a chance to play. That changed everything. Immediately after that game it changed. For a guy like that, who loves the game as much as he does, to not get a chance to play at all? That was the first time he didn't play at all. It was a shock to him and it kind of hurt him.

"You know, I kid him about being a crybaby, but his attitude's not going to change until he retires. Then he'll sit back and appreciate everything he's done. He's starting to appreciate a lot more now, but he's still in the heat of the battle."

✦ ✦ ✦

GREG LLOYD left the Steelers with bitterness in his heart. He was bitter with the media and bitter with the coach who cut him. But it's since given way to a new source of bitterness: his ex-wife Rhonda. An ugly divorce resulted in a 2004 trial in Fayetteville, Georgia, in which Lloyd was accused of putting a gun in his then-12-year-old son Greg's mouth because of poor grades. The jury deliberated for three days before a mistrial (11-1) was declared. Lloyd had testified and denied it happened. He was held for another trial 11 days later, and the result was another mistrial (8-4). The key testimony came from Greg Jr.'s girlfriend. She told the court that Rhonda Lloyd had urged Greg Jr. to convince a counselor that he wanted to live with his mother instead of his father. This was perceived as an attempt to slant the facts and it tainted the prosecution's case.

The Hartford Courant talked to Greg Jr. about his dad in the spring of 2007, after Greg signed to play football at the University of Connecticut, but the university prohibited me from speaking with the freshman about his father. That would've been an easier interview than this one.

FAYETTEVILLE'S NOT COZY like Clinton, nor is it the mean streets of Florence. It's your common, middle-America morass of shopping centers. I maneuvered through the unnamed streets of these plazas to find the Oh Do Kwan Martial Arts Center. Lloyd pulled in on time and his fit, young, beautiful wife jumped out of the SUV with her two young children – Lloyd's stepkids – running out behind. Lloyd stepped out and with a limp headed inside. I looked to Stephanie, who had arranged the interview.

"Honey," said Stephanie. "This is Jim Watson ..."

"Wexell."

"... Jim Wetzel, and he's here to interview you."

Lloyd didn't stop. Still thickly muscled, maybe 10 pounds over his playing weight, Lloyd limped toward his office. It's a small office with a big desk, and there was nothing in the room that said he was one of the great players of the 1990s.

"Stephanie, please close the door," said the man known here as Master Lloyd. "What can I do for you?"

"Tell me about this place," I started off. More than 1,300 words later, I asked my second question.

MOVING FROM athlete to athlete was not the initial plan for this book. I envisioned sitting in fan bars and talking to displaced steelworkers and, really, bouncing funny thoughts off the reader, personal thoughts, intimate thoughts, as I careened around the country without a plan.

The vacation hotspots off the Carolina coast certainly held the promise of not only Steelers Nation, but my own mini-vacation. A friend in the business, a retired scout of 35 years, said I had a place at his table in Wilmington. The stories would've entertained me – us – for days, but I have this thirst for news after spending some 25 years in the business. So instead of sunning on a beach deck with a retired scout who's giving me more legend than fact, and me not caring about the difference, I'm staring into the eyes of Greg Lloyd somewhere in the suburban sprawl of Atlanta on a hot September afternoon as he's talking non-stop about the importance of discipline. All I could think about was finding the right time to ask him about his son, so I just blurted it out. Lloyd expected the question and didn't blink.

"I don't blame my son for what has taken place," he started. "I think everybody around me and everybody over there realizes it was a lie."

Lloyd recounted his son's girlfriend's testimony, the testimony at the second trial that cast doubt over the case.

"I think what happened," Lloyd said, "is Gregory loves his mom and he didn't want to disappoint her. So I understand why he did what he did. As a father, he's kind of like the prodigal son. He has spun his wheels, said some things that I think and I know that he doesn't believe. I have put myself out there to let him know that he's forgiven, but I can't be sure the message gets through because there are so many people trying to block it, which I never understood. How can somebody stand in the way of a father-son relationship? Who would want to do that? So I've waited until he's become a man, and I think the best thing for him is being at UConn, being away from his mom, growing up and understanding life. I think that's going to open up his eyes to what really went down, and I think in time that'll do it. I tried to make the initial contact by saying, 'Hey listen I'm here. My number hasn't changed the last 10 years. You know where I live and you know my values and my views won't change.' They won't change. I am still the same person. I still believe in discipline. I still believe in doing things the right way because that's the way to do it. I still believe in honor. I still believe in children honoring their parents. I let him know that, but I also let him know that he's his own man. That's really all, as a father, I can do.

"You know, when I stopped playing football I gave up my old life. I stopped drinking. I gave all that up. I haven't drank since then. I'm not that same person. She still wanted that lifestyle and I didn't, so when I retired, I retired to do everything: Get my kids up in the morning, take them to the private school, pick them up, help them with their homework, and then get them here in time to do tae kwon do. I became mom and dad. For me, it was almost like I was trying to make up for all that time I missed. You can't do it, but the thing was I was resented. I was resented. You would think most women would say, 'Wow, dad's home. Now I get to rest.' But she liked that power. She liked that power of 'Look at my house.' I'm like, 'Well, you didn't play football. You don't have any bruises or broken fingers or bad knees or screws in you, so don't do this.' That's what most of the arguments sprang from. Then she started doing stuff, having people at my house without me knowing, and it became very disrespectful, so one of us had to go. I brought my children downstairs and just explained to them what was going on, and that they probably weren't going to see dad for a while. I still didn't want them to let that be an excuse for bad behavior or for bad grades in school. My son was right there, and he was, 'Aw, dad, we're going to be sad.' That was really kind of it, and I was like, 'OK, they understand,' because they had friends who had been through it before. And then I go hunting one day and I came home to warrants, just like that, and I've got some judge down here who says, 'Oh, I believe it.' Well, here are receipts of where I bought stuff that can prove that I wasn't home. Do you think he wanted to hear it? They don't want to hear it because he wants to make a name for himself in this little ol' bitty little town. That's how it went. They didn't want to hear that I'd never been arrested. They got this woman screaming, and then I'm saying, 'Listen, baby, you can kiss my behind because I haven't done anything and I don't care who you think you are.' See, they were not used to that. Believe it or not, this is still a prejudiced little town. I had never been in trouble. I stayed in my house. I played golf. I went and did my little autograph sessions. I didn't mix. I came here. How many times have I been pulled over out here? I can count on this hand and toes how many times I've been pulled over, and they'd say, 'OK, sir, have a nice day.' Didn't say why they pulled me over or nothing like that. I didn't go down there and file no police report because I expected it. I did. I expected it to happen."

Lloyd said teaching and working out helps him relieve stress.

"If I wasn't doing this, to be totally honest with you, I would probably be suicidal," he said. "It's either that or I would hurt somebody. I would really hurt somebody. But it's calming.

"My thing is this: I've spent probably half of my adult life trying to prove to people and coaches and everybody that I was a good person. But I don't need anybody's approval that I am that because I am a child of God. I changed my life. I've got friends now that I played football with that don't even bother to pick up the phone and call me because they know I'm not running the streets. I used to. I did. See now, if my wife wanted to get a divorce based on my infidelities and things of that nature, then, yeah, that was true, but the way she went about it, trying to make me out like I was a bad father, when never, anywhere, did my kids ever go to school with bruises on them. There were no teachers or nurses calling my house or calling the police, but nobody ever wanted to hear that. It was basically, 'There's a mean guy. She said he did it. You know how he played football. He could've done it. He did it.' And that's what they ran on.

"I didn't expect that from this woman I'd been married to for 15 years and who had known me for 19 years, who'd been to my house, who'd seen how I was brought up, who knows I had no mother and father, who KNEW that I would never abandon my children. So the only way that she could stick that knife in my side and twist it is to try and change my children against me. The people that she's convincing don't have kids. The judges don't have kids, so how can they relate? So no matter how many people came in there and said, 'I've known Greg since he's been here in this business right here and he's upstanding,' they didn't care.

"In court, I told my attorney, 'If my son looks me in my face and he says that, then he believes it. But if he never looks at me, you'll know and I'll know he's lying.' He walked in there and he was looking and talking, looking and talking, and he couldn't look at me, because I'm just standing there staring at him like, 'Why are you saying what you're saying?' But that's life."

Was it painful?

"It was. Initially it was. To be sitting in somebody's jail for five and a half months just because you said I did something. You don't have any evidence, but YOU – YOU don't even know me – YOU said I did something and they came and put me in handcuffs and arrested me and took me to trial based on what (looks down to check my name) Jim said. That's how it was. Five and a half months. Zero evidence."

How did the authorities get away with that after the second mistrial?

"Because they're Fayette County," he said. "Who's going to come in here and question them? Are you? Are you going to come in here and say, 'You know, y'all shouldn't be holding Greg Lloyd here in jail.' They'll arrest you. That's how they work. And it's not so much as that, Jim, my thing is that I'm not the only guy that's going through that.

"It was the biggest show. She took everything, every piece of furniture, everything I had, stuff that belonged to me. I have to go back to court to get it, even after the judge had ordered her to give it back to me over the last three or four years. We shared investments but somehow they've got this thing set up where she gets the check, like she played football. It goes to her first and she's supposed to send me money. The last three years, haven't seen one thing. So I've got to go to court. That's the kind of stuff I've been dealing with, but every day I wake up and I smile, because most people couldn't deal with it. The thing of it is, I have confirmation. I have confirmation from my God that He's going to give me no more than I can bear, and that He's going to supply all of my needs according to His riches and glory. I have the faith and I believe that, and so that keeps me going.

"When I get up in the morning, I'm constantly doing something, because if I have time to sit down, and think, well, you know what I'm thinking about? I have a 15-year-old daughter. If this woman has remarried and there's some man fondling my daughter, if he is, and I'll say it right now (taps desk twice), graveyard dead. There's nothing that could stop me. There's not a SWAT team or anything that could stop me from putting my hands on him and doing what I need to do. That hurts more than anything.

"Before my (second) wife and I were dating and this thing had gone down, my kids were coming to see me. No problem at all. But I could tell after a while my daughter kind of started clamming up. I didn't know what was going on, but what it was is she'd seen her mom with somebody else in that house and it was tearing her up. I told her, 'Listen, I'm there. I'm never going to change. I love you. My love is unconditional regardless of what you say or what you do. It's never going to change.' We sit down and we do our Bible study every night and every morning and we pray for our family. We pray that (Greg Jr.'s siblings) Jhames and Tiana are safe. We pray that they understand that their father loves them and that they long to be with their father just like I long to be with them."

LLOYD WAS BORN in Miami, the youngest of nine children. He never met his father and his mother dropped him and four of his brothers and sisters off at her sister's house in Fort Valley, Georgia. It created one angry young boy who — he told *The New York Times* in 1993 — took it out on the other Pop Warner football players.

How much anger does he still carry around?

"I have my own devils and demons that I have to fight," he said. "But it's not anger anymore. It's more controlled. It's not anger because I've been healed of that. When I was playing football, the anger that I had back then was that I didn't have parents. As I got older I was the best kid in everything, but there was nobody there to go, 'Way to go, Greg,' other than a coach. All my other friends, they sucked. They sucked at football and their parents were there saying, 'Hey, way to go.' And I'm going, 'You sucked.' And so when I went to play football, and I see this parent jumping up and saying, 'Come on, Johnny!' I'm finding out who's Johnny. I'm looking around for her boy because she's making an awful lot of noise, and I would look at him and say, 'I'm going to knock hell out of him. I can't wait to knock hell out of him.' And I'd go and knock him out and my whole demeanor was, 'Clap about that.' You wouldn't think that at age 8, 9, 10 a kid would think like that, but that's how I was. And I carried it right on through high school and I carried it right on through college.

"I went to college in Fort Valley, which is about an hour and 15 minutes from where we're sitting right now. My home was 1.35, no, 1.36 miles from my college, and my aunt never came to see me play football. I played baseball in my backyard. The high school baseball field was in my backyard. She never came to see me play. I always had to prove myself to people that, regardless that I have no parents, not only am I a good player but I'm a good person. After a while you get tired of it."

WITH STEPDAUGHTER running calisthenics, Greg Lloyd's tae kwon do class was underway. We'd talked for an hour and Lloyd showed no signs of losing interest, so we went in another direction. Lloyd had recently been named to the Steelers' all-time team. Did it mean anything to him?

"I don't know," he said. "To be honest with you, when people hear me say I don't watch football and I don't care too much about football, it doesn't mean I forget that football has provided for me and opened a lot of doors for me. But I don't watch it because I don't think the game is at the level where we played it. I don't think there's enough integrity. I don't think the guys understand that just because you hear your name on ESPN and you're going to pimp your ride on MTV, that's not football. When we were there, we tried to carry ourselves no different than the CEO of PPG. That's the way we took our job. We showed up for work and we worked. We didn't show up for work to put on airs and to sell stuff. That's why me and the media there didn't get along. I'm not here to kiss your ass. I don't care if you don't invite me to your little parties or soirees that you have, because I don't want you in my personal life like that. I want you to understand that I was hired to be an outside linebacker, and that's where the shirt came from: I Wasn't Hired For My Disposition. I was hired to be an outside linebacker, and for 60 minutes all hell is going to break loose. I have no friends – not even my own teammates. I will fight my own teammates because they're not pulling their own weight. That's how I played the game of football. That's how I brought that to the rest of my teammates and they had that mentality.

"Being on the All-Steeler Team, I mean, I've met every one of the linebackers and I'm humbled. When I'm in the same room as Lambert, Ham and Andy Russell, I take a backseat. We measure everything by a ring now in the NFL, and these guys won four Super Bowls. Not only did they win four Super Bowls, but look at the stats. Look at how many times they went to the Pro Bowl and things of that nature. But, yes, I was up there with them when it came to that. Tenacity and the way the game should be played, I think that's how people identify with me and the old Steelers because I did not care. I played with an I'll-step-on-you, I'll-spit-on-you kind of mentality. I thought that's the way everybody played, but I came to find out that, no, that's not the way everybody played and everybody didn't have that passion for the game that I had. So, I wanted to step my level up to let my teammates around me know this is how we're going to play, and if you're not playing with that you're going to be on my you-know-what list.

"That anger was there. That anger was there because I came from a little old black college right here in Fort Valley, a sixth-round draft pick, and then I've got these big jokers coming from these big schools and they are wimps and they suck and they're getting millions of dollars and they're there for two years and they're gone. They're set for life if they take care of their money, but I've got to make that up. I can play three years and not make that up. But I'm going to do it in practice. I'm going to find out if they breed them the same way as they do in Fort Valley. Do you think you can play this game better than me? Well let's strap it up. Let's do it. The thing about it is I'll fight you till I got no fight left in me. And I think after a while my teammates began to appreciate that and they respected that and they realized that, 'Don't come over here and line up in front of Greg in practice and not buckle your chinstrap up, because he's going a hundred miles an hour.' And when everybody adopted that mentality, guess what we did? We were in three AFC Championship games and a Super Bowl."

Lloyd paused for a moment, and then said: "There's no way that we shouldn't have won two Super Bowls."

KEVIN GREENE once called the loss to the Dallas Cowboys in Super Bowl XXX his greatest pro disappointment. He called the previous year's team, the 1994 team, the best he ever played on. Lloyd agreed on both counts.

"The '94 team was better than the Super Bowl team," Lloyd said. "There's no way that we should not have won at least two Super Bowls. And we come back in 1997 and lose to Denver in Pittsburgh in the AFC Championship game; one of the best runs I ever had in my life. And who do you blame it on? We give all the glory to the quarterback when we win. We give all the glory to the coaches when we win. But when we lose, who gets it? Who are you going to put it on? Are you going to put it on the back of who? I never said, because the fact of the matter is they're my teammates and what happens in-house stays in-house. We can sit back and look at the film and let the country and all the readers and the writers make the decision, but the fact of the matter is we won as a team, we lost as a team. That's how I saw it.

"When I'm talking to my class this is how I get," he continued. "I had the opportunity to talk to Marvin Lewis, who was my linebacker coach in Pittsburgh. The Bengals came and played the Falcons here Monday night, preseason. He called me up and left me a message. He wanted me to come talk to his football team

Sunday night. And so I got my (step) son – he's a big Chad Johnson fan – and we got in my truck and drove downtown. They were in their meetings so I went in the meeting and sat there watching and I'm going, 'Wow, I remember that play.' And I lean over to Marvin, and I said, 'Inside fire zone?' And he said, 'You didn't forget.' Just little stuff like that. Then they went to individual meetings, and then defensive and offensive meetings, and then I came in and spoke with them in the team meeting. When I talk football, sometimes I have to go back home and get on my knees and ask God for forgiveness because it's a passion, but I told them that when I was with Pittsburgh, we didn't care about our offense because defense wins championships. And I was trying to tell them that they have young guys and I guarantee what's going to happen: One guy's waiting for somebody else to step up, and what if that doesn't take place till the ninth game of the season? Now you're regretting that you didn't step up early. Now is the time.

"I relayed a story to Chad Johnson. I told him that we had a guy by the name of Andre Hastings. He grew up right here in Atlanta in Morrow High School. In fact, he went to school with my wife. But when Hastings first came to Pittsburgh, he made our defensive backfield look so bad. I remember at practice he had Rod Woodson turning all kinds of ways, catching balls, making our defense look bad. It ticked me off. When we went to seven-on-seven, I held them up and I told them, 'If he catches the ball across this middle, I'm going to knock him out. He's showboating and he's not going to do that to my defense.' And lo and behold, I dropped back into pass (coverage) and he cut across the middle and he caught it and when he turned, all he saw was 95. I hit him right there. I hit him, the ball went one way, ear pads went another way, and the whole team's going, 'Ohhhh. Ohhhh. Ohhhh, Greg.' And I said, 'NOBODY is going to come out here and show my defense up. NOBODY.' I took my helmet off and talked to the whole offense. I said, 'Anybody else think they can come out here and show my defense up?' The offense just mumbled to themselves.

"They'd be at practice and our (scout) defense is running the other defense's stuff and they'd tell these guys where to go so the offensive players can't hurt them. I was like, 'Listen, y'all not getting it done.' I would come in there and Marvin would be, 'Greg, get out of there.' I'd say, 'Listen, this dude needs a break and I'm in here to give him a break.' I'm running second-team defense against our first offense. They hold them little cards and Marvin came over and said, 'Greg, you go here.' And I'd say, 'Marvin, you're in my way. Go ahead and yell at me but I ain't following that card. I'm going to the football.' I told him I was going straight to the football. I look up and – Pow! – I messed the play up. Bill Cowher, I could see he was upset: 'Do it again!' he yelled, and I said, 'Hell, man, I'm going to be right there again.' I run in there again — Pow! He goes, 'Coach! Get him outta there!' I said, 'You know what? What if you got Ray Lewis running up in there on Sunday? You going to tell them to get Ray Lewis out of there?' That's why me and Bill started having our little tiffs then."

Lloyd stopped to catch his breath and noticed his pupils looking around. It was time for Master Lloyd to get to work, so he put on his white robe and black belt.

"This is not the end of life," he said. "This is where God has me right now. I enjoy it. I would love to be able to share that motivation that I have for the game. I think I can motivate players to reach beyond what their potential is. I really do. It's in me. God gave it to me. That's what makes me who I am, and not everybody likes it. But I know that God loves winners. He wants all of us to win in whatever we're doing. These are the tools that He's given me. To be doing anything less than what I'm doing right now would be a failure, a failure to Him and me. So I'm not going to let Him down. If I let Him down, then I let all the people around me down."

Chapter Six
Deep South

BACK IN THE RV, Jan put the shopping centers and traffic of Atlanta in the rearview mirror, but I was wishing he'd put a cold beer in my hand. It's been about 10 years, and I hadn't really thought much about getting drunk until spending 90 minutes with Greg Lloyd. But the mood passed and I slogged on with the tea.

We were covering a little more than eight miles for every gallon of gas as we pulled into Mobile for lunch at a downtown Steelers bar. The time-zone change threw us and we arrived an hour before the joint opened. We didn't figure it out until we were in Mississippi. There, we found ourselves in one of the more underrated football states in this great football nation.

"Jerry Rice, Brett Favre and Walter Payton all came from Mississippi," Deshea Townsend told me one day. "So did Steve McNair and L.C. Greenwood and a bunch of others."

Townsend's from Mississippi. That's where he went to high school, at state power South Panola High. You may remember Deshea, before Super Bowl XL, introducing himself as "Deshea Townsend, South Panola University."

It's a big-school prep power in the northern part of the state, just south of Memphis. South Panola won its first state championship in 1993 with Townsend – the Steelers' right cornerback – at quarterback. Townsend played with Dwayne Rudd and they kick-started a dynasty that in 2007 won its 75th consecutive game and seventh state title.

Townsend's proud of the Mississippi football heritage, but even he left the state to play college football at Alabama.

Why?

"There's not too much to do in Mississippi," he said. "And a lot of struggles with racial battles that people went through down there, that's still going on. It makes guys hungry to get out."

On that front, Townsend said he experienced "nothing major, but you knew it was there. There's still some division down there."

So how do the Steelers go over in Mississippi?

"I used to hate the Steelers," he said. "My entire family was Cowboy fans. We were brought up on the Cowboys, and the Steelers used to always beat the Cowboys, so you had to not like them."

✦ ✦ ✦

SANTONIO HOLMES heard me talking to Casey Hampton about this trip, so in the locker room Holmes walked past and whispered "Belle Glade, Florida" in my ear.

He did the same thing the next day as I was plotting Colorado with Aaron Smith. Santonio knew I couldn't swing it, so the Steelers' speedy deep threat talked about his hometown.

"There's nothing in Belle Glade. Nothing," he said. "There's no mall, there's no movie theater, there's like one grocery store." He paused. "There's no Wal-Mart, there's no Target. There's nothing there. Nothing."

According to statistics, Belle Glade is a good place to get your ass kicked. A 2003 FBI report listed the town of 15,000 as having the second highest violent crime rate in the country. Belle Glade has also ranked among cities with the highest cumulative per capita incidence of AIDS. The town sits on the southeastern shore of Lake Okeechobee in the middle of sugarcane country.

"I grew up right in the heart of where all the drugs are sold in our town, where everything went down," Holmes said. "When I was eight my mom moved us away. I still went back there because that's where all my friends were. I went back till I was about 12."

Holmes has no fear in his eyes, but an innocence remains. He's not hard-edged, but is fearless. "My dad had me in the streets with him, as a kid, all the time. I saw what was going on, but I never felt like I wanted to be a part of it," he said. "As a kid in Belle Glade, either you go rabbit hunting during the cane season or you just stand on the corner."

Holmes chose rabbit hunting. In the spring of 2007, *ESPN The Magazine* ran a feature on the young rabbit hunters of Belle Glade. Holmes and his cousin Fred Taylor, the great Jacksonville running back, were among those interviewed.

Belle Glade is called "Muck City" because the fertile soil provides the country with nearly half its sugarcane. To get to the sugarcane, farmers burn the leaves off the stalks and make a stinky, smoky mess. When the tractors harvest the cane, the rabbits run and the kids give chase. ESPN theorized that the 28 pro football players turned out by Glades Central High School in the last 29 years learned how to run in those smoky fields.

"I think it was preparation for training," Holmes said. "But I did it because that's what got money in my pocket. My grandfather would go out and hunt rabbits. Everyone knew him because he sold rabbits and sold fish from our house. That's the way we lived. We went out fishing early in the morning, or we'd go rabbit hunting early in the morning, bring it home, clean 'em up, put 'em in the freezer. People come by the house and buy what they wanted and granddad would give you your share.

"I didn't look at rabbit hunting as something that would get me ready for the NFL, but that's probably where it came from. Like I said, I think it was preparation. It prepped us for speed; it prepped us to run faster to chase the rabbits. But I wouldn't say I went out and chased rabbits for training. I started rabbit hunting when I was about six and I stopped when I was about 14, in ninth grade."

ESPN pointed out that cottontails are more difficult to catch than the standard "muck rabbit." One boy was photographed and praised for catching a cottontail.

"I saw that," Holmes said. "I saw this kid and I'm like, 'How come they never did this for us?' We were the ones that started this stuff and now these young guys are taking all the love. But I guess if you're the guy holding up the rabbit you're pretty happy."

Are cottontails tough to catch?

"They are. They're the most elusive rabbits."

Ever catch any?

"A lot of them. You didn't really chase them. If you did, you chased them with a dog or you chased them with a stick. When you chased them with a stick, and you're letting them run in a straight path, it's easier to throw that stick, break both his legs, bring him down, catch him. It was basically like a survival game. Like how we chased rabbits is how people in other countries chase animals to kill for food. That's what we had to do."

✦ ✦ ✦

JAN AND I weren't exactly walking to New Orleans, but we weren't busting our tails in the RV, either. We set up camp in Gulfport, Mississippi, just off Interstate 10. Jan unhooked my car and waved goodbye as I set off for a city I'd never seen. Jan stayed behind to catch up on his reading.

If you know Jan, you're shocked. And really, I wasn't all that excited to see New Orleans, either. Twenty years ago, the two of us would've planned a lengthy stay there, but the city ain't what it used to be, and frankly neither are we.

Herman Francois was my New Orleans contact. He's the uncle of Ike Taylor, the Steelers' left cornerback. Herman owns a beautiful home in Harvey, Louisiana. The town is southwest of New Orleans across the Mississippi River. Uncle Herman's house in a gated community was spared two years ago from Hurricane Katrina, as was most of the town of 22,000 people.

"My sister, my brother, they had trouble during the hurricane," said Herman. "God spared this house, I think, so everybody could go there till they got back on their feet, and most of them came and worked for my wife's company."

Herman and his wife Judy, or "J Lo" as she's called, fittingly, took Ike in as a small child. Herman's sister had Ike in North Carolina but struggled with finances, and once Ike visited New Orleans he didn't want to leave. So he was the first to call and offer his help to his aunts and uncles after the storm.

"He did that from his heart, Mr. Jim," Herman said. "He found them, helped them, and they will never forget that."

Herman is a few years older than me, but calls me "Mr. Jim." He tells me this display of respect and friendliness is a New Orleans staple, and he was right. This city might be in tatters, but no one walks past without a smile and a hello. I noticed this when Herman took me to the Kings & Queen Hair Salon in Marrero.

You've heard of Steelers bars, well this is a Steelers barbershop. Head barber Anthony Bell, the "A-Train", had on his Ike Taylor No. 24 jersey with a Terrible Towel in his back pocket. Taron, cutting on the right, also has a friend with the Steelers in Ryan Clark. "My dog," Taron said.

A group of guys who didn't need haircuts sat in the waiting row of chairs just to shoot the breeze. That's where I picked up an undercurrent in the room. Something was abuzz, and it was about to be my hair.

"Come on, Mr. Jim. Let's get you a little seat right here."

I resisted.

"Come on," said the A-Train. "This'll impress the ladies."

I could resist no longer. I buckled up and the A-Train dug his shears deep into the back of my head and plowed upward. The rest of the guys laughed as they watched. I just grinned and pretended to like it.

"It looks good, Mr. Jim," Herman said when it was over. "Go tell the world this is the spot. Kings & Queens, where all the players come, like you, Mr. Jim."

Yeah, that's me, a real player.

Oh, it was short all right. But I'd be on the road another month or so. And I had a hat.

HERMAN FRANCOIS raised Ike Taylor in the city's 9th Ward. The house remains, but Ike's high school, Abramson High, is shuttered. The schooling now takes place in a network of trailers in the back parking lot. Trailers also fill the playground where young Ike played basketball till the streetlights came on. The gym and pool at the facility were destroyed. Herman and I drove around the area. He showed me Fats Domino's home and adjacent office. He showed me the old house in the upper 9th Ward where he and J-Lo raised Ike.

"You have the lower 9th and the upper 9th," Herman said. "The lower 9th was considered a bad neighborhood and the upper 9th was all right, but it all wrapped around each other and it all could get pretty bad. But the flood came in and wiped everybody out. People lost everything down there."

How did Ike make it out of here?

"Ike had a mind made up," Herman said. "He just said, 'Look, I'm not going to hang with these guys. I'm going to go to school and make something out of myself.' A lot of his friends didn't make it. That's just how it goes. Some of those kids had some difficult lives."

Herman and I drove on, past the neighbors out front working, or – being that the sun was setting on a Friday – drinking. They were either moving piles of debris or looking at piles of debris. There were a few tourists driving past with their video cameras. We drove into the lower 9th Ward, which had no debris at all.

"Everything, all this, on both sides, gone," said Herman. "There were houses here. See, all this."

I swung my camcorder from one side of the street to the next – nothing but grass.

"There's a frame," Herman said as he pointed to a block foundation. "See all this, and all this, and all this here. All of this, these were residences and now nothing. See how they fly?"

Where's the rubble?

"It's gone," he said. "It's blown away. It's no more. The 9th Ward's no more. A lot of football players came from here; a lot of bankers and lawyers, too. It's gone."

EXCEPT FOR the guys at the barbershop, there didn't appear to be much of a Steelers presence in New Orleans. Herman said otherwise.

"I run into Steeler fans all the time," he said. "It surprised me at first. I remember when I came back from the hurricane. We didn't have no TV, no cable, so we had to go to this place in Metairie here and, boy, they were all Steeler fans."

Herman drove us to another bar in town — Bruno's, in the uptown section of the city – that's owned by a Steelers fan, a guy Herman figured could answer any question. But the owner wasn't working that night. The barmaid called him at home and he told the barmaid to "just ask anyone there."

"Well," I said, to Herman, "how about that guy?"

We closed in on a fifty-something with the thick neck of a football fan.

"Yes I am a Steeler fan," he said. "How can I help you?"

His name was Alden and he was born and raised in New Orleans.

Why would a New Orleans man root for the Pittsburgh Steelers?

"My first memory of the Steelers," he said, "was in 1967. That was the first year for the Saints, and the Steelers played them here and beat them, 14-10. It made me feel good that my team could give them such a good game, and I guess I was just left with a good feeling about the Steelers. And then they drafted Bradshaw in 1970. That brought the whole state into it. Then came the Immaculate Reception and I was hooked."

Alden went to the Steelers' first Super Bowl in January 1975. The Steelers beat the Minnesota Vikings, 16-6, at Tulane Stadium.

"It was the first Super Bowl in New Orleans," Alden said. "I remember they sent a guy up in a balloon. It was cold out and the balloon crashed into the north end zone. But I was there. I saw the Pittsburgh Steelers win the Super Bowl, so, Go Steelers."

IKE TAYLOR runs a website called FaceMeIke.com. He does this little palm-in-front-of-his-facemask shimmy after he makes a play. "Ike says that sooner or later, if you're a player in this league, you have to face him," Herman explained.

At Abramson High, Ike once stepped in for an injured kicker and booted a 30-yard field goal at the gun to win a game.

"He was a kicker, a wide receiver, a running back, a defensive end. He's just an athlete and he'd do whatever the team wanted him to do," Herman said.

Ike went to college at nearby Louisiana-Lafayette because his high school coach told him it'd be the best fit for him. However, Ike didn't play cornerback until his final season, and even then he didn't see much action. Opposing quarterbacks looked the other way to pick on the injury replacement for another future pro cornerback, Charles Tillman.

"He's still learning," Herman said. "What people don't understand is that Ike had no experience at cornerback until now. He's learning as he plays."

Herman explained why it's more difficult to play left cornerback, like Ike, than right cornerback.

"If you look at a right cornerback," Herman said, "a quarterback has to turn and throw over his shoulder. So, a right cornerback has a chance to break on that ball. The other way, boom, the ball's out of his hand."

Early in the 2007 season, Ike appeared to be out of the malaise that forced him to the bench in 2006. On opening day in Cleveland he intercepted a pass and had his first career sack.

"I was drinking a glass of lemonade and I dropped it. I did," Herman said.

Neither of us had dropped our O'Doul's that night, but it was still time for me to get back to Gulfport. Herman gave me a going away pep talk that went something like this:

"You've *been* to the Ninth Ward, Mr. Jim. You've *seen* where Ike Taylor grew up. You *know* Ike can come back from anything. It's like Willie Parker; you *know* these guys now and you *know* they'll never quit. You've been covering them before, Mr. Jim, but you are just now getting to know them."

Somewhere, the great David McCullough was smiling.

✦ ✦ ✦

WHAT I THOUGHT was a night game at Death Valley – (aren't they always night games?) – was instead a 1 p.m. Saturday game between No. 1 LSU and visiting South Carolina. The traffic grew thick with each passing mile before I finally arrived, late for my interview in Baton Rouge with Uniontown, Pa., native Jack Marucci.

Punch that name into an Internet search and this is what you'll learn about Marucci: 1.) He makes baseball bats for the greatest stars in the game; 2.) He's a Pittsburgh Steelers fan; and 3.) He's the LSU trainer.

Marucci might also have the world's greatest sports memorabilia collection, and he groomed what he calls a professional whiffle-ball field in his backyard, replete with grass infield, base paths, pitching mound, an outfield wall modeled after Fenway's, a scoreboard, and foul poles on top of the wall. Jack and his wife watch their kids play from seats yanked out of Comiskey Park and Cleveland Municipal Stadium. Marucci asked me to get the interview rolling because it was four hours till kickoff and there were ankles that needed to be taped. He's been doing that here since Alan Faneca was a senior.

"Faneca," Marucci said. "I remember Tom Donahoe calling me and asking me about him and I promised him he was not making a mistake because he's one of the best guards that I've seen, and he ended up taking him a week later. I'm sure it wasn't because of my recommendation, but it didn't hurt. I told him he'd be a good anchor for them."

The only other LSU player with the Steelers is Ryan Clark. Marucci compared the free safety to one of his old favorites.

"Ryan Clark was a guy who's probably more like a Mike Wagner if you want to go back, because Ryan Clark's a very smart player, like Wagner, very intelligent, someone to line guys up. He's not the biggest guy. I mean, he'll hit you, but Clark's a very, very smart, intelligent player. He was very good for us when (Nick) Saban was here. Saban had very complicated defenses so we relied on Clark lining up our guys. Clark's the type of guy who's a grinder, probably a little bit of an overachiever, and fits the Steeler mold perfectly."

Marucci has been a Steelers fan since spending his childhood in Uniontown and his summers at St. Vincent College where the Steelers train. He was thrilled to help Donahoe before the 1998 draft and was hoping to help Mike Tomlin when the two sat down for dinner before the 2007 draft.

"He was looking at some players," Marucci said. "At the time he didn't know much about Pittsburgh. He knew some, but he didn't know the fans and what exactly was involved, so we were talking about that. He understands that as long as he wins he'll be popular there. There's a give and take, but that's part of the passion of Steelers football. That's what makes it so great. But I really enjoyed talking to him. I think he's going to have great success. He's a solid guy. He's a guy's guy and that's what Pittsburgh needs."

Jack takes pride in former Steelers, like Tony Dungy, guys who have an affiliation with the team and/or the city. At his office, Jack sees them come and go.

"Fortunately we have a lot of good players at LSU and we are always talking to NFL scouts," he said. "At least a third of the guys who come through have a connection to Western Pennsylvania. In my opinion, they're your best scouts, GMs, coaches."

Dan Rooney once said there are more NFL coaches, scouts, and officials from Pittsburgh than anywhere else. Marucci already knew that.

"People don't realize the population that's out there, throughout the NFL, that has ties to Western Pennsylvania," he said. "They grew up watching the Steelers and they wanted to be part of NFL football. That's the thing a lot of people miss out on. They're transplanted all over the place. I think that's the big thing. We even have people on our staff who didn't grow up in Western PA but they like the Steelers. Our strength coach grew up in Tennessee and he's a huge Steeler fan. So what he does, he talks about them to his son. He talks about Joe Greene. He talks about Terry Bradshaw. He talks about Franco Harris. He talks about Lynn Swann. I think that's another element of it, and that's what I've seen.

"If you just look at our team, LSU, at the coaches and players who don't have Western Pennsylvania ties but who still root for the Steelers, I would say they're more America's Team than the Dallas Cowboys ever could be. And that's just not being a homer. I'm removed from Pittsburgh and I'm saying that because I see it in other people. Our players would like to play for the Steelers because it does represent a college atmosphere, they do have a winning tradition, and their football looks like it's supposed to be played. People see black and gold and they associate that with success and winning, and that's why these players would love to play for the Pittsburgh Steelers."

Jacob Hester, the tough LSU tailback, is one fan. He's related to Terry Bradshaw. And Bo Pelini, the LSU defensive coordinator at the time, is a devoted Steelers fan and it's reflected in LSU's physical play.

Before I left, I asked Jack if I should buck the traffic to snap a shot of the Faneca plaque over at LSU's Hall of Fame.

"Right now it's going to be nightmarish," he said. "In fact, I'm going to have a nightmare. It's a CBS game and these fans here are like Steeler fans. Wait till you see. It's insane."

✦ ✦ ✦

I DROVE OUT of Baton Rouge as the rest of the bayou was driving in, and eventually found Jan at a rest stop off Interstate 10. We scrubbed the love bugs off the front of the RV and then bounced our way over the swamps of Lafayette and southwestern Louisiana. We hit the Texas border that evening and Jan's mood changed as suddenly as the road surface. The distant sign for gas at $2.32 a gallon also helped. We were in such a good mood we laughed at the sign telling us El Paso was a mere 889 miles away.

"God, I love Texas," Jan said as he bumped the cruise control up to 68 m.p.h. I broke out the tea and settled in for my big Saturday night on the road.

Chapter Seven
SUNDAY AT THE HAMPTONS

CASEY HAMPTON stared at me in disbelief.

"You want to drive down to Galveston to watch a game that's being played in Pittsburgh?"

"Well, yeah," I said.

"What the *fuck* you wanna do that for?" he said.

Casey laughed, of course. He can't keep a straight face. I told him about the plans I'd already made with Willie Parker, Heath Miller and James Harrison.

"James said OK?"

"Yep."

"My mom's number is … "

Guys are figuring that if it's cool with James, then it must be all right. So I made arrangements with Casey's mom, Ivory Anderson, who invited us to Galveston, a city of 57,000 off the gulf coast of Texas, about 60 miles southeast of Houston. We drove over the causeway to Galveston Island and turned right along a row of palm trees. To our left was the 17-foot high Seawall that protected the people and to our right was the upscale neighborhood into which Casey had recently moved his mom.

Casey's brother Nassaval, his adopted brother "Sweets," his sister Sha, another friend, a girlfriend or two, and four nephews showed up for the party that kicked off at noon, or when Sweets, with his shades and gold chains, walked through the door with a wide grin.

"My grandmother gave me that name when I was my kid's age," said Sweets. "Me and Nassaval have been friends since elementary school. When I turned 15 or 16 I was living a little rough at that time and so they took me in. I'm 28 now, so she's my mom away from mom."

Sweets calls Ivory "Momma," as in, "Me, Nass and Momma got a U-Haul not too long ago and went up to Missouri City to help Casey move into his new house. On our way up there, we see this nice Range Rover. Some lady had a flat on the side of the road, and we passed by. We get down the road a little bit and I said, 'Man, let me call Casey to see if that was him.'" Sweets learned that it was Casey changing the woman's flat tire.

"This was on a Sunday, probably at about 3 o'clock, dead heat, and he got out there and helped that lady," Sweets said. "You don't find people that do that kind of stuff, especially when they've got their own stuff to do.

"He's just a good-natured kid. When you're raised right as a kid, you kind of live by life's rules. You've got to do good deeds. That's how we earn our way up to the head of the gates."

Casey warned me not to visit his old neighborhood in Galveston, where the legend of Mighty Casey was born. One newspaper had him, as an eighth-grader, fighting off two armed burglars and saving his family. The story reached Pittsburgh for the draft in 2001, when the Steelers picked Casey in the first round.

"He didn't fight them off," Nassaval said while shaking his head. "He took off running like everybody else."

Four years younger than Casey, Nassaval was on the same path in football. He was a sophomore who could squat 500 pounds, the strongest player at tradition-rich Ball High School and the starting nose guard. But he got his girlfriend pregnant and stopped playing.

Was he as good as Casey?

"Just about," he said.

What's it like being Casey's brother?

"It's great," he said. "But people ask you a lot of questions."

The room broke up. Nassaval smiled and continued talking as he watched his children playing in the pool.

"Seriously, it can't get no better than this. Casey's the friendliest person in the world. You see how big he is in Pittsburgh. Everybody loves him."

EARL CAMPBELL was already a local legend by the time Casey Hampton started playing football in Galveston. Campbell, the Texas PR department once calculated, racked up over 1,000 yards *after* contact during his senior season at UT. Those tough yards made Campbell a legend on both the college and pro levels, but the punishment exacted a toll.

"Earl's beat up, man," Casey said. "Every time I see Earl in Austin he's just out of it. He works for the university. I see him all the time and each time he seems like he's worse."

Does Casey worry about such a future?

"I don't get hit hard like that," he said. "I'm not taking that pounding. You watch me play; during the course of a game I might get one hard hit. I use my hands. My fingers and stuff might be messed up, but I don't put my head in there too much, unless I really, really have to."

Casey once dreamed of becoming the next Earl Campbell. An Oilers fan, young Hampton played running back through middle school.

"He was pretty good," said Sweets. "Back in middle school he was real fast. He just blew up one summer and got big. That was that."

Casey flashed his old style when he picked up a fumble in 2002 and rumbled 36 yards. He not only put the ball in the correct hand, he straight-armed a would-be tackler before the Cincinnati running back chased him down from behind. Thereafter, Hampton pleaded with Bill Cowher to use him at the goal line, but to no avail.

Mike Tomlin arrived in 2007 and thought it might be a good idea to use Hampton as a blocking back during a goal-line drill in training camp. The object of the defense's pre-snap jeering, Hampton stood up — without the ball — as he went through the line, and linebacker Clint Kriewaldt crushed him. Hampton's helmet turned sideways, covering half his face, as his buddies on defense howled in delight.

"That shit's a rap, man," Hampton said after practice. "Everything's hurting. I can't go in there and give my body up like that."

What about the dream?

"I've been begging to do it," he said. "But I don't want it no more."

THE 49ERS and the Steelers put their 2-0 records on the line that afternoon. Game analyst Daryl "Moose" Johnston set the tone in Galveston when he said of the Steelers' base defense, "… a key ingredient to the 3-4, the nose tackle, Casey Hampton, one of the best in the NFL." Momma – a big, sweet lady who spoke softly and smiled easily – was beaming. She turned that to a cheer when her son stuffed Frank Gore on the second play of the game. In fact, the 49ers ran between the tackles six times in the first quarter and gained only seven yards. This prompted Johnston to amend his comment about Hampton to "*the* best in the NFL." Johnston also mentioned San Diego nose tackle Jamal Williams, which struck a nerve with Sweets.

"I was watching a game last week and one of the announcers was trying to say Jamal Williams was the best nose tackle in the league," Sweets said.

"Well, he is pretty good," I said.

"Casey's the best nose tackle in the game!" Sweets snapped back.

If this game was the measuring stick, then, yes, Casey is the best. On the 49ers' first pass attempt of the second quarter, Big Hamp looped around the right guard to pressure the quarterback into an incompletion. He stuffed Gore again on the next play.

"Casey Hampton has to love that San Francisco keeps running right up the middle," said sideline reporter Tony Siragusa.

Casey Hampton's family certainly loved it. In the first half, against the Steelers' base 3-4 defense, the 49ers ran up the middle nine times for 18 yards. Meanwhile, Willie Parker had put together a 79-yard first half. On one sprint draw to the left, tackle Marvel Smith pushed the defensive end one way and hustled to the second level to smother a linebacker. Parker gained eight yards behind him. Marvel repeated the double-block on the next series. This time he was joined at the second level by Alan Faneca and Parker ripped off a 17-yard run.

Marvel owned his competition on this day as he and Parker shredded the 49ers. Then, as the running game was proving unstoppable, Ben Roethlisberger faked a handoff and threw an easy 9-yard touchdown pass to Jerame Tuman to give the Steelers a 14-6 halftime lead.

In went the Steelers; out came the smoked ribs, baked beans, potato salad, jumbo wings, mini burritos, tortilla rolls and nachos. One of the wives took a timeout to log onto a web site called drunkathlete.com. She'd heard about a photo of Casey, and there he was in all his glory: standing on a chair, shirt up over his neck, bottle in hand, upraised Longhorn salute. Kids.

The 49ers snuck an 11-yard run up the middle on their first play of the second half, but the Steelers pulled away and the 49ers would run only two more plays (for 2 yards) on Casey the rest of the way. A 50-yard interception return for a touchdown by Bryant McFadden cemented the 37-16 win and the Steelers were 3-0.

Optimism ran amok in Galveston. Ivory predicted a 14-2 finish. Sweets went with "11-5 or 12-4." Nassaval, the calm one, was so moved he predicted an undefeated season.

"Nobody will beat them," said Little Hamp. "The defense is great; we knew that. But the way Roethlisberger's playing, I don't think anyone will be able to stay with them."

✦ ✦ ✦

HOUSTON HAS a mad crush on the Steelers, too, according to Dan Ferens.

Ferens was once a star quarterback at Connellsville (Pa.) High. He negotiated contracts for the Steelers during the 1990s, and after a stint at IMG took a similar position in the Houston front office when the Texans entered the league. Ferens came back to work for the Rooneys in 2007 and talked about Steelers mania in the Houston area.

"The one thing that stood out," he said, "was the interest in the Steelers at the speeches I'd make. Every year I'd have to make speeches out in the community. They'd give them my background, and after I was done giving my little spiel the first two questions or so would always be about the Steelers — every time. It was a joke."

As Jan and I headed back up north through Houston that Sunday night, we talked about the underlying reasons for the popularity of the team. Jan's was pretty good.

"There's an ethic – hard work and hard hitting," he said. "It's an ethic that's identifiable, and I think if I were a working man in any city I would really relate to the Steelers.

"Really, I think Pittsburgh has a unique, hard-to-beat work ethic. I think anybody who was raised in Pittsburgh has that work ethic. You're expected to do your part. That's important. The Steelers signify all of that."

✦ ✦ ✦

AT THIS POINT we had some options. We could shoot into Houston, or even Austin, to sample Steelers bars. Ernie Holmes was in nearby Wiergate, but I wasn't getting any help with his number. Joe Greene's birthplace of Temple was further north of Austin, and Bobby Layne's birthplace of Santa Anna was 140 miles past that. Gabe Rivera and Bam Morris reside somewhere in this massive state, but a visit to San Antonio won the vote. Jan knew of a campground outside of town and we needed the break. After all, we didn't need to be in Phoenix for the next game until Friday. I tried to get tickets for Jan, but was told by Steelers management that none were available.

"Any other game," I was told. "But the whole world's coming to this one."

Jan didn't mind. He wanted to visit his cousin anyway. We decided on a Friday morning parting in Tombstone, which seemed symbolic enough.

✦ ✦ ✦

BACK ON THE road Thursday morning, I returned a call to Phil Kreidler. He's the Steelers' pro/college scout, a position that allows him to work mainly from his office and raise a family the way most scouts can't. Perhaps Phil misses the road a bit, because he's been interested in this trip from the start. I told him we were heading west on I-10 into West Texas.

"The roughest rednecks in all the land," he said with a laugh. He wondered whether we were nearing the spot where Bobby Layne's father had died long ago in a car wreck. Young Bobby was six years old at the time, and the legend goes that the youngster was thrown in a ditch and wasn't found till the next day. "Some say it's the reason he lived the way he did," said Phil.

I thought about the way Bobby Layne lived his life to the fullest as I sipped some nice Chamomile tea – decaffeinated, of course.

It was noon and we were already bored. Jan spotted a cop on the side of the road and figured he was bored, too. "He probably pulls people over just to say 'How 'bout them Cowboys?'"

At 3:30 p.m. we merged with I-20 on the right. The FM rock station invited us to listen to Pecos High Lady Eagles volleyball action on Saturday – "LIVE!" shouted the pitchman. While it promised to be an exciting contest, Jan said we couldn't stick around for it, but he did spot the first cattle west of San Antonio.

"If you could get a cow to eat dirt you could make a lot of money out here," he said.

At 7:30 p.m. we reached the New Mexico border. We hit the first exit, parked and raided the cupboards for food. I called my dad and reported that the sun was setting on the toughest part of the trip.

Chapter Eight
THIS DESERT LIFE

WHAT WOULD Ed Hochuli do?

That's not only an important philosophical question, it's the bumper sticker on Bird Martine's car here in Phoenix.

Bird's an old friend from home and my host for the weekend. And his answer to the question concerning the well-known NFL referee would be this:

Drive faster.

That's what Bird does, he drives faster, and so we arrived at the Arizona State University campus just in time to talk to Dan Cozzetto.

Cozzetto is to ASU what Joe Moore was to Pitt: a legend of an offensive line coach. The Steelers' West Coast scout, Kelvin Fisher, a former running back at ASU, directed me to Cozzetto to gain a better understanding of Steelers left tackle Marvel Smith.

Smith was part of Cozzetto's best line at ASU. Smith and five other future pros paved the way for a Sun Devil running attack that averaged 172 yards per game in 1999. After that season, Cozzetto left ASU to coach with old friend Dennis Erickson at Oregon State. Because Cozzetto left, Marvel also left and the Steelers drafted him in the second round.

Prior to the draft, word had leaked that Marvel had tested positive for marijuana. The Steelers asked Cozzetto about it and he convinced them Marvel was worthy of a high draft pick. Marvel eventually repaid Cozzetto by giving him his Super Bowl jersey.

Cozzetto returned to ASU in 2007 with Erickson. The team was 4-0 and on this Friday morning was finalizing preparations for its first road game of the year – at Stanford. The staff was low on time, but …

"Whatever for Marvel," said Cozzetto. "He's one of the great success stories we've had."

Cozzetto first heard about Marvel from Phil Snow, who's now Rod Marinelli's linebackers coach with the Detroit Lions. Snow was ASU's defensive coordinator at the time and told Cozzetto to head to Oakland's Skyline High School to check Smith out.

"Marvel, he didn't have a whole lot," Cozzetto said. "Mom drove a bus. His brother was in and out of trouble. I got to know him real well, as far as where he came from. When we got him he was overweight, wasn't a very good student, and so it was a challenge. We had to work right to the end to get him eligible in order to come to Arizona State."

Why recruit a guy like that?

"He was athletic," Cozzetto said. "I watched him play basketball. He was a big man at the time and he was carrying too much weight. His coach, John Beam, guaranteed that he was the kind of kid we were looking for, because he knew the kind of players I had at Cal-Berkley, like Todd Steussie and Troy Auzenne and Eric Mahlum and all those guys that went on to play in the NFL. John had never sold us a bad bill of goods, so I bought into it. Plus the fact that I'd talked to Marvel and knew how important football was to him. With his environment and how hard his mom had to work, it was a big deal to him to get her out of there and get his brother out of there."

Cozzetto introduced Marvel to the strength coach and the two formulated a game plan. Marvel began a regimented program and watched what he ate. Cozzetto then had Marvel work with a tutor on his grades.

"To make a long story short, he did everything we asked him to do," Cozzetto said. "After his first year here, he was about 280, down from 320, and he became a running fool. Athletically, he was a new man. Academically, he was on the Dean's list – 3.0 every semester he was here."

Cozzetto huddled with head coach Bruce Snyder in the middle of the 1997 season and they decided to move Smith and another freshman tackle, Victor Leyva, into the starting lineup. Soon they were joined up front by future first-round picks Todd Heap and Levi Jones.

"Levi was like a cat on a hot tin roof," Cozzetto said. "He had a fiery temper and defense didn't want him anymore. I made Levi the left guard and told Marvel to get him under control every game, so Marvel basically taught him the game. I think Levi owes a lot of his development to Marvel. Two different cats. Two warriors, but two different cats."

Cozzetto said Marvel's best performance was the 1997 Sun Bowl when he was a redshirt freshman.

"It was against Hayden Frye's last team at Iowa," Cozzetto said. "There was a big challenge between one of the defensive ends (Jared DeVries) and Marvel, since he was a young player, but Marvel destroyed him, just destroyed him, and we went on to win the game."

The Steelers obviously scouted that bowl game. In addition to Smith, they drafted cornerback Jason Simmons (held Tim Dwight to 3 catches) and defensive lineman Jeremy Staat (3 sacks, defensive MVP).

What about Marvel as a pro?

"I think he's the best in the business," Cozzetto said. "He just totally developed, but he struggled at first. I think Russ Grimm was a terrific help. Marvel always had a bad habit of putting his head in there, and he told me that Russ had him do the same things with him that I used to do. Marvel's matured, he knows his game, he knows where he's at with his body, he knows what he has to do. He's grown up so much. I had my last conversation with him last night and he said he wants to get into coaching at the high school level. I told him when he's ready to let me know."

Cozzetto coached Marvel through a second pot infraction a few years ago. Marvel paid for a hotel room in which marijuana was smoked. He took the rap for a friend and was later exonerated.

"He called me and we addressed it," Cozzetto said. "He asked for my opinion and I said, 'What are you doing? Is it that important to you to screw up an opportunity of a lifetime? That you worked so hard to get? Over that? Figure it out.'

"But he's come a long way. I remember when he came here in an old broken-down blue Camaro. He was so big he kept breaking the seats. It's funny, because I just dropped my car off over here at the dealership to have it painted and the guy said, 'How's that one guy from Oakland who always had to get his seat fixed here?' I said, 'Well, if you turn on your TV his name's Marvel Smith and he's doing rather well for himself. He's played in a Super Bowl and a Pro Bowl.'"

The hand-signed Super Bowl jersey hanging in Cozzetto's office serves as proof.

"I was flabbergasted," Cozzetto said of the gesture. "I'll tell you what, he's my favorite. He's one of my favorites out of all the kids that I've coached and sent on."

One of the favorites? Or *the* favorite?

"People ask me that all the time. There were a lot of tough guys. Mark Schlereth was a tough guy. I had him at Idaho and he played with a dislocated elbow and too many knee operations, but he beat the odds. Todd Steussie's going into his 14th year or whatever. Just say that Marvel's right up there as being *the* guy."

Cozzetto paused for a moment and nodded his head in the direction of an autographed picture of Marvel Smith. On it, Smith had written, "Cozzetto, Thanks for getting me here."

"There've been a lot of good guys that I've had," Cozzetto said. "But that's my man, right there."

OUTSIDE COZZETTO'S office, in front of a bank of elevators, stood a familiar face, but the name didn't come. Bird and I walked over and the man turned, smiled and extended his hand.

"Hi, I'm Dennis Erickson," he said, and he made comfortable small talk until his ride showed up.

"Everyone's so happy around here," I said to Bird.

"They just watched the Stanford tape," Bird said to me.

Bird's about a year younger than me, and a certified Steelers fan. But on this day he was more interested in West Virginia University. Bird studied ornithology there, I suppose, and the Mountaineers were putting their undefeated record on the line that night at South Florida. It gave Bird a sense of urgency that even Ed Hochuli couldn't imagine, and it got me to my next appointment in record time.

✦ ✦ ✦

JAKE ROSS lives in Phoenix's upscale Paradise Valley neighborhood along with the Goldwaters, the Barkleys, the Hardaways and the rest of the desert ruling class. What makes Ross different is that he's held Steelers season tickets since Three Rivers Stadium opened in 1970.

Ross was born in the Pittsburgh suburb of New Kensington, raised in Natrona, and educated at St. Vincent College and WVU. He went from a government job in Washington, D.C. to a banking job in San Francisco and then back to Pittsburgh where he and his wife, his high school sweetheart, had two children. He started a private practice in Pittsburgh and purchased season tickets. Later he took an executive position with Citicorp and moved to Rochester, N.Y., and then Phoenix, where he retired. He now spends much of his time following the everyday minutiae of his favorite team.

"I still have my season tickets," he said. "My brother uses them and I go back to Pittsburgh for a couple games and take my boys and it's boys' night out."

Until he left Pittsburgh in 1983, Jake had missed only one game. He even saw the Immaculate Reception.

"Saw it with my dad," he said. "I saw the ball passed and said, 'Oh, hell.' And I saw the ball go up in the air. When Franco picked it up off the ground I was yelling at him to run out of bounds and kick the field goal so we would win. But he kept running."

Franco picked it up off the ground?

"No. Absolutely not. I misspoke. It was clear as day," Ross said. "If my dad were alive he'd tell you the same thing."

Jake saw the dynasty of the '70s unfold from the 50-yard line, and his office overlooked Mellon Square in Downtown Pittsburgh, where football season was a five-month holiday. I asked Jake for some memories.

"I remember when middle linebacker Henry Davis got knocked out and they brought in Lambert," he said. "Friends and I wondered how we were going to win the Super Bowl with a broken linebacker. Guess what? Lambert took over the team. He was a unique rookie. I get goose bumps when I think about those times.

"Watching Oakland and the Steelers in what I call the Ice Bowl, it was freezing cold. We had garbage bags; she had a fur coat. The wind was whistling. That's when Noll and the grounds crew were accused of icing the sideline so Branch couldn't get outside of Blount. He couldn't anyway.

"And one of the fantastic things I remember about that time was that during the year those players lived in Pittsburgh and you would see them on the street. One time I walked up to Joe Greene and said, 'Great game, Joe.' It was a Monday or Tuesday, and he said, 'Well, how'd you think I played?' And I said, 'I thought you were great.' He said, 'Well, what are you doing?' I said 'I'm just going out to get a sandwich.' So Joe Greene and I went down to The Press box in Market Square and had lunch.

"Joe Greene was my favorite. You could always count on him. He got off the ball so fast it was unbelievable. As soon as the ball was snapped he was gone. He looked offside all the time but he wasn't. And I loved Ham. No one ever got outside Ham. The guy who taunted Roy Gerela? Cliff Harris? And Lambert went in and threw him to the ground? It's classic. We looked forward to going to those games. My wife, I don't think she missed a game. My boys are diehards. One's in San Francisco and one's in L.A. and they're still Steeler fans."

Jake said he's been to most of the big sports bars on the West Coast and wasn't surprised to find they're filled with Steelers fans on Sundays.

"My friend Jay owns two sports bars in L.A.," Jake said. "I have never seen such rabid fans. My son went to L.A. and indoctrinated his friends. His girlfriend was a helluva Dallas fan. She's a Steeler fan now."

In Phoenix, the best-known Steelers bars are Harold's Cave Creek Corral and the Sugar Shack, where Pittsburgh's KDKA-TV set up shop during Super Bowl week in January 1996. Jake's brother back in Pittsburgh spotted Jake at the bar during one segment.

"How cool is that?" Jake asked.

"Pretty damn cool," said Bird.

The interview was being hijacked by a couple of WVU fans who were already in tailgate mode.

"The people at these bars are a lot of people from Pittsburgh," Jake told Bird. "But there are a lot of converts because they like the brand of football."

Dan Rooney said he first noticed his team's national appeal in 1994 in Phoenix. The national media took notice at the end of the 1995 season when the Steelers played the Dallas Cowboys in the Super Bowl. What had been "Cowboy

Country" for years seemingly became a Steeler Nation stronghold overnight.

"On Friday night and Saturday afternoon, before Super Bowl XXX, we went down to Mill Street, the big street in Tempe," Jake said. "It was total black and gold. That's all there was. The Dallas people may have been somewhere else but they sure as hell weren't in Tempe.

"During the game it was unbelievable, the yelling, the screaming. I thought they were going to kill O'Donnell. I mean, we had two chances to beat them. We had them on the ropes. But that whole week this town was going crazy and it was mostly black and gold."

Jake predicted the breakdown for Sunday's game would be a 50-50 split between Cardinals and Steelers fans. That sounded high – for Cardinals fans. Jake explained.

"There are a lot of people out here who really want to see Whisenhunt and Grimm do something good," he said. "The Steeler fans here are very angry with what happened with the coaching change in Pittsburgh – very unhappy. They think it was all about the Rooney Rule. Go to the Steeler bars here and ask around. They just don't like it."

We'd passed one Steelers bar on the way to Jake's house. It welcomed fans with a huge sign on the roof of the building:

You're in Steelers Country

From a businessman's perspective, is that wise? Jake laughed. "A lot of people here do not like the Bidwills, and thus don't like the Cardinals," he said.

Jake also answered this question: Could Phoenix, with all of its Steelers fans, host a proper victory parade should the Steelers return in February and win the Super Bowl?

"If you want one, I'll get you one," said a guy who just might have the connections to get it done. "If they win the Super Bowl, I'll get you a parade here. I'm serious."

✦ ✦ ✦

WE MUST be in Steelers Country. That's what the sign on top of the Celtic Curtain told us. Three flags jut from the front of the building: The Irish flag flies on one side, the American flag on the other, and a Steelers flag sails in the middle.

Is that legal?

"I don't know," said owner Kevin Mannion. "My crazy Irish cousin works here. He put them up there."

Mannion, 36, grew up in West Mifflin, Pa. His bar is adorned with more modern memorabilia than most Steelers bars, and there's the Irish angle: A Jerome Bettis-autographed No. 6 Notre Dame jersey is mounted next to a poster trumpeting Gaelic football. It's a place the younger Rooneys could call home. A framed quartet of *Steelers Digest* covers made me comfortable as well.

"I've read your columns in there," Mannion said. "They don't suck."

Thanks. I think.

"I went on quite a run a few years ago," he continued. "My buddy and I got tickets to the playoff game in Indianapolis. We had so much fun there we had to go to Denver. And then he ended up going to the Super Bowl."

How much did it all cost?

"About a thousand bucks."

Not bad.

"And my marriage."

Oh.

So, why not appeal to the locals and make this a haven for Cardinals fans?

"That's possibly the worst question I've ever been asked," he said. "That would be the equivalent of opening a Jacksonville Jaguar bar, so, no. Nobody likes the Cardinals out here. I guarantee you it'll be 80-20 Steelers fans at that game Sunday."

✦ ✦ ✦

BIRD WOKE UP Saturday in a funk. His Mountaineers had lost the previous night, so he thought it might be a good time to call Todd Lawson.

This act of self-loathing could only mean one thing: My interview with a Cowboys fanatic was at hand.

Born in the West Texas badlands, Todd and half of his family moved to Phoenix back when Roger Staubach was the Cowboys' quarterback. Todd's favorite player was Walt Garrison. That's like saying your favorite Steeler is Rocky Bleier. It's to be respected, yet Todd has problems that needed to be worked out.

"I've just always hated the Steelers," said the 45-year-old who drove to the interview in his new Corvette.

He's the vice-president of a financial start-up. He has a wife and daughter. Yet, he has an anger deep inside that can't be sated.

"My dad didn't care too much about any sport but football," he said. "He was a good ol' boy raised in Lubbock, Texas, so he taught me at a real early age. But he and my mom divorced and I've grown up my whole life in Arizona. We really didn't have a team to follow, so, yeah, I became a Dallas Cowboy fan."

Todd's not a typical Cowboys bandwagoner. Steelers fans can respect him for that, too.

"Well, I have to admit I respect that about Steelers fans," he said. "Steeler fans are very passionate, very loyal, whereas it seems like a lot of the Cowboy fans are jumping on the bandwagon and jumping off, jumping on and jumping off. It seems to me if a guy tells you he's a Steeler fan, he's got some pretty deep roots."

It seemed that Todd's hatred of the Steelers could really just be love.

"Uh, no," he said. "My dad is old and pretty sick and he still hates Pittsburgh. He hates them probably worse than I do, so, no, because my hatred has been passed down to me and I won't be changing teams anytime soon."

Todd spends much of his time as a Fantasy League commissioner. The position affords him the opportunity to e-mail propaganda to the rest of the league.

"I give my polluted vision of what's going on," he said. "Stuff like, 'What a great day for America. America's Team's back on top after beating the Chicago Bears.' I just do it to get them upset."

Todd sent out a particularly hate-laden e-mail after the Steelers beat the Seahawks by 11 points in Super Bowl XL. He took the opportunity to blast the game's hard-working officiating crew.

"That was bad," Todd whined. "But it wasn't as bad as the Super Bowl that was 35-31. That was the game when Jackie Smith dropped the touchdown and the pass interference call."

Didn't the Steelers have an 18-point, fourth quarter lead in that game? Wasn't that a natural ass-kicking that only became close late?

"Yeah, I know," he said. "I guess it's just that the Steelers beat my team. I didn't like it and I didn't like them."

Todd, of course, attended Super Bowl XXX in Tempe. The Cowboys were favored by 13 points over the Steelers, so Todd walked in with great expectations.

"For me it was just a given that the Cowboys were going to win," he said. "They were heavily favored and they had their triplets and the whole deal. I thought it was going to be really fun to get the ghosts out. But the game was tight and the Steelers were ballsy with the onside kick and they were only down three until what's his name, O'Donnell, threw his second timely interception."

Dallas had touchdown drives of 18 and 6 yards in the second half thanks to Neil O'Donnell's absurd interceptions to cornerback Larry Brown. It allowed the Cowboys to hold off a Steelers rally and win 27-17.

"The Cowboys certainly didn't play all that well," Todd said. "And here I was hoping to forget the ghosts of Super Bowls past. Next thing I know I'm on the edge of my seat and I'm thinking, 'Ain't no pep rally here.' Eventually it got to the point where I was thinking, 'Oh, my God. If this happens again …'"

✦ ✦ ✦

THIS TOWN can't hold all these Steelers fans. The dust cloud was visible from Cochise's mountain stronghold overlooking Tombstone. I noticed it right before I met Al Kenna.

Al moved to the desert in 1980. He's a Steelers fan who wants to become a Cardinals fan because of Ken Whisenhunt and Russ Grimm. Al said that's the reason he believes Cardinals fans might actually outnumber Steelers fans on Sunday.

"I went to training camp and Russ Grimm was chewing out one of his linemen for something," Kenna said. "An older lady said, 'I can't believe the way that coach talked to that player,' and I said, 'Hey, lady, that's football. That's Steelers football.'"

Steelers football rules the desert these days, and their fans packed into Harold's Cave Creek Corral on Saturday. Harold's is a 100-year-old biker bar located 33 miles north of Phoenix. It's out in the wilds, where the coyotes call the shots. We arrived at 8:30 Saturday night to find the ranch crawling with Steelers fans. Men on the street directed us to the upper-level dirt parking lot. Even the patio surrounding the two-storied bar was packed. A row of Harleys lined the side of the building and each sported Steelers flags. I tried to find the owner, but the guy raking in the cash at the front door didn't know where he was. Inside, the action began to percolate. The chant "Here we go, Steelers, here we go!" was being led by a man wearing number 69. Why number 69?

"Maybe he's an Ariel Solomon fan," I said to Bird.

"I think that's David Opfar himself," Bird said.

The chant went up again, this time with more vigor. And I began to tremble.

"I gotta go," I said, and Bird agreed. We needed something to eat, so we left at 9 o'clock.

The Celtic Curtain wasn't quite as packed, but it was busy with black and gold. Most watched Arizona State finish its 41-3 rout of Stanford to put the Sun Devils at 5-0.

"Steelers fans are adopting ASU," I told Bird.

"So am I," he said. "I need a new team after last night."

He needed a girlfriend, too, so Bird began chatting up a lovely over at the next table. I, of course, struck up a conversation with Ed Pons.

"The last 10 years my main focus has been to travel about the country and take in as many Steelers games as possible," Pons said. "That's why I'm here today."

Born in the Pittsburgh suburb of Greensburg and raised in West Newton, Pons had just driven in from his vacation home in Utah.

"The biggest sports bar in the city of Salt Lake City is a Steelers bar," he said. "I thought it might be a Broncos or 49ers city, but there are more Steelers fans in the state of Utah than any other."

Ed owns a Steelers bar in Bradenton, Florida. He was merely a customer when it opened 18 years ago.

"I made a bet with the owner," he said. "Whoever brought in the most fans in the first two weeks could have control of the big screen TV. Well, the first couple weeks there were like 200 Steeler fans there, 10 Dolphin fans and about 10 Buccaneers fans, so it's now a Steelers bar, the biggest sports bar in Bradenton. It's called Fanatics."

My cell phone rang. It was a frantic call for me to come to a bar in Scottsdale; there were people I needed to talk to. One was Dan Ciarochi, a Steelers fan from Uniontown who now lives in Dallas. We watched the Psychobilly Rodeo Band finish their set before walking outside to chat.

"At the game in Dallas in 2004 it was about 40 percent Steelers fans," Dan said. "The next morning on sports radio they were saying that at the end of the game it sounded like a home game for the Steelers. They were talking about it all day. Randy Galloway said there were a thousand Steeler fans at the main gate who couldn't get in, and that Jerry Jones wheeled out a couple of big screens for the Steeler fans who couldn't get tickets. Randy Galloway said that on the radio. There were busloads of Steeler fans from Mexico."

Dan's friend Jeff Mills once traveled from Long Island to Miami for a Monday night game. The night before the game he visited the hotel where the Steelers were staying.

"My neighbor made me this great Steeler flag and sure enough Mr. Rooney signed it," Jeff said. "As we were standing on the sidewalk talking, Dan Ferens came off the elevator. He has cousins in Uniontown and sure enough I went out with his cousin in high school. Now I've got Mr. Rooney and Dan Ferens talking on a sidewalk just like we are. They're the greatest people in the world. You can't sell that. You can't fake that. How do you not love it?"

✦ ✦ ✦

THE HOSTILE takeover of the Cardinals' stadium never materialized, on or off the field. Estimates put the Pittsburgh attendees at less than 50 percent and the Cardinals won the game, 21-14. And it wasn't that close.

The Steelers took the lead with an early 3rd-and-26 Ben Roethlisberger prayer to Santonio Holmes, but didn't score again until 1:54 was left. The second touchdown pass from Roethlisberger to Holmes was too late and the Steelers had their first loss of the season.

The Steelers played without Hines Ward and during the game lost Troy Polamalu, Casey Hampton and Chris Hoke. They also – for about the 114th consecutive game – played without their special teams. Pittsburgh kid Steve Breaston returned a punt 73 yards for a Cardinals touchdown – their first TD return in 14 years – to give the Cards a fourth-quarter lead. They followed it with a Steelers-like 7-minute, 15-second, run-heavy drive later in the quarter to close the door. Instead of kicking a 41-yard field goal to go up by 10, Ken Whisenhunt gambled on 4th-and-1 – with two Steelers nose tackles injured – to win the coaching battle and the game.

"I didn't think twice about it," Whisenhunt said after the game. Family and friends surrounded Whisenhunt at the Cardinals' tailgate party. He couldn't say much more, but the guy next to him, special teams coach Kevin Spencer, could.

"Tell your reporter buddies thanks for ignoring me before the game," Spencer said with a beer in his hand and a smile on his face.

Spencer was the Steelers' special teams coach from 2002 to 2006. He too had ridden off into the desert to coach with Whisenhunt, but his presence was lost in the pre-game media fuss being made over the head coach and Russ Grimm. Spencer was assured that Breaston's TD return wouldn't allow reporters to ignore him after the game.

"I guess that's better," he said.

The tailgate was Grimm's idea; it's something he did in Pittsburgh for the sake of camaraderie. And he hasn't looked this healthy in a long time. Grimm lost weight since leaving Pittsburgh, but not his sense of humor.

"Genie, genie, give this baby a weenie," he said as he rubbed the pregnant belly of the wife of Todd Haley, the Cardinals' offensive coordinator.

"He used to be a ballboy for the Steelers," Russ said by way of introduction. "He's Dick Haley's son."

Russ offered free license to his cooler, but it held only three beers.

"This builds a little camaraderie with the players," he said. "And it lets the traffic clear. No matter how the game turns out they don't have to walk out, get in the car with the wife and a bunch of kids, and listen to all the bullshit. It gives everybody a chance to just relax."

The tailgate is part of an attempt to "change the culture" surrounding Cardinals football. But can the new coaches "change the culture" of the hordes of Steelers fans in Arizona?

"It's a big market that hasn't been winning," Grimm said. "It'll change. Once we start winning, those tickets won't be available."

He sounded confident.

"I haven't been anywhere where I don't win," said the guy with four Super Bowl rings. "Losing is not an option. We sat there the last two weeks and listened to people say, 'Well if you play good you may stay close with Pittsburgh' Well, you know what? If they play good, they may stay close with us. That's the mentality you've got to get and you've got to keep pressing the issue. It's a different type of attitude, believe me. You treat guys right, they're going to play for you. The guys in Pittsburgh played for me. The guys out here are going to play for me. It's an attitude."

I told Grimm that he looked healthy, but I didn't say what I was thinking, that being rejected by the Steelers may have been the best thing to happen to him. It's obviously motivated him. *Only three beers in the cooler!?*

"I like it here. I'm getting used to it," he said. "I lost about 20 pounds since I got here. Christ, you don't have a choice with this heat."

Was this a circle game?

"It really was," he said. "I looked forward to it."

On top of the world?

"No. I mean, we're 2-2. After the game I wished them all the best of luck. I hope they all stay healthy. They're a bunch of good friends of mine. I want to see them have success. I hope the next time we meet will be out here in February."

✦ ✦ ✦

HEARTFELT HUGS dominated the pre- and post-game action, but the announcing crew of Greg Gumbel and Dan Dierdorf made a bigger deal out of a hug that never was between Ben Roethlisberger and Ken Whisenhunt. It allegedly stemmed from Whisenhunt telling a reporter that, in retrospect, the Steelers did rush Roethlisberger back too soon from his motorcycle accident. Ben took umbrage, but told me this:

"I got along just fine with the old staff. A big deal gets made when I say that I have more input with this staff. It doesn't mean I didn't like the old staff or they didn't like me. It just means I have more input with this staff. I'm up in the meeting rooms more and they have a trust in me that the other staff had every right not to, because I was such a young guy. Now that I've grown and they've seen that I've put the work in, that's why they have the trust in me. As for the big deal they made about Whis and me not shaking hands after the game, well I was disappointed. We lost the game. I was off the field. People don't realize that I texted Whis after the game. We talk many times. We talk quite frequently, but I didn't go up and give him a big hug right after the game. I'm a competitor and am hurt after a loss. I had texted him a message as soon as I got on the bus. People don't know about that, so they make a big deal about it and say whatever they want to say. That's fine. And people made a big deal about me saying that I like Tomlin and I didn't like Cowher, but I never had a bad relationship. I feel honored and privileged to have played for a Hall of Fame coach in Coach Cowher."

"The thing Kenny did well," Bruce Arians said of Ben's early years, "he simplified things for the young quarterback, but he made it look complicated. To do that, he had to put a lot on the offensive line, with the calls and all, and to tell you the truth that's when we'd run into problems at times getting everyone on the same page."

Chapter Nine
CALIFORNIA STARS

TROY POLAMALU was in the middle of a classic Polamalu performance against the Cardinals until he tore cartilage in his ribs and had to leave the game.

In the first half, the Steelers' All-Pro strong safety: forced a fumble on the second play of the game; knocked the quarterback into throwing a short pop-up that was dropped by James Harrison; clocked a wide receiver to force an incompletion and a punt; and recovered a fumble and made a frenetic 13-yard return that didn't end until four Cardinals gang-tackled him.

The injury may have occurred on the interception return, but no one was sure. However, the impact of Polamalu's loss was clear.

Another key loss occurred when Steelers nose tackle Chris Hoke — in for injured Casey Hampton — was smacked in the helmet by the Cardinals' left guard in the fourth quarter. Hoke's head snapped back, but he continued into the backfield where he butted heads with runner Edgerrin James, whose own head snapped back. Hoke went straight to the ground and temporarily lost consciousness. He came to and wobbled off the field with the help of the training staff.

In the locker room Hoke seemed fine. He at least knew his dad's address in Los Angeles.

"Make sure he tells you the funny stories," Chris said. "Otherwise he'll get all serious with you."

◆ ◆ ◆

ED HOKE looks, sounds and acts just like his son: a down-to-earth people person who smiles easily. Ed has five other children and a wife named Kim, Chris' stepmom.

If it takes a neighborhood to raise a child, Ed Hoke figured he may as well build the neighborhood. He's a general contractor and built all five houses that form the cul-de-sac of his upper middle class street in Fountain Valley, an Orange County suburb about 35 miles south of Los Angeles.

"I don't panic until I know all the facts," Ed Hoke said of watching his son drop like a rock the previous day.

"When Chris was little he got hit by a car," Ed said. "He was running across the street. This was when he was 5 or 6. Chris was running across a semi-busy street and he hit the middle island with his foot. The car thought he was going on through, but Chris went back and the car hit him. Paramedics came; we went running over there. You don't want to panic until you know everything. There was a big group around him and I looked over and he looked at me and said, 'Daddy,' and I knew he was going to be fine. So, yesterday, same thing. He went down, clump, so you're wondering for a moment, and then when he brought his arm around you were relieved. I anticipated a stinger and that's probably what it was."

I relayed Chris' plea that Mr. Hoke tell me funny stories.

"That was one," he said.

Getting hit by a car?!

"Not a funny story, but that was one story," he said. "Funny stories of Chris, let's see … when I think back about all the kids I don't think of funny stories, I think of life-changing stories. There are stories where whatever happens had an impact on their life, rather than something they did that was embarrassing."

OK, bring it.

"Chris is a member of the Church of Jesus Christ Latter Day Saints. We're all Mormons, so one of the things you do growing up is to serve a mission. It's something you look forward to for a long time. When they turn 19 it's a choice that they make, to serve a mission for two years. I went to Italy on my mission. Chris was in Brussels, Belgium. So it's a big deal and he was right at the point: He was a senior in high school and was ready to start looking at colleges. Knowing he would be going on a mission, he sought advice from his high school coach, and the coach told him, 'If you go on a mission, you'll ruin your career. No teams will take you.' He was being recruited by UCLA at the time, so he had a decision to make: Would he follow what he believed and knows is right for him to do, or would he listen to his coach?

"So it came time for one of those father-son sit-downs, and we went out. As I did with Chris, I would always take him somewhere to eat, so we went to a restaurant and had a plate of ribs and a steak; whatever, give me the whole left side of the menu. We were eating and talking and it was a real serious conversation because it was a time when he needed to make the choice for himself. So we talked and a little bit later he made the decision he was going on the mission, so he lost UCLA. But his whole life his dream was to play for BYU. That was the natural thing. But next he went to visit the University of Utah and the stadium's up on the hill and you can see the scoreboard, or the display, from downtown Salt Lake, and up there it flashed 'Chris Hoke' with his number. It'd stay for a minute and a half. Then you'd go into the locker room and see his Hoke jersey. Even at that point he wasn't sure about the choice. Ron McBride was the coach for Utah and they really wanted Chris, and he said to Chris, 'You need to ask yourself these questions: If you got hurt, where would you want to continue your education?' In his head, Chris answered BYU. 'And number two: Where does your heart lie?' Well, BYU, again. Wrong questions, Ron.

"Still, Chris came away from there really indecisive because the hype had really pumped him up. On the way home, he talked about it. I said, 'Well, you still have to visit BYU and then you can make up your mind.' We went to BYU and that was the deciding factor. Now that was a life-changing decision for Chris. It was really a moment where Chris decided for himself what direction his life was going to take.

"I think keeping the church, keeping his belief and his religion in the forefront of his decision, from then on, has been tremendously beneficial in his life. I think that's been an asset to him as he was going into the NFL. As they learned more about Chris and who he was, one of the great selling points was his character, his teachability, his willingness to learn, his following-direction-without-attitude, his work ethic. Those were big things at the beginning with the Steelers. There were several comments made about his dedication and that stems from following what you believe is right."

HOKIE, AS HE'S KNOWN in the locker room, made the Steelers as an undrafted free agent in 2001. He started a family and began saving as much of his minimum-wage salary as he could.

Chris' breakthrough came in 2004, when he replaced an injured Casey Hampton and started 10 regular-season games and two playoff games. The Steelers finished with the league's No. 1 defense, primarily on the strength of their No. 1-ranked run-stopping unit, of which Hoke was the new anchor. Ed Hoke made the trip to Heinz Field for the Halloween game against New England in 2004. It was his son's first start.

"We didn't know which side of the ball would be introduced," Ed said. "All of the sudden, Aaron Smith was first, so it was the defense. And then you hear, 'And starting at nose tackle, from Brigham Young University, No. 76, Chris Hoke,' and he came charging out with that loud pounding music. I looked over at his wife, Jaimee, and everybody had tears. I had tears. It was just that moment. Ever since he was a little boy he'd dreamed of this and here he was starting for the Steelers."

Mr. Hoke fought back tears as he re-told the story.

"I get emotional, sure," he said. "There's no greater joy than to see your kid succeed. There isn't. And there's no greater sadness than to see him fail. As parents, that's what you go through. So that moment, everything was right. I still get goose bumps thinking about it."

✦ ✦ ✦

UP IN HOLLYWOOD, Paul Sams took a lunch-time break from his duties as the world's king of PC gaming. Sams is the chief operating officer of Blizzard Entertainment, the group that turned "World of Warcraft" into a cultural phenomenon. Blizzard has turned out six of the top 11 PC games of all time and every game it's launched since 1995 has been named Game of the Year. The company has churned out 11 No. 1 "hits" in a row and Sams is responsible. He's also been a Steelers fan since the age of 5.

"The first play I saw of football my whole life was the Steelers versus the Vikings in the Super Bowl and the touchdown pass to Larry Brown, the tight end," Sams said. "It was love at first sight."

After Sams' business fortunes skyrocketed, so did his attendance at Steelers games. He first made it to Three Rivers Stadium to watch the Steelers edge the Patriots 7-6 in the 1997 playoffs, and he had tears running down his face. "I kept telling everyone it was like I was going to Jerusalem," he said.

Sams also attended the Super Bowl in Detroit and scalped a ticket in the Steelers' family section, where he got to know Ike Taylor's mom.

"She was standing next to me after the game," Sams said. "I was on an aisle. I took her hands and congratulated her, told her her son had a great game. I told her that it must feel incredible to know her son sealed the game with his interception in the fourth quarter, and I asked her how that feels. She's got my hand and she started saying, 'I don't know. I can't put it into words …' and she just went down, fainted in my arms."

SAMS GREW up in Ventura, just north of L.A., and went to college at Cal-Santa Barbara as a business major. He hoped to become an architect, but began working in an educational software company his junior year. That company eventually acquired Blizzard, and Sams was moved over to head-up that portion of the company.

Blizzard now has three main franchises: Warcraft, Starcraft, and Diablo. The most popular is "World of Warcraft," a massive multi-player on-line role-playing game. It's the world's largest subscription-based game of its kind, with over 9 million paying subscribers in 2007. The game grew into such a hit that several movie studios bid for the rights to the story. Warner Brothers sent the head of Legendary Pictures, Thomas Tull, to Blizzard to negotiate a motion-picture deal.

"One thing that's not very typical in Hollywood," Sams said, "is for the executives to actually take a road trip somewhere out of Hollywood to meet with someone, and these guys all drove down to Irvine, which is a hike, especially since they had to sit in four hours of traffic. So it was a nice signal."

Blizzard employees wear an ID tag fastened to a lanyard, and Sams' "is a Steelers lanyard that I wear every day." So when Tull, another lifelong Steelers fan, walked into the room, he noticed Sams' Steelers lanyard. Tull thought he was being set up, that this was being done to gain his favor. He was a bit miffed before realizing it was no set-up.

"We ended up hijacking the first 45 minutes of the meeting talking about the Steelers," Sams said. "I've got executives from my company and he's got his top executives all there, but it was like there was no one else in the room except me and Thomas. All we were talking about was the Steelers.

"Honestly, we joke about it now, but really what pushed us over the edge, to feel like we could have a trust, was because we had this bond of being Steelers fans. Everything after that came very easy because there was an immediate trust."

The result will be a 2009 motion picture based on Blizzard's "Warcraft" game property. Will it contain a hidden salute to the Steelers?

"We talked about that," Sams said. "We joked about having a character called Lambert. It's a fantasy-based movie, so you really couldn't have the Steelers' logo emblazoned anywhere, but we've talked about putting in some character names. People who know we're both Steelers fans would watch it and know it, but the normal moviegoer, it's not going to take him out of that kind of fantasy the game creates."

THOMAS TULL read my e-mail and immediately left the room.

"The Steelers are the only topic that could get me out of a board meeting," he said.

Tull, 37, is a lifelong Steelers fan who's produced the movies "300," "We Are Marshall," "Batman Begins," "Superman Returns," and the new blockbuster "The Dark Knight," among others. He's the CEO of Legendary Pictures, which signed a 25-movie contract with Warner Brothers in 2005.

"It's a dream come true," he said. "Every day I pull into the Warner Brothers lot and see that water tower and I realize I'm making movies with them."

Not all was cheerful on this day in Hollywood. Tull is a diehard fan who takes Steelers losses personally, so he was a bit cranky a day after the loss to the Cardinals in Phoenix.

"As a former athlete I was never a good loser," he said. "I hated to lose worse than anyone I know. And now, when they lose, especially when they've got a good thing going and it's somebody they should beat, that to me is the worst. I am not proud to say it but it has a material affect on my mood for the rest of the week until they play again."

Tull grew up "very, very poor" in Binghamton, New York. Raised by a single mother, Tull made good grades and excelled in sports so he went off to play football at Hamilton College, where he studied law and played wide receiver. He had become a Steelers fan the same day Paul Sams had – January 12, 1975.

"The Steelers vs. the Vikings in the Super Bowl was the first football game I remember watching," Tull said. "I remember that year, and then the next year when they won again, and I remember thinking these guys – Lynn Swann, John Stallworth, Terry Bradshaw – were from Mount Olympus. They were unbelievable and tough, and ever since I was a little kid I've loved the Steelers and would wear the jersey, my little yellow wrist bands, all that stuff. Binghamton is right on the Pennsylvania border. I'm not sure that had anything to do with it or not. A lot of Giants and Bills and Jets fans are in the area, and I used to get so angry because I'd be forced every week to watch those teams and read about the Steelers later. That's why I was very pleased when Direct TV came up with their Sunday Ticket."

Bradshaw is Tull's hero. As a boy he'd emulate the unique way Bradshaw threw.

"It didn't work out very well," said Tull, who spoke for all of us once-young hopefuls who tried to throw with their index finger on the point of the ball.

Tull didn't play football after college, but he came out of Hamilton with plenty of business savvy. He bought and sold a small Laundromat chain and learned how to raise money. So, being "a total film geek," he took his game to Hollywood.

"The way Legendary happened," he said, "I was at dinner socially in a group with the chairman, at the time, of MGM, and we were talking, talking about how movies got financed and I had some ideas, and I said, 'Well, if you would do things differently …' and he said, 'Well, if you're so smart, how would you do it?' And I guess about $1.6 billion worth of financing later we have Legendary Pictures."

Since he's married with two children, Tull doesn't get involved with the stereotypical Hollywood lifestyle. His "partying" consists of sitting in his TV room once a week with his wife and the Steelers.

"I don't answer the phone, my Blackberry's off, there are no meetings or screenings planned, and I don't watch the game with friends," he said. "It's a very intense, very focused experience for me. It's just a part of what makes me happy. There's nothing better than watching the game. And because I'm so enamored with the personality of the team, I have not missed a snap since 1993 or '94."

There was a visitor once.

"When I had a house in Atlanta years ago, Takeo Spikes, who lived on my street, wasn't in the playoffs so he came over to watch the game, and he turned at one point and said, 'You're more intense than we are on the field.'"

Why the Steelers?

"What I love about them," Tull said, "is it's hard to name another team in any sport with the continuity the Rooneys have provided. And it's not just the organizational stability and class, it's about intimidating defense, running the football, playing Steeler football. You look at other organizations and the continuity of the Steelers is pretty amazing and I just love what they stand for, and the fact that when the guys put on the uniform there's a responsibility that goes with that. The city loves the team so much. I think it's like nothing else in sports."

THE PREMIERE of "Superman Returns" remains one of the biggest moments in Tull's life. When the credits rolled up, the sense of arrival smacked him in the face. And then he took a trip to Pittsburgh to show "We Are Marshall" to Dan Rooney, Bill Cowher and the Pittsburgh Steelers and he experienced a similar feeling.

"That was truly being on hallowed ground," he said. "I sat at the Chief's desk in the trophy room and was a complete geek about it."

Tull makes speeches in front of thousands of people and said he's never been nervous, but he was nervous when he met Dan Rooney.

"Because he's been a constant since I was a little boy," Tull said. "And when I went into his office, I turned to my wife and said, 'This is the coolest thing ever.' He was nice and gracious and we've talked numerous times since then and he's just as advertised. That day was something I won't forget. It was a real privilege."

Tull's favorite all-time Steelers are Bradshaw, Jack Lambert, Greg Lloyd, Carnell Lake, Dermontti Dawson and Jerome Bettis.

"Bettis was just a force of nature, the way he could move and carry the team," he said. "There's nothing better, to me, than getting into that fourth quarter, up 10, and it's just Steeler football. You just hand the ball to the Bus and pound it and you watch the other team get demoralized having to tackle the guy.

"Right now my guy's Hines Ward. For me, as I look at each era as to what defines the team, Hines Ward is not only getting the most out of his talent, he's one of the toughest guys in the NFL. His blocking is unbelievable and he's just got that attitude. He has fun playing the game. He will be a Hall of Famer and should be. He just personifies toughness. That's one of the reasons I tune in every Sunday. A guy like that, fans will remember for years. Every Sunday he laid it all out on the line. I'm a huge Hines Ward fan, and Troy Polamalu obviously is a human missile all over the field. I had a chance to spend some time with him when I was in Pittsburgh. I always heard he was soft spoken, and when you sit with him in person he really is unbelievably soft-spoken and quiet. I thanked him for everything he does and how important it is and how much it means to people all over the country. We talked about him being from Southern California, and I told him if he ever wants to go to a premiere or tour the studio, let's do that. That's one of the things I told Mr. Rooney and the team: 'I don't know if any of this matters, but look, I don't care if you're recruiting a free agent or trying to sign one of the guys, if they're out here and they want to come to a premiere or do anything, if I can help in any way I will.'"

PAUL SAMS explained why he and Thomas Tull can't slide Steelers propaganda into the "World of Warcraft" movie, but Tull needs to make 25 movies by 2010. Couldn't he make one about his favorite team?

"At some point I'd like to make a smaller film or a documentary and talk to the guys about what it means," he said. "There are things like that, projects I'd love to do on that front."

What about the players themselves?

"Absolutely. I talked to a couple guys on the team when I was up there who said they wanted to be in a movie. Now, we put a lot of money on the line, so it can't be a vanity moment that's ridiculous, but if it's within the confines of the story in a cameo or the right thing, the appropriate feel, I'm going to do that. There's a movie we're developing that's kind of an all-quadrant big movie and the main character has a parrot. The parrot's name is Jack Ham. "Believe me, there's always a way I'm looking to put the black and gold in there, without being obnoxious about it. But, yeah, if it makes sense I'm happy to do it."

Chapter Ten
THE POLAMALU TRAIL

IT'S A DIFFERENT place, Southern Oregon. It unfolds from the border via the I-5 roller coaster through the mountains. Up the road a bit is the Oregon Vortex. It's billed as a phenomenon where objects roll uphill or balance at odd angles. A few more miles north is a place called Tenmile. It's 20 miles west of the Interstate and 67 miles from the coast. It's the place Salu Polamalu visited as a man and wouldn't leave.

A native Samoan, Salu met his future wife Shelley in Hawaii and the two journeyed to Tenmile to meet her parents. Salu loved the climate, the atmosphere, the serenity, and of course Shelley, so he stayed.

Salu and Shelley had three sons: Joe, Darren and Brandon. The Polamalus didn't have many neighbors on their country road in this town of 539. They moved into a double-wide trailer next to Shelley's parents, who'd moved to Tenmile from Texas. The kids loved to fish in the creek behind the house with Salu, and they played basketball all day and night on a court he cemented to their land. They put hoops at both ends of the court and installed a set of lights that kept the game going till exhaustion. The kids built a press box that still stands like a patchwork tree house. It's a thickly wooded area, mountainous and green, much like Western Pennsylvania, only more: more trees, more mountains, more rain. It's greener, has fewer people, and better roads.

Into this setting came a boy from the violent streets of the Los Angeles suburb of Santa Ana named Troy Aumua. His father had left him soon after he was born. His mom had to work to support five kids. Troy fended for himself much of the time. His cousins from Oregon would visit on occasion, but the first time he returned their visit to Tenmile, Troy refused to leave. He eventually took his mother's brother's last name and Troy Polamalu became the next phenomenon from Southern Oregon.

TROY POLAMALU is the most challenging interview in the Steelers' locker room. Perceptions aren't allowed. Some days he'll tease reporters and say things like "I went out with another woman" just to see who overreacts. Here's a quick interview I had with Troy in preparation for my visit to Tenmile:

What was high school ball like?

I played tailback in high school.

How good were you?

I play safety now.

You wanted the ball against Indianapolis in the playoffs at the goal line, didn't you?

Oh, yeah. I definitely wanted the ball. I wish I was a running back still.

Weren't you bugging Cowher to get the ball?

We've always kind of joked around, and I ran a couple scout-team plays and I knew a couple calls on the offense, just the ones that I like. USC was one of the few colleges that only recruited me as a safety.

So why did you go there?

USC? Compared to going to Washington State or another school like it?

OK. How good was your high school team?

We were all right. My junior year was my best year. We were unde-feated and ranked No. 1 in the state. We had our first-round bye and in the second-round we lost. We were an extremely, extremely small town. I remember our first practice in preparation for the playoffs, a lot of the guys missed it because it was the first day of hunting season. It's that small of a town. My family was one of the few minorities that lived in that area. It's definitely a different lifestyle. You're talking about living in the middle of nowhere, you know, where there's two miles between each house, farms all over the place. When I came from California to there it was kind of a culture shock.

Were there problems for you as a minority?

There were. There were, definitely.

Any bitterness?

No, not at all. It kind of adds up to my whole experience of my life. I think I've been very blessed. I think I can really sympathize with a lot of people growing up in an inner city; I can sympathize with a lot of people growing up in the south with racial persecution. So I think it's really added to my outlook on life in general. It's blessed me in different ways in that I can sympathize with a lot of different people.

Were you a hunter?

I was always playing sports, but I did go out a couple times. I remember sleeping in the back of the truck and my uncle asked me to open a beer and I opened it up. He had shaken it up while I was sleeping. Dumb little hunting tricks like that they played on me.

Do you hunt now?

Oh, no. I fish every once in a while, but that's about it.

Is Tenmile an interesting place to visit?

Yeah, definitely. There's a place where there's some weird magnetic point where you can put a marble on a hill and it will roll uphill. People are in awe. They have shows about it on the Discovery Channel. They have a wildlife safari right in the city where I went to high school, which is like a Jurassic Park where you drive and they shut a gate and there are lions. You could roll down a window and pet a lion if you wanted to.

What do you remember about Santa Ana?

My mom worked so I was basically on my own. I'd stay out till 12 or 1 in the morning. I'd go out late at night with 15 cents in my pocket and walk a half hour to get some candy. I loved candy so much my front six teeth were black. But I'd walk down the middle of the road so no one could jump out at me.

Did your instincts tell you to stay in Oregon?

Not really. I just fell in love with the place – so green. Horses, cows, I'd never seen anything like it. Also, I always enjoyed my cousins whenever they'd come to visit.

"HE CRIED and cried and cried," said Shelley Polamalu.

She's Troy's aunt who became his mom.

"They came up to visit and he didn't want to leave, didn't want to leave, and it was the end of July and I told his mom to come back and get him on Labor Day weekend. So Labor Day came and he didn't want to go. He never wanted to go back. His mom didn't come up, so we went down there on spring vacation to see them all and he was so afraid we were going to leave without him that he wouldn't unpack his little suitcase."

Troy was enrolled in Tenmile Elementary School and so he asked Shelley – an administrative assistant in the school district – if he could take her last name. "He's gone by it ever since," she said.

And the transition?

"I'm sure he'll tell you it went well," Shelley said. "He had seen his older brothers and friends have problems, gang related, drug related. It's all down there. Troy's direction? He wasn't headed anywhere. He couldn't even play sports because he didn't have anybody to get him there. His mom and dad were split. He got up here and saw how uncomplicated our lives are here compared to what he knew."

"When you get to their house, you'll kind of understand," said Jason Dickover, the athletic director at Troy's alma mater, Douglas High School. "Troy could just get outside and play on acres and acres and not worry about anything."

When Troy entered fourth grade, his oldest "brother" Joe was away at Oregon State, where he played linebacker. Darren was in Douglas High and Brandon was in middle school.

"My younger brothers spent a lot of time with Troy," said Joe Polamalu, a guidance counselor at Douglas. "He was a young kid who just really kind of fit right into our family. So many of the games we were playing we made up in the yard and he kind of fit right there. With the old man (Salu) it's pretty simple to understand. We all walked that tightrope making sure we did what we were supposed to do, and Troy followed suit. He took care of school. He was respectful at other people's homes. We all got along pretty good. Darren and Brandon pretty much took him in and made him a country boy for a while."

The elementary school, now closed, stands next door to the family's church – Tenmile Methodist – and the community ball fields. Troy loved baseball but he couldn't see the ball.

"We found out he was blind," said Salu.

Troy's coach at the time approached Shelley and asked if Troy ever had his eyes checked. "He's blind," the coach said.

"But he hits the ball," said Shelley.

"He feels it coming, or hears it," said the coach. "He doesn't see it. Do you realize how much better he would be if he could see the ball?"

So Shelley took Troy to the eye doctor, who confirmed what the coach had said. "He's almost blind," the doctor told Shelley, so she bought Troy contacts in the fourth grade and he's worn them ever since.

Troy began playing football in the fifth grade. His best friend Erick Stookey and his best friend's dad, Curt Stookey, a lifelong Pittsburgh Steelers fan, coached the local little league team in nearby Roseburg. It was tackle football, and Troy scored a touchdown on one of his first plays.

"He jumped up and he was smiling," Shelley said. "He looked at us and he was just so happy."

But Salu wasn't so happy. "Don't you ever do that again," Salu told him. "Don't celebrate."

That year, the worst team in the league became the best. The team sensed what was coming the first time Troy played.

"By about the end of the first quarter," said Curt Stookey, "those kids, who'd never won a game, were really starting to feel like maybe they could play football. It was a big turnaround for that whole team. It was the same thing in basketball."

Opposing parents complained when Troy's youth basketball team beat their kids, 40-1.

"People wanted to know who those jerks from Tenmile were," said Curt's wife Kerri. "People thought they were dragging kids in from everywhere."

"I was trying," Curt said with a mischievous grin.

"They just dominated," Salu said in his distinct Polynesian accent. "Sometimes they yelled, 'Take that kid out! You guys score enough points.' There was one guy, he was asking me, 'I hope you're not bringing more Polamalu from California.'"

ONCE AS A CHILD, Troy went out with two friends and was told to stay away from the field that held "the mean bulls." But Troy went to the field and the bulls chased him up a tree.

"He ended up with 12 stitches in his head," said Shelley.

"He's been up a tree more than once," said Curt. "We were pheasant hunting. He and my son were kind of like my dogs, and as dogs they weren't that good but they could point. But somebody's bull got out and put them up a tree. They never even told me the bull was coming till they were up the tree. I just left them there."

The Stookeys own Treats Cafe, a coffee shop/restaurant they opened early on this particular day for a group interview. Older brother Joe was asked about the shaken can of beer on the hunting excursion.

"Troy was probably with Uncle Jerry," Joe said of Shelley's brother. "He was in the wrong pickup. You don't go to sleep with Uncle Jerry around."

JOE POLAMALU went to Oregon State on a football scholarship, one he accepted because the school promised he could also play baseball. But he tore up his knee playing football and jumped into coaching soon thereafter.

"I'll never forget dad calling me," he said. "Troy must've been in junior high in flag football, but my dad said, 'You've got to watch him, man.'

"Now, he could run with us when he was 10 years old, but I remember that junior year when I came back and helped coach. Some of that stuff, I can remember it like it was yesterday. His moves, his sidesteps, it was almost effortless. You just don't see that stuff, and nobody's seen that around here for — I don't know if they've ever seen a guy like him. I had seen some athletes up at college, and I came back and saw him and knew he was the real deal."

Tenmile hadn't seen anyone like Troy Polamalu, but he's actually the third NFL player out of the tiny town. Dennis Boyd played on both lines for the Seattle Seahawks from 1977-82, and Josh Bidwell broke in with Green Bay in 2000 and is still punting for Tampa Bay. But Douglas couldn't make the playoffs until Troy came along. What was he like on the field?

"One time he had a penalty for too hard a hit, or something, and I'd never heard of that," Joe said.

"It wasn't a blow to the head or anything," said Jason Dickover, the AD. "It was, 'Personal foul. You hit the kid too hard.'"

"I used to cringe when I saw a quarterback throw that lazy pass over the middle," said Joe. "You do not want to do that because you'll see a blur coming through there. He was quite a safety."

Troy's football skills took a backseat to his baseball skills in many minds around Tenmile. In fact Douglas High recognizes Polamalu – and Bidwell, for that matter – in its Hall of Fame as a baseball player. A switch-hitting outfielder, Troy brought 16 scouts out to one game. Douglas coach Rod Trask remembers Troy's tryout at Dodgers Stadium.

"He really did well," said Trask. "He was already signed to USC but I thought they'd draft him anyway. I was really surprised they didn't. They were coming in for cross checks and all that kind of stuff."

"He could cover any ground that needed to be covered in the outfield," said Dickover. "And any ball he hit to the left side of the infield was a single. They weren't going to throw him out."

Troy once hit a home run that the folks at Douglas say is still orbiting the planet. He'd dropped a fly ball in center field during an American Legion game and came in to lead off the next inning: Pow! To the moon.

"I always thought baseball was going to be his sport," said Dan Bain, a TV sports reporter from Roseburg. "I thought, well, he was a good football player in high school but he was probably too small to play major college ball. I thought he really had a chance to play pro baseball."

"Yeah, we all kind of thought that," said Dickover.

"And that was my thought and prayer," said Shelley. "Please, baseball, because I already lost one son's knee to college football. It's a brutal sport."

IN THE spring of 2007, Troy made a pilgrimage to Mt. Athos on the coast of Greece. Mt. Athos is the center of the Greek Orthodox Church, the religion to which Troy converted. His wife Theodora studies the religion but wasn't allowed on Mt. Athos.

"A female hasn't walked there for a thousand years," Troy said.

Troy spent his time there in meditation with the monks and came back refreshed and called it one of his great thrills. Those who've seen him bless himself before every play might understand the joy Troy takes in his spirituality.

"It was always there, but never spoken," Shelley said.

Jason Dickover remembers when Troy first discussed religion with him.

"I was driving a van to a tournament down in Medford," said Dickover, then an assistant basketball coach. "We were taking the boys out to the buffet after the game to eat, and I was driving my van and one of the kids said 'Jesus Christ' or something like that. And I said, 'Hey, you guys knock that off. I don't want to hear that.' And pretty soon the quiet voice from way back was Troy, and he said, 'Coach Dickover, do you believe in God?' I was like, whoa, this is a little heavy for a post-game discussion. And of course I'm driving and I look in the mirror, and I said, 'Yeah, Troy, I do.' And he said, 'Well what do you think about …' and he started up a discussion then. That had to be his sophomore or junior year. The rest of the drive to the restaurant, we talked about God and where He belongs in our life. It wasn't the typical post-game discussion you have in a van full of teenage boys."

Fans and reporters wonder how Troy mixes the violent world of pro football with the quest for spiritual transcendence. Dickover heard Troy raise his voice only once at Douglas.

"Actually, it was one of the saddest days in Troy's high school career," Dickover said. "It was the day Salu had the heart attack."

Salu suffered a "non-damaging" heart attack in 1999, but Troy didn't know it was "non-damaging" then. He just knew it was a heart attack. "He didn't want to go play his basketball game," said Shelley. "Salu made him go."

The game was to be played the next day and Troy spent the night in the hospital with Salu and didn't get any sleep.

"I didn't expect Troy to show up, but he did," said Dickover. "We talked a little bit. He was so heavy-hearted, so sad. He was just not Troy. And we got over there to Bandon and there was an incident in the game. Again, he stole the ball late in the game and he went in, dunked the ball, and this little freshman from Bandon, who didn't know any better, undercut him and Troy ended up landing hard on his head and his shoulder. I know it scared him, and when he got up the whites of his eyes were all I saw. He was going for it. I got out there on the floor and it was hard for me to hold on to him. He was close to out of control at that time. He wanted to do something. That was the only time I'd actually come close to seeing him lose it."

Salu has since rebounded, as has Troy. His skirmishes are minor at worst. Steelers fans expected a Polamalu eruption in 2006 after running back Larry Johnson tackled him by the hair during Troy's interception return. But Troy bounced up from the ground and pointed skyward.

"My mind was above," Troy said later. "My mind was on God then. I was praising and thanking God for a gift like that." He cradled an imaginary football and again gave thanks.

THE HAIR. A young Samoan walked past the Douglas football field as Shelley Polamalu and Jason Dickover were showing me around campus. The young man's name was Isaiah Taylor, cousin of Jacksonville Jaguars guard Vince Manuwai, and he was on his way to practice. A Samoan who'd just moved into the school district from Seattle, Taylor is a big fan of Seahawks LB Lofa Tatupu.

"Without Lofa and Troy Polamalu, the NFL wouldn't be the same," Taylor said.

Why Troy?

"He represents our people, the Samoans, with his long hair," the teenager said.

Troy hasn't cut his hair since 2000 when he was at USC.

"He always had it cut as short as possible here," said Dickover. "You'd be lucky if you saw one little curl on the back of his neck."

"This curl stuff just started his junior year at USC when he had concussions and didn't know where his barber was anymore," Shelley said.

She noted the look of disbelief on my face.

"That's what he said. He didn't know where his classes were. He had to have somebody take him to classes and he said, 'I have to forget about haircuts.' He'd call me several times a day and ask me the same questions during that period. He didn't have any memory. He had three or four (concussions) that year and only missed a month. He was recovering and said, 'Maybe I'll leave my hair to cushion my helmet more.' He didn't get another concussion until last year, a mild one. That was his first one with Pittsburgh, so I don't mess with it."

What does Shelley think of the long hair?

"I'm getting used to it," she said. "If he cut it now he'd probably have five million people coming after him with shotguns. It's kind of become his trademark. It amazes me that old women love it, but my brother, he is such a redneck. He hates it. He almost doesn't even like Troy anymore, honestly, just because of his hair."

That would be Uncle Jerry, the beer-drinking hunter. He probably enjoyed Larry Johnson's tackle in 2006. What did Shelley think of the play?

"I thought it was pretty interesting," she said. "Not just tackling him, but pulling him back up and hanging him in the air for a while. But I liked Troy's reaction, which was no reaction. It was first class."

AS A BASEBALL player, Troy Polamalu was named to the Oregon All-State team twice, but only once as a football player. He injured his kidney his senior year and Douglas didn't make the playoffs. The big year was his junior year, when he made his name as the Douglas tailback.

"The first time I saw him," said Dan Bain of KPIC-TV in nearby Roseburg, "he scored five touchdowns and had two called back."

Joe Polamalu — like most of Troy's coaches since — was mesmerized by Troy's speed and aggressiveness on defense when he joined the Douglas High staff for

Troy's junior year. The rest of the town preferred to watch Troy run – like his ping-ponging interception return three days before against the Arizona Cardinals.

"He was literally untouchable when he got the ball on offense here," said Dickover. "He'd just run all over the field, kick returns and punt returns and everything. It seemed like we spent too much time on defense."

Dickover recalled one particular run Troy made in which he was "ahead of the pack by about 30 yards." The only player close to Troy was his team's tight end, who'd never scored a touchdown. Troy turned around and handed him the ball. The teammate scored easily as Troy finished the run as a blocking escort.

"The crowd just went crazy," said Shelley.

The crowd went crazy many times that year. Douglas made the state playoffs for the first time but was eliminated after the aforementioned hunting party had decimated practice that week. Was it a factor?

"Hunting still is huge here, but I think probably more so then," said Joe. "When you've got half the lineup gone it makes it tough. But a lot of those guys were pretty good about it. They loved the game, too. It wasn't like we shut down practice."

"All of our linemen were big into that," said Dickover. "That may have been the last real hard-nosed football group we had here. They'd knock you down and make you like it. Troy was the superstar on the team but he had a lot of complementary parts that went with it, the line in particular."

Joe Polamalu was fast – as any major college player would be – but he wasn't Troy fast.

"I don't know if we ever knew how fast he really was," Joe said. "I don't know if you can measure that game speed."

Where did Troy get the speed?

"His Uncle Kennedy was pretty fast. He clocked out at a 4.3 or 4.4, which amazed me for his size. The old man (Salu) had pretty good speed, too, when he was chasing us."

BASKETBALL WAS, according to Dickover, Troy's "fun sport" because it offered him a break from the football/baseball recruiting wars. Dickover was an assistant then, the head coach now. Troy's head basketball coach at Douglas was Steve Fisher.

"Troy brought athleticism to the game," Fisher said. "He would put pressure on the ball, get the rebound, lead the break, finish it, that sort of thing. He was unselfish. I BEGGED him to shoot the ball. I couldn't get him to shoot much but he made everyone around him better."

Was he a good shooter?

"Marginal," Fisher said. "But I wasn't afraid to ask him to shoot. He'd lead the team in scoring at times but a lot of that was athleticism."

The leading all-time scorer at Douglas is Erick Stookey, Troy's best friend who's now raising a family in Cleveland. Even though Douglas had no one taller than 6 feet, the two friends developed chemistry on the court that paved the way to a 20-win season.

"My favorite memory of Troy on the basketball floor was actually our first home game his senior year," said Dickover. "Erick stole the ball and threw it ahead to Troy and all 5-11 of Troy dunked the ball and it really kind of broke open the game for us. We had a capacity crowd and it just went nuts. I looked at my assistants in disbelief. Then I looked up in the balcony and Salu, a huge man, was doing a little Samoan tap dance up there. I couldn't hold it in. I had to start laughing."

"We were at a 16-team tournament down in Medford once," recalled Fisher. "We get to the finals to play a team that had blown everybody out. They were loaded. It was a parochial school and we were not a large school. They were loaded, nobody shorter than 6-foot. We were outmanned at every position. I think they scored the first 13 points. We called timeout. I remember during the timeout saying, 'Stick with the program. Stick with what we're doing. Maybe we'll get back in the game.' That sort of thing. Well, anyway, the next time the ball comes down the floor, we're fronting the post and they lob over the top to their 6-7 guy and he's on the block and he turns and he's going to lay it up. Troy covers down from the point and this kid turns like it's an everyday lay-up. Troy slaps it up into the seats. And then all of a sudden everybody on our team, me included, thought, 'He's on our team and guess what fellas? You're in for a ballgame right now.' And that's what happened. They became a little deflated and our kids got all puffy and everybody elevated at that moment and guess what? We had a halftime lead and were within a point with a minute to go. We lose the game but we would've been blown out. That one moment right there changed the entire face, color of that game. It just elevated everyone here. That's the one I remember the most."

THE SUN peeked in and out of the rain clouds on this Wednesday in Tenmile, Oregon. KPIC's Dan Bain said, "This is real Oregon here. It's raining and the sun's out. We need a little hail mixed in with it."

"Yeah, pretty soon we'll get that, too," said Shelley.

Shelley, by my estimate, is in her 50s. She's pretty and slender with a keen eye and alertness about her. In fact, she probably gave my visit more attention than it deserved since I'm sure I wasn't the first reporter to come through asking questions about Troy.

Out of respect for Shelley, several businesses in the area welcomed me on their outdoor reader boards. She left no stone unturned. I was provided access to just about every one of Troy's coaches, the local sports reporter, and all available family members (except Uncle Jerry) and friends. Troy's football coach had moved to Montana, but I had access to …

… the current football coach at Douglas, Rick Taylor, who left the school before Troy and came back after. "You should see some of the stocks I bought," he joked of his timing.

… Troy's woodshop teacher, Jim Anderson. "Troy made a lot of beautiful projects, but I think he used woodworking mainly as an escape. In high school he would come to the woodshop where he just got lost in his work and forgot about what was going on in the rest of the school."

… the current principal, Kevin McDaniel, a former coach at a nearby school. "I've been in Southern Oregon my entire career and I've seen two athletes – Troy and Danny O'Brien, the decathlete – who were remarkable." McDaniel added that: "Troy is very much involved in our center for educational partnerships – disabled students, kids with Downs syndrome, mental retardation, autism. He sneaks into town and that's one of the first places he goes, down to visit that program."

… and some of the current players. Isaiah Taylor was one. David Ingram is another. I asked David if Tenmile is the kind of small town from which teenagers hope to some day escape. "Some people say that," he said. "But it's really nice out here actually. You're away from everything, the city life. It's nice being out in the country."

Standing outside the school that day, I couldn't doubt David Ingram. The spectacular view from the Douglas Trojans' stadium reminded me of the first day of my trip, when I stood at Honaker High stadium and looked out over Heath Miller's hometown.

"We hosted a big track meet here not too long ago," said Dickover. "An opposing coach looked out at this view and said, 'This is the most beautiful place I've been.' It's one of those things we take for granted."

SALU POLAMALU grew up in Samoa playing soccer, rugby and cricket, but he moved to the states when he was hired to perform at the New York World's Fair in 1965 as a fire knife dancer (a dance Troy, Darren and Brandon later perfected). Salu was spotted in New York by Royal Hawaiian and was hired to perform his Polynesian dances in Hawaii, where he met Shelley.

Salu has five brothers and four sisters spread out from American Samoa to Florida. His brother Kennedy coaches running backs for the Jacksonville Jaguars and another brother, Aoatoa, played nose tackle for Penn State's 1986 national championship team before settling in Pottstown, Pa.

Salu was a highway maintenance man for the Oregon Department of Transportation before becoming a surveyor and project inspector for ODOT. He received his certification from Umpqua Community College and has spent the years since his heart attack exercising and watching his diet. On this early October day, Salu invited me into his new Ford diesel pickup truck to visit some of the sights before meeting the rest of the gang at Treat's Cafe.

Salu, what do you think about the Steelers this season?

I'm excited. When Bill Cowher left I had questions but I'm very impressed with Tomlin. I like his attitude toward things and the way he treats the player and his seriousness. He doesn't baby them. I like that part of his character.

What about Troy?

Well I like what I saw this last game. He's coming out and he was flying like the old days. When he comes out and makes those plays, I thought wow. It's a matter of staying healthy, but he looked like he was playing with that reckless (laughs) … when he makes those hits I said, whoa.

Does the injury concern you?

When I talked to him he assured me that it's sore but he will be fine.

When did you know Troy would make it in football?

Right out of high school. When I saw him play in high school he was like a man against kids. He was just a standout athlete. This whole community was so impressed with him. He was just everywhere. His speed stood out.

His brother said you were a big reason for his character.

Well like he always say, I'm a disciplinarian. All the four boys, I don't separate them. Once he moved in I just say all four are my boys. I don't tolerate that rah-rah-rah type of thing. Play the game like it is and be humble. Give the ball back to the official. Everybody knows who scored. It's something I am so against when I see that, the pounding of the chest. Come on. Everybody knows you made a good play; when you pound your chest and all that you're just showing off. So that's something I absolutely just don't ever want to see. Just play the game the right way.

As a fan of football, thank you.

(Laughs) I enjoy games when they are played right and played with class. Maybe just a little celebration, but when you overdo it I don't like it. They say games are getting longer, well that is one thing they need to get rid of.

What do you like most about Troy's game?

Aggressive. I like his style of playing. He's aggressive and moves on. Make the play and walk away and make another play. That's what I've always told him, just go out, button up your mouth and do what's good.

Like the interception reversal against the Colts in the 2005 playoffs?

Yeah. That's a really good example of what I tried to teach him. That just showed what Troy is. He never complained. They had a camera on him, when they come out, the decision to make was not his. He just put his helmet on, never complained, and went right back onto the field. To me that was an example of a gentleman. Let the officials and all that do the talking, which they did, and later they said they made a mistake.

What's your most proud moment with Troy?

The proudest moment I had of Troy is when he asked my wife, 'Can I use the Polamalu name?' And my wife said, 'Yes.' There's no explanation. All the boys and me, we are all Polamalu. For such a young kid to ask for that, to be part of my family here, that, to me, will always stand out.

Do you ever make it into Pittsburgh?

The last time we were there they played the Jaguars about a year ago. It was lost on the interception, the game Maddox was playing. They would've won the game by running down the field and kicking the field goal. What I really enjoyed when I was there, I drove from Pittsburgh to see my brother in Pottstown. We flew to Pittsburgh, had a room at the Hilton and we were a week early so we went to see Ao and his family in Pottstown. He used to play for Penn State. He's my youngest brother. They beat Miami with Testaverde when they played for the national title. He was a nose. Ao Pola. He's a pretty wide boy, about 5-11. He was a fullback when he got there."

Salu turned off the main road and into a parking lot.

"This is Tenmile Store. Shelley's brother used to own this and he sold it and retired. There's the little post office and this is it. Tenmile is not much. When Troy was at USC, he always told everyone he's from Tenmile, Oregon. Well, Jim, now you see it. No stoplight, nothing. But this is highway 42. It takes you to the coast. It's almost like you're going down highway 30 in a small little community outside Pittsburgh. That's what I did. I took that old road. I was in no rush, just stayed right on the old road. Got in a little town, got a hotel, had dinner. I stayed there. Next day we got up and we drove again.

Are you a small town guy?

Yep. I am.

Both you and Troy fell in love with Tenmile. Why?

I like the greenery. I was in New York for a year, in Queens, New York, when I was 19. I was 190 pounds. I said, 'Wow, too many people.' And then I lived in Hawaii and then L.A. and San Francisco, and I just wanted to get away from the crowd. When I came here I just said, 'Oh, my God. This is what I've been looking for.' The weather is excellent. It's a little warm and a little winter. The fall and spring are just gorgeous. I like the change of seasons.

Kind of like Pittsburgh?

That's what I was just about to say. When we were in Pittsburgh the leaves had just started turning. It was gorgeous.

That's why Troy likes Pittsburgh, isn't it?

I think that's a reason. The area's very similar with the hills and the green. Look, there's a beautiful rainbow. OK, this is our little gathering place.

LOVE THE big family morning sit-together. It's a cheerful childhood memory, probably because they were always wrapped around cheerful events, like a wedding or graduation. Well, that's pretty much the scene here today at the Stookey's Treats Café. Shelley brought Troy's family and friends and the stories flew fast and furious:

Jason Dickover: Right now, this is Steeler country. There've been a lot of people converted to it because of Troy, but I grew up with friends of my family and there was a pretty strong Steelers contingent going on already. I'm used to the Steeler fans around here. There's a sports bar here that was first opened by a Raiders fan and he got a dish to get all the Raiders games. But now there's a huge contingent that goes there and they have the Steelers game on every week.

Shelley Polamalu: Joe wanted to be Lynn Swann when he was little. I had to buy him the whole number No. 88 uniform.

Big Shot Writer: *Joe told me all his friends wanted Jack Lambert "and his missing teeth" for president. He said it was kind of weird when Troy signed with them.*

Curt Stookey: I've been a Steelers fan since I was a kid. It was the uniform that did it for me. But when Troy signed it gave me an excuse to finally go to a game there. We flew back to watch Buffalo two weeks ago and there were a lot of people from California and Oregon on the plane going to watch the game. We had to go to Georgia for a layover and they were picking up more fans. We were pretty amazed by that.

Kerri Stookey: We expected to be the only Steelers fans on the plane. What was more amazing was the game and seeing all the people wearing the No. 43 and the Polamalu Power banner. It's amazing that such a quiet kid from this small town can touch so many people.

Salu Polamalu: Quite a few guys come in on Mondays and sit around and talk about the game. It's Oregon, Oregon State, Steelers here.

Does everyone in Tenmile know each other?

(All laugh.)

Or is this group here the town of Tenmile?

Salu: Used to be a lot closer. There are quite a few new people moving in.

Shelley: Kerri, tell a story about what it's like in here all the time.

Kerri: Every day, especially after a game, everybody has to rehash everything. I hear a lot of the same stories over and over again (slight laugh). It's just that Troy gives a lot of hope to a lot of people. You're here and there's not a lot. You basically become a teacher, work at the school, or you work at the mill (in Roseburg). There's just not a lot, and for young kids, having three pro players – Boyd, and then Josh and then Troy – it's just kind of incredible. And of course Troy is the No. 1 and everybody wants to know him. They might've just passed him on the street or went to school with him and never even spoke to him, but they know him. Everybody has a Troy story. A lot of them are cute and some of them I just get really tired of hearing.

Shelley: And some of them aren't even true (laughs).

He couldn't have done much wrong, could he?

Rod Trask: The only time that I really had to reprimand Troy, we were up north for a baseball tournament. This was summertime. We had just checked into a hotel and their room was up about three stories. We played the next day, so I went out to eat with the coaches, and we came back, went into the lobby, and the person at the check-in calls me over. 'We've got some problems here.' Of course, I didn't know what to expect because they were great kids. They never

(LEFT) *My partner for the first half of the trip, Jan Jones, poses with his baby, The Dutch Star, a 35-foot RV.*

(BOTTOM LEFT) *A portrait of Steelers legend Bill Dudley greets students as they enter his alma mater, Graham High School, in Bluefield, Virginia.*

(BELOW) *Doug Hubbard, coach at Honaker High, with the sign that renamed the street circling Heath Miller's former high school.*

(LEFT) *Bill Archer on the site of the former North-fork High football field. The defunct West Virginia prep powerhouse turned out former Steelers defensive lineman Tom Beasley.*

(RIGHT) *The fellas at Kings & Queens outside New Orleans: Herm Francois (left), Anthony (barber) and Taron (right). The "player" in the middle is me.*

(BELOW RIGHT) *LSU trainer and Steelers fan Jack Marucci stands with the pride of his collection: a helmet signed by the Steel Curtain.*

(BELOW) *Herman Francois raised his nephew Ike Taylor in this house in New Orleans' Ninth Ward.*

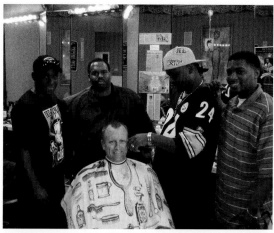

(ABOVE) *Ike Taylor's school in New Orleans, Abramson High, has been shuttered since Hurricane Katrina.*

(RIGHT) *Partying on game day with Casey Hampton's crew. From left, sister Sha, mom Ivory, buddy Sweets, aunt Diane, brother Nassaval.*

(LEFT) *Denise Miller holds the first masterpiece drawn by her son, famous artist and Steelers tight end Heath Miller.*

(BELOW LEFT) *Clinton, N.C., lawyer Greg Griffin in front of a shot of the record Super Bowl run made by favorite son Willie Parker.*

(BELOW) *Willie Parker Sr. and his necklace with the words his son once told him: "We're going to make it."*

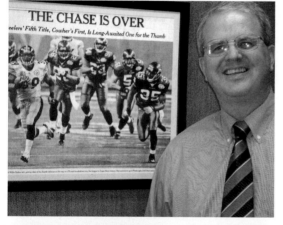

(ABOVE) *Lawrence Timmons' family in front of their home in Florence, S.C.: mom Audrey (left), sister Lakendra, and dad Lindsey.*

(ABOVE) *Greg Lloyd, former linebacker of the Pittsburgh Steelers, smiles in his office in Fayetteville, Georgia.*

(RIGHT) *Jan and I pose in front of The OK Corral in Tombstone, Arizona. Jan left me for dead in the legendary capital of the Wild West.*

(BELOW) *My Phoenix host Bird Martine (right) with Cowboys fan and Steelers hater Todd Lawson and his new Corvette.*

(RIGHT) *Arizona State University tight ends coach Dan Cozzetto, Marvel Smith's former mentor, in his office inside Sun Devil Stadium.*

Steelers fans in Hollywood, Thomas Tull (left) and Paul Sams, gave the world "The Dark Knight" and "World of Warcraft," respectively.

(TOP) *The Celtic Curtain, a Steelers bar with the best jukebox in Phoenix; and insert photos of fans at Harold's Corral in Cave Creek, the Steelers bar play-by-play man Bill Hillgrove calls "the best in the country."*

(RIGHT) *Leaders of the NW Steeler Nation Fan Club, Shawn Bell (left), Walt Cavalier (center) and Will Kohn, orchestrated the Seahawks-Steelers game day party at Hooters in Tacoma, where (below right) Steelers fans celebrated and (bottom right) Seahawks fans cursed.*

(BELOW) *Treats Café welcomed me to Tenmile.*

(RIGHT) *Inside, the family and friends of Troy Polamalu gathered. First row center is Rod Trask with Curt Stookey on the right. In the back, from left to right, are Troy's sister-in-law Anna, Jim Anderson, Kerri Stookey, Jason Dickover, Salu and Shelley Polamalu (2nd from right).*

(LEFT) *Ed and Kim Hoke show off their Lombardi Trophy and a Super Bowl jacket with every autograph except Duce Staley's. Look closely below at the very first autograph Hines Ward signed as the Super Bowl MVP.*

(BELOW LEFT) *Salu Polamalu on his couch in Tenmile. Those are his sons in the photo on the wall, with young Troy in the middle.*

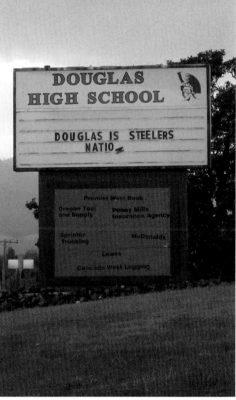

(ABOVE) *The woodworking shop at Douglas High in Tenmile, Oregon, where Troy Polamalu sought shelter from the storm.*

(RIGHT) *Douglas High School near Tenmile welcomed me to their corner of Steeler Nation.*

(RIGHT) *Sa-mantha Wexell with a snowball in Winter Park, Colorado, on Oct. 15. Below she's with her mom, my beautiful wife Lydia.*

(BELOW) *That's my reflection in the photo of a Byron "Whizzer" White plaque at Colorado University. White was the first great Steeler.*

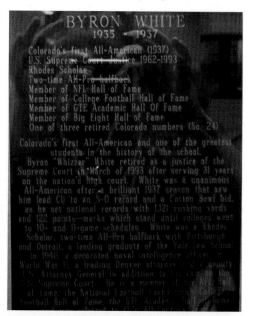

The Brett Keisel jersey and journey are chronicled here in the Greybull High School trophy case.

Former Steelers center Ray Mansfield commemorated in Kennewick, Washington.

(ABOVE) *In a bar in Greybull, Wyoming, with high school Coach of the Year Mike McGuire (left), and Brett Keisel's in-laws, Patty and Steve Johnson.*

(LEFT) *Brett Keisel and future wife Sarah before the junior prom.*

(RIGHT)) *The statue of former Steelers draft pick Johnny Unitas stands in front of the Football Museum at Papa John Stadium in Louisville.*

(BELOW) *The Joey Porter Locker Room at Colorado State University.*

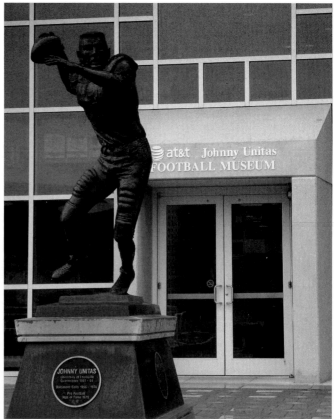

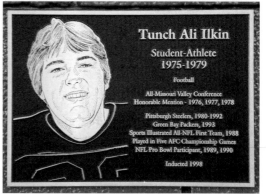

(ABOVE) *A Hall of Fame plaque of former Steelers Pro Bowl right tackle Tunch Ilkin at Indiana State University's Hulman Center. That's John Mellen-camp playing in the background.*

(ABOVE) *Annette Slack and Carey Davis Sr., parents of Steelers fullback Carey Davis, inside Annette's downtown St. Louis office.*

(LEFT) *Young Aaron Smith in the bottom row with his Steelers gear. He's with brothers Dave (left), Kevin (right) and Steve (center, also in black and gold).*

(ABOVE) *Dale Dodrill and his wife Jan hold a sign the grandkids brought to Heinz Field to honor the Legends Team.*

(ABOVE) *A few years later, from left to right, Kathie, Dave, Shelby, Kyler, Steve and Brandon Smith. Shelby's brother Daniel just missed the photo.*

(ABOVE) *Steelers center Sean Mahan, when he was the left tackle at powerful Jenks High, holds the Oklahoma state championship trophy.*

Ben Roethlisberger and Miami
University president David
Hodge retire Ben's college jersey.

(ABOVE) *Anthony Smith's brother Donny
and great uncle Homer pose outside the
family home in Hubbard, Ohio. At right,
Donny is No. 50 with brothers Matthew (1)
and Anthony (10) on the Hubbard Middle
School team.*

(ABOVE) *A Rooney family photo with the Chief in the middle and great granddaughter Katey Rooney to the left. Katey again, at the top, with the Chief and cousin Clare Galterio. At top right, it's Hollywood actress Kate Mara in a Gilles Toucas photo.*

Dallas Cowboys owner Jerry Jones secretly adores the Steelers. Here he's caught wearing his Steelers cap.

(ABOVE) *A man tidies up around the project building in the South Bronx where Steelers right tackle Willie Colon grew up.*

(RIGHT) *Homer Smith's backyard, where his "son" Anthony mowed the grass every Saturday.*

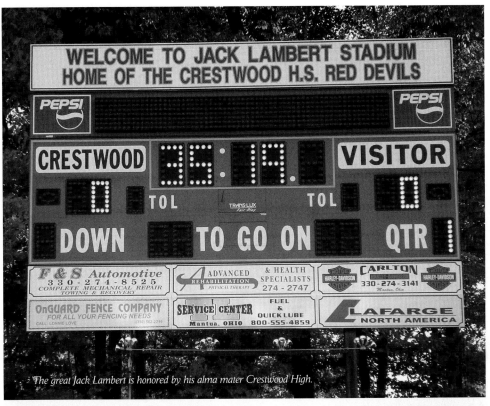

The great Jack Lambert is honored by his alma mater Crestwood High.

(ABOVE) *Brandon LeBeau and his dad, Steelers defensive coordinator Dick LeBeau, in Cincinnati.*

(ABOVE) *In Cincinnati, famed Steelers bar Martino's On Vine. From left, Bill Weisberg, Glen Campbell, owner Marty Angiulli, Kurt Emmert, Steve Condo.*

The myth that James Harrison's a mean guy is obliterated by this photo of him holding a baby and signing autographs. (Chaz Palla/Tribune-Review)

Ben Roethlisberger's friends at Tony's Restaurant in Findlay are Chaz Hatfield (left), Rick Hatfield, Mayor Tony Iriti, and Tim Tagliapietra.

caused a problem. But we went upstairs and the police were up there. Lo and behold it was Troy's room with these two other guys. They had gotten some balloons and filled them up with water and they were dropping them out the window on the people down below. One person called the cops so they had to come in. I told them I'd take care of it, and then I called the three down to the baseball field and they had a big track right there and I had them run 100 laps on this quarter-mile track. And I drove off.

Twenty-five miles?

Trask: Twenty-five miles.

And they did it?

Trask: They did it.

Isn't that excessive?

Trask: It was either that or not play. And, you know, I never had any more trouble from any of them.

Is that the only case of Troy getting into trouble?

Salu: As far as I know. But I don't know much because Shelley always makes deals with the kids before I come home from work. They butter up to her so she don't tell me about pulling the girl's bra or something.

Shelley: Troy got suspended in grade school — grade school! — for doing that. (Room breaks up into laughter.) I said why did you do this, Troy? He said, 'I really don't know why I did that.' He said she must've just got it because it wasn't there yesterday, and he said he was just curious and pulled it and it snapped and she went 'Oh!' He got in trouble. He got suspended three days and he had to stay home with my dad for three days and my dad wouldn't let him do anything. He was ready to go back to school, and he didn't do THAT ever again either.

Salu: That's the kind of thing she wouldn't tell me.

Shelley: Oh, he knew about that. There's no way to keep that from him.

How did you react?

Salu: I thought it was cute.

Did you tell him that?

Salu: No. But you know, boys are boys.

Shelley: But he didn't mean anything by it.

Why did Troy go back to USC to play football?

Salu: Well, that's always his dream to go back down south. When my brother was in Colorado, at the time (Rick) Neuheisel was hired by Washington and he didn't want to go to Washington even though he was being recruited by Neuheisel.

Did Troy switch from Colorado to USC because his Uncle Kennedy changed jobs?

Salu: He grew up watching Kennedy play. (Looks at photograph) That USC jersey was Kennedy's. That's why he has it on.

Dickover: Troy told me at one time, when (Mike) Bellotti was really putting the pressure on, he said if U of O had a baseball program, he probably would've gone there.

Salu: He would. Yes.

Shelley: He could've played baseball at USC, and they would've let him, but after his first year they changed football coaches and Troy didn't want to miss spring football with a brand new coach. He was ready to go, but the football coach quit and here comes Coach Carroll. What a great find that was though. He and Troy were so intense about football.

Why doesn't Troy watch football on TV?

Anna Polamalu (Darren's wife): He won't. One time, it was Christmas and USC didn't make it to a bowl game and Oregon State did, and we were all up at Uncle Jerry's house in Tenmile, and the Oregon State game was on and after dinner everybody spread out and watched the game. But Troy refused to watch the game. He slept on the floor the whole time the game was on.

He once said he lets his wife make one comment about the game.

Anna: Oh, he doesn't like to talk about it either.

Curt: Yeah, he'll ask about work. He always wants to talk about fishing or going out, but never about football.

Aren't you curious about the Steelers?

Anna: We know not to ask. You can call and leave a message and congratulate him. He'll call my husband and talk about fishing. He does not like to talk about football.

Never?

Anna: Well, one time Darren and I and Brandon and his wife and their baby went to the USC-Notre Dame game. After the game we were standing waiting for Troy and tons of fans were outside the stadium waiting and we see Carson Palmer come out and jump in this car and take off. Troy comes out and we were standing there for four hours. He signed every single person's autograph after the game. People waiting for Carson Palmer and other players said, 'Oh, we'll take Troy.' And he didn't mind. He just stood there and signed and talked till midnight. When we got in the car and drove off, the first thing he said was, 'Wasn't that great?'

Everyone likes Troy.

Anna: Maybe not everyone (laughs). When Taele was first born she was two months old and we went to the Pro Bowl, Troy's first Pro Bowl. He had never seen Taele, and we were just having banter back and forth about kids and how our lives have changed having this baby, and Troy would joke, 'I'm going to have 10 kids.' Theodora would kind of smile, like, 'Yeah, OK,' and he goes, 'No, we're having 10 kids at least.' And then Taele woke up and Troy said, 'Let me hold her.' As soon as Troy took her she just started wailing and bawling. Troy said, 'Well maybe we'll just have eight kids.'

Anyone else not take to Troy?

Steve Fisher: Everybody around here is — I don't know how to say this — rural America, genetically challenged, and so here's this kid who can do a lot of things. His senior year in basketball, there was a coach in our league who didn't vote him on first or second team at all. We got to the state tournament that year. Without him we're OK but not very good, so here's this coach who didn't recognize his impact on every single aspect of the game. Of course, that kind of speed is fun to play with. We had a great time with that. But that coach understands basketball; I just think he was jealous.

Or maybe racist?

Fisher: It's interesting that you bring that up. Politically right now immigration's this big thing, and Salu, he comes into this country like about 30 years ago and this community here is rural America. For someone of Salu's stature to come in this community and to add parental guidance, moral guidance, he coached all the sports and he and Shelley have been pillars of the community. So here we are in this area with the No. 1 immigrant. It was fortunate he happened to land in this area, and of course Troy's connection. It's pretty neat.

Shelley: Joe kind of paved the way for all the boys. He kind of broke the water, made Samoan, the great Samoan race, something to be proud of as good people, and it made it a little easier for each one down the line.

Fisher: There were something like 52 sawmills in this area, within 10 miles of this area at one time. You didn't see anybody of any color here for the longest time. Salu, did you struggle?

Salu: In '69, but I was tough enough to take care of myself.

Fisher: This is what I hear, too. I'm a bar owner, too, see, so everybody tells me these legacy stories: 'I knew Salu when he first came to town.' The story pretty much is, 'You can piss us all off, but don't piss off that big Samoan, man. You'll get in trouble.' Those stories still linger around from when he first got in this community. I don't know if you knew that or not.

Salu: Yep. I still hear them.

Shelley: Most Samoans, I think you can say, are very good-natured, easy going, but, man, don't make them mad.

Curt: That's like Troy, he'd look like he was moping around out there, but then once you give him the ball he's a whole different kid. Salu said, 'Oh, that's just how us Samoans are.' Once they start doing something, they would get it done.

Salu, do you sense how Polynesians everywhere are looking up to Troy?

Salu: Yes. They respect Troy.

Curt: A lot of that was Salu raising him.

Salu: They call it an iron fist (laughs). Also, that story Steve told about the coaches' voting, football's the same way. Coaching around here, we were new to the Coastal League, and I second Steve about the coaches. Now, look where he went. And you were sitting there with your little pencil and said he's not good enough. THAT's what really ticks me. Like Steve said, there are some. Remember the one kid they voted for instead? I wonder where he's at. I heard he got charged for robbing.

Fisher: I think Salu's the only one in town who knew Troy was going to be an All-Pro. We were all hoping. But, really, unless you have any experience in that regard, you just don't know how far a kid can go.

Chapter Eleven
Super Bowl Redux

I KNOW, I know. Setting the scene for the 2007 Seahawks-Steelers game requires yet another review of Super Bowl XL, so I'll keep it short:

Waaaah …

Waaaah …

Waaaah …

Yes, the Steelers beat the Seahawks 21-10, and Seahawks coach Mike Holmgren broke down and cried.

"We knew it was going to be tough going up against the Pittsburgh Steelers," Holmgren said with tears running down his shirt and pants. "I didn't know we were going to have to play the guys in the striped shirts as well."

Within 14 weeks of the game, Holmgren met twice with the NFL director of officiating. This elicited much sympathy from Peter King of *Sports Illustrated*, who gave Holmgren a forum in which to sob, again. Holmgren cried long and hard, but never once talked about his game plan — which featured the ridiculous Jerramy Stevens — or his clock-management debacle at the end of the first half that cost the Seahawks at least three points. That would've at least made the game close enough for Holmgren and the rest of Seattle to even begin blubbering.

Waaaah …

Waaaah …

Waaaah …

✦ ✦ ✦

THE SPACE NEEDLE wasn't exactly awash in tourists. No, the sky was overcast and the mercury checked in at 51 degrees on this early-October afternoon. So it wasn't easy to find Seahawks fans with which to engage in debate about Super Bowl officiating.

"I'm afraid I won't be much help to you," said the first person at the base of the Space Needle. "I'm a Steeler fan."

And the next guy: "Yes, I'm a football fan," he said. "But, I hate to tell you, I'm a Steelers fan."

As Vince Lombardi would say, What the HELL is going on around here?

I ran into a Bears fan, another Steelers fan, and an Appalachian State fan who was absolutely giddy that someone recognized his t-shirt and wanted to talk football. So I asked him how his team could lose to Wofford.

"Wofford!" he said. "I thought you were going to ask me about beating Michigan."

Then it happened: a true blue and green Seahawks fan. I asked him if Sunday's game was a big game.

"They're all big games," he said.

But don't you hate the Steelers?

"I absolutely hate the Steelers," he said. "And I hate the refs in Detroit."

Still bitter?

"I'll be bitter until we win a Super Bowl," he said.

Were the Seahawks cheated?

"I don't think they were cheated. They could've played better. But I definitely thought there were some calls that were completely ridiculous."

✦ ✦ ✦

THE ACTION at Pike's Peak Market was furious, but, again, where were the Seahawks fans? Where's the Seahawks garb? In fact, where's any NFL garb? This bustling marketplace was certainly not the Strip District in Pittsburgh. I had to ask one of the clerks if she knew of any Seahawks fans. She steered me to Casey, who was distinguished in his corner of the market by his Seahawks cap.

"Every game's a big game," he said.

Don't you want to beat the Steelers?

"Yeah, but it's at their home – again," he said.

Of course, Detroit, the site of Super Bowl XL, was Steelers territory. I asked him for his feelings on that game.

"The worst officiated game I've ever seen," he said.

Which call was the worst?

"The pylon call," he said. "One foot in, the other one hit the pylon. It should've been a touchdown. Simple call."

Except a receiver must have two feet in bounds before he can score one of those pylon touchdowns. That's the rule.

"Well, what about the two refs that were from Pittsburgh?" he asked.

Even though, as Dan Rooney said, there are more NFL officials from Western Pennsylvania than anywhere else, only one Super Bowl XL official, back judge Bob Waggoner, was a Pittsburgh-area resident or native. Casey might've been confused by head linesman Mark Hittner, who went to college at Pittsburg State in Kansas. Like so many of the Seattle complaints, this one was just a bit outside.

"That's kind of fishy," said Casey.

Will this game make up for it?

"No," he said. "There's a big difference between the Super Bowl and Week 6 of the regular season."

✦ ✦ ✦

AFTER THE Arizona game, and before Ben Roethlisberger sent a text message to Ken Whisenhunt, he limped slowly from the shower to his locker. His sore foot didn't make the injury report, but the Steelers would miss Troy Polamalu, Casey Hampton and Hines Ward because of injuries.

"Yeah, we've got players hurt," said Steelers fan and Seattle resident Will Kohn. "But since they're in our house, and the whining has been so intense, and we're coming off an embarrassing loss to the Cardinals, I think Santonio Holmes will step up and we'll win. I don't think I'll be wrong."

Kohn and Walt Cavalier and Shawn Bell run the Northwest Steeler Nation fan club out of a Hooters Restaurant in Tacoma, and they explained the presence of an inordinate amount of Steelers fans in a region that's 2,500 miles from Pittsburgh.

"It's a simple explanation," said Shawn. "The military brought us out here."

And they're passing the word along to the next generation.

"I didn't have a choice," Shawn Bell's daughter said of her favorite NFL team.

"I thought it best to give her her team until she's old enough to make a rational decision," explained Shawn.

The Bell family was featured by KDKA-TV back in Pittsburgh during Super Bowl XL week. Shawn is a Steelers fan and his wife is a Seahawks fan, so they dressed their toddler in a Steelers shirt and Seahawks hat to the delight of the reporter.

"My wife and I didn't talk the week of the Super Bowl," said Shawn. "I watched the game here (at Hooters) and she watched it with her friends somewhere else. Whenever something happened, I called her cell phone and let the crowd cheer and hung up without saying anything."

A Super Bowl XL party was held at the Tacoma Hooters, long a Steelers bar. More than 200 fans packed the place. Since 170 Steelers fans showed up a week ago for the Cardinals game, Shawn and Will expected Super Bowl levels for Sunday's rematch with the Seahawks.

"This restaurant will be packed with Steeler fans," Will promised on Saturday night. "You'll see the intensity and the kind of camaraderie you'd see at Heinz Field."

Will had sojourned to Heinz Field for the 2004 AFC Championship game against the New England Patriots.

"I was in the end zone," he said. "Deion Branch was stretching and some guy near me said, 'Deion, your momma's a bitch.' Deion stopped stretching, just turned around and looked at the guy and didn't say anything. I looked at Deion, looked in his eyes, and was thinking, 'That guy probably shouldn't have said that.' And guess who scored the first touchdown? Deion Branch. And he ran right to the spot and threw the football at the guy and ran away. And the next touchdown, Corey Dillon ran it in, went to the same spot, and threw the football at the guy. You know, you can say a lot of things, but leave the moms out of it."

Shawn Bell laughed. So did Will. The Steelers lost that day, but, one ring later, all is well. They were confident of a win over the Seahawks the next day.

"It'll be 90 percent Steeler fans in here," Shawn said, "and if the Seahawks make a first down you'll hear a little roar from the other 10 percent."

Shawn had heard more than "a little roar" that week from Seahawks fans who've come to despise the Steelers.

"All week I heard how they got cheated in the Super Bowl," Shawn said. "So I've got a picture of Big Ben with the ball crossing the goal line on my computer. I'd bring it up, and they didn't know what play it was, but they'd say, 'Yeah, that's a touchdown.' And then I'd say, 'If I'm running a route and I push you and catch the ball, what do you call that?' And they'd say, 'Pass interference.' OK, 'If you're rushing and I'm holding your shoulder and pulling you down, what do you call that?' And the answer they'd give me: 'Holding.' Some of them didn't even know what I was talking about. The only really bad call was when (Matt) Hasselbeck threw the game-clinching interception, in an 11-point game, and he was called for a penalty he didn't deserve. Really, it was one bad call: The way the quarterback tackled the guy who intercepted his last-chance pass."

✦ ✦ ✦

IT MUST be Sunday, otherwise the banner on the roof of the Tacoma Hooters – You're in Steeler Country – wouldn't be allowed by law.

By law?

"We win the Super Bowl," Shawn Bell explained, "and all of the sudden, the following year, there's an ordinance that says you can't have a banner bigger than whatever size our banner was up on a building during the week. So our banner can't be up during the week; on game day only."

But it's not all latte-sipping computer geeks out here. The guy walking into Hooters on this morning wore a Julian Peterson jersey and had a neck right out of the Iowa cornfields. I asked him if he wanted revenge.

"Wouldn't you if you were cheated?" he said.

Another Seahawks fan, a guy who looked like a former high school tackle, didn't really care that Steelers fans had taken over the bar.

"I go to games, where the action is," he said. "I just hope these Steeler fans feel stupid today when they lose because the refs won't be working for them today."

A woman stepped to the front of the bar and proclaimed, "Hawks nest over here; Steeler Nation over there." But two guys broke the rules. They sat their mixed allegiances down at the same table and appeared to enjoy each other's company. "Just don't tell anybody," said the Seahawks fan.

"Yeah, he's a reasonable man," said the Steelers fan. "He's also come to the realization that as long as he lives in Seattle, he'll never see a championship team."

THE ATMOSPHERE intense, as promised, and every first down was hotly contested at the packed Hooters, where Steelers fans only slightly outnumbered Seahawks fans.

Ben Roethlisberger complained about wearing black on a hot day back in Pittsburgh, and he could've complained about his depleted receiving corps. Santonio Holmes was a late scratch, yet Roethlisberger was hot. Scoreless late in the first half, he threw to Heath Miller to convert a third down, and Najeh Davenport tore off a 45-yard run. Miller converted another third down before catching a 13-yard touchdown pass to give the Steelers all the points they'd need.

The Seahawks' response was meek. Their late-half foray into Steelers territory was their first of the game, but Hasselbeck was intercepted by Ike Taylor at the goal line and the Steelers went into the locker room ahead by 7-0 at halftime.

Taylor was the star of the half for the Steelers. He had a chance for two other interceptions as the Steelers sat back in a cover-2 defense and gambled that Shaun Alexander wouldn't hurt them, and he didn't. The Seahawks' back had only 15 yards on eight first-half carries.

The banter between the fans bordered on intense, but trouble was never imminent. Restaurant manager Will Powell approached Shawn Bell to express his gratitude. I asked Powell about managing a Steelers bar in Seahawks country.

"We do get a lot of negative feedback from Seattle people living in Seattle, but Seattle fans don't show up consistent enough to make it worth giving them designated seating," he said. "Steeler fans are loyal and we appreciate them being here. They're good people."

Is it all about the money?

"No, not necessarily," he said. "We want to fill the seats. The biggest expense in a restaurant is an empty seat, so if we have people who want to fill every seat, we'll give preference to them, and they show up every week."

THE STEELERS opened the second half with a 10-minute and 17-second drive that ended with a Davenport touchdown. A three-and-out by Seattle was followed by another Steelers touchdown drive – this one lasting 8:06 – and that was the ball game.

Steelers fans serenaded Seahawks fans with "Na Na Hey Hey Kiss Him Goodbye" as the latter filed out before the 21-0 win became final. Willie Parker had 102 yards rushing to put him at 507 through five games. Roethlisberger completed his final 13 passes to finish with a passer rating of 120.8, nearly 100 points better than his last game against the Seahawks. One scary moment for the offense occurred when right guard Kendall Simmons was driven into the legs of left tackle Marvel Smith during a pass play. Smith went down and left the game, but returned a series later, as did the team's health going into a bye week. In two weeks, the Steelers expected to be at full strength in Denver.

The 4-1 Steelers had yet to allow a first-half touchdown, and on this day allowed only 144 yards, the Seahawks' lowest output in five years. Alexander carried 11 times for 25 yards.

"I can't wait to get back to work," said Shawn Bell. "I'll walk in and say, 'I didn't see the game. Who won?'

"It just solidifies the fact we beat their ass in the Super Bowl. We had three Pro Bowlers out and our deep-threat receiver out. We beat their asses."

✦ ✦ ✦

SEATTLE'S TOP-RATED sports talker is a guy named Softy of KJR Radio. Here's his Monday morning show already in progress:

"... after a scum bucket of a game in Pittsburgh. What the heck was that? Let's hope by the time they're on Monday night they play better than yesterday. Oh, God. I don't even have anything to say. Let's go to Dane in Bremerton."

Dane: "What a game, huh? God. I've got lots to say but we're on the radio and I can't use some of those words. Maybe Mr. Holmgren should get a running back that's not weighed down by his wallet."

Softy: "It took us 20 seconds to pin it on Shaun Alexander. Let me tell you something, part of the reason why Shaun had a terrible day is because the offensive line SUCKED. That line couldn't block you. Let's go to Dave in Snohomish."

Dave: "Thank God I was watching that game with a hot chick yesterday."

Softy: "Oh God I was watching that game with about 200 people at a casino who all felt the same way I do. We had a group hug after the game was over it was so bad."

Dave: "I wanted to throw up, too. Everybody sucked."

Softy: "Ike Taylor had the big pick to end the first half and the Pittsburgh papers are in awe. They're shocked, because this is a guy who's been known to drop a pass or two."

Dave: "He's the guy that killed us."

✦ ✦ ✦

FINALLY, MT. RANIER. It appeared in the rearview mirror 100 miles out of Seattle, on my way to Kennewick in the southeastern part of Washington. In Kennewick, a giant wall mural of No. 56, Ray Mansfield, in his black and gold, brightens the downtown landscape.

Mansfield was a star at Kennewick High and then the University of Washington. He centered for the 1961 Rose Bowl champs and was drafted No. 18 overall by the Philadelphia Eagles in 1963 as, writers surmised, a replacement for center Chuck Bednarik. But the Eagles used Mansfield on defense, and were disappointed. The week of the 1964 opener they sold him to the Steelers for $100.

"The same day I joined the Steelers," Ray once told Dave Ailes of the *Greensburg (Pa.) Tribune-Review*, "old Buddy Parker fired six players, including a pair of All-Pros (Lou Michaels, John Reger). You should've seen what it was like in those days. I'm convinced Parker was a neurotic."

Mansfield played defensive tackle for the Steelers his first two years, but was needed at center late in 1965. In his first game he blew a long snap in a loss, but remained at the position all the way through 1974, when he began alternating with Mike Webster. Mansfield played in a then-Steelers record of 168 straight games, but nearly had it broken. He told Ailes about that early 1970s moment:

> "It was late in the game and the Rams were beating our tails. I hadn't been in the game, but when they lined up to kick off, I ran out to replace Fats Holmes in the blocking wedge to keep my streak alive. I didn't want to bother Noll about such things as streaks, so I ran out on my own. Then, I made sure I threw one hell of a block at midfield so the films would prove that I was in the game."

Mansfield died of a heart attack in the Grand Canyon. Here's a beautiful tribute from bobspixels.com:

> *Former Pittsburgh Steeler star center Ray "The Ranger" Mansfield died in the Grand Canyon on Saturday, November 3, 1996. Ray had been hiking with his son and another companion when problems with an ankle caused him to fall behind. He told the others to go on ahead and that he would catch up with them later that evening at the campsite. He never showed up. His body was found the following morning sitting with his back against a big rock, cigar in hand, facing a magnificent vista where the sun would have set the previous evening.*

Chapter Twelve

WHERE THE BUFFALO ROAM

THE 1313 Club in northern Idaho was recommended for its food and its wall-mounted, big-game trophies. The brochure didn't mention football, but the busty blonde barmaid arguing with two patrons that "my Steelers wouldn't have done it that way" sure did. So I asked her – Dawn – which team the fans up here in northern Idaho root for.

"I don't know who *they* root for," she said, "but I root for the Pittsburgh Steelers."

The story was told at my next stop in Polson, Montana. My aunt and uncle run a ranch in the wide-open spaces a mile outside of Flathead Lake. I told them how I'd instantly found Steelers fans in Idaho without even trying. So my aunt suggested we check out the only sports bar in Polson, and off we went to The Sports Page Bowl. I approached a woman named Glenda as she was putting up Halloween decorations.

Me: Do you run this place?

Glenda: Yes I do.

Me: Is this a sports bar?

Glenda: Yes it is.

Me: What teams do you root for here?

Glenda: May I ask what you're doing here?

Me: I'm gathering research.

Glenda: On?

Me: On football.

Glenda: For who?

Me: For myself. Do you watch football?

Glenda: You'd better talk to the bartender.

Me: Are there any Steelers fans here?

Bartender: Yeah. You were just talking to one.

Me: Glenda? You're a Steelers fan?

Glenda: Yepper.

A bit more relaxed with her inquisitive new customer, Glenda pointed out memorabilia and pennants on the walls and the "This is Steeler Country" sign lording over the barstools from the ceiling.

"Back in the 70s," she said, "and I'm dating myself, but my girlfriend and I were big Steeler fans. Still are. We had Jack Lambert jerseys – yeah, living in Montana – and we would hang signs up all over our high school 'Steelers will beat ...' whoever. But if they lost we wouldn't go to school on Monday. We couldn't stand it if they lost, so it's a good thing they won a lot. We had so much fun with that."

✦ ✦ ✦

ABOUT 185 miles due east of the Montana town of West Yellowstone – the west entrance to Yellowstone National Park – is the small town of Greybull, Wyoming. Steelers defensive end Brett Keisel said that if I wanted to visit his family in Greybull, I had to camp in Yellowstone Park. Well, the closest I came was the leak I took on the side of the road in pitch-black surroundings. It's truly a spooky place.

"Camping outside at Yellowstone? That's just crazy. Brett's never even done that," said his mother-in-law Patty Johnson.

Patty and her husband Steve stopped in Greybull while moving from Chicago to California. They stayed 30 years.

Steve, with his gray ponytail, has the look of an old hippie, and I told him so.

"Right on," he said as he flashed a peace sign and a smile.

"We are old, yes," said Patty. "And we are from the sixties."

Steve said he didn't remember much from the sixties, and that gave an opening to the young man sitting with them.

"Kind of like Super Bowl night," said Mike McGuire.

McGuire is one of Brett Keisel's oldest and best friends. He quarterbacked the Greybull Buffs to the state semifinals in Brett's senior year. Brett was the tight end and middle linebacker, easily the best player in this state of 515,000.

The play Greybull fans remember best is an interception Brett made while playing with a broken hand. With his good hand, Keisel pinned a deep pass next to his helmet and made a diving catch.

"It was so fun playing with him because we knew every week, no matter who we were playing against, we always had the best player on the field," said McGuire. "He was just kind of a freak. I never saw anyone like him before or since. They don't come along very often in these small towns."

McGuire graduated from Greybull High and attended the University of Wyoming, as Brett went to BYU. When Brett turned pro, McGuire turned to his dream: coaching. While working at Fort Hays State University in Hays, Kansas, McGuire received a call from another buddy who asked Mike if he wanted to go to Denver to see the Broncos play the Steelers in the 2005 AFC Championship game. McGuire had just watched the Steelers beat the Colts and "was a mess" after the emotional win, but he took his buddy up on the offer and began planning for the trip that weekend.

"Now, I grew up worshipping the Denver Broncos," McGuire said. "I've just always been a huge Bronco fan. So that next week I made the drive from Hays to Denver, about four hours, and proceeded to dress up in all my Steeler gear and I went into Invesco. That was when I officially joined Steeler Nation. And I heard about it from my friends, too, but it was pretty cool, especially as good a game Brett had. It was his breakout game."

Keisel sacked Broncos quarterback Jake Plummer two times that day. The sacks occurred on back-to-back plays as Keisel substituted for Kimo von Oelhoffen at right end in the fourth quarter. The first sack, on 3rd-and-3, with the Broncos trailing by 10 with 5:27 left, put the Broncos in 4th-and-10. Keisel then sacked Plummer on fourth down and forced a fumble that the Steelers recovered. Hello, Super Bowl.

"He doesn't remember the Super Bowl," Patty Johnson said of McGuire.

"I remember the Super Bowl," McGuire said. "It's just parts of the party afterward that are a little hazy."

McGuire partied with the team after it beat the Seahawks in the Super Bowl and called it "the greatest 24 hours of my entire life. I mean, just going to the Super Bowl as a fan would be good enough. To watch your best friend play is pretty amazing. I still get goose bumps thinking about it."

McGuire has since coached Greybull's rival, Riverside, to the state championship game. He did that as a rookie high school coach in 2006, proving he could change loyalties quickly and with great success.

"It wasn't quite like that," he said with a snap of the fingers. "Changing from the Broncos to the Steelers was gradual over a couple years. After I went to a few games at Heinz Field and just saw the fans there, there's nothing like it on the face of the earth. It's hard to describe, being a fan of one team and going to another, because I never thought it would happen. I was going to bleed orange and blue until I died, but just being out there and seeing all the Terrible Towels and the tailgating: The Steelers are Pittsburgh and everything about Pittsburgh says Steelers on it. It was pretty cool."

And what if his best friend is, say, traded to the Broncos tomorrow?

"I'd obviously be pretty happy," McGuire said. "But after the experiences that I've had in Pittsburgh and with the Steelers, I'm probably going to be a Steeler fan for life."

MIKE McGUIRE quarterbacked the football team at Greybull High and Jeff Hunt quarterbacked the basketball team as the point guard. The two athletes came up though the ranks with Brett Keisel and by the time they reached high school the town of 1,815 was ready for the big time.

"That group came along after a long drought," said Ted Menke, a teacher and coach at Greybull. "They hadn't won a game for years and years and years and then finally these kids, who played together since they were little, tiny kids, they got here and everybody's expectations kept creeping and creeping to the point where we kind of expected to have our state championship. In basketball, it happened."

The turning point for the group occurred in the regionals when Keisel sparked a rally from 15 points down.

"He just kind of went crazy for about a quarter and a half," McGuire said. "He just took over the game. He got every rebound and we kept feeding him and feeding him and feeding him the ball. We were juniors on a senior team, but he stepped up and said, 'We're not going out like this.'"

Greybull won the game, lost the regional championship, but won the state title the following week in Casper.

"You just get it up in the air and he'd go get it," said Hunt, the point guard. "There wasn't a person in the state who could play with him. We took state our junior year, but our senior year I kind of messed up. A few of us messed up. I broke my thumb skiing on Christmas break. We should've won the state again that year, but Brett didn't look down on me for that. Brett wasn't the type to yell at me. Some of the other kids were pretty upset. They wouldn't even talk to me for a few weeks. Brett wasn't like that."

THE KEISEL family visited Greybull from their home in Provo, Utah, in 1990. They came to lend grandpa a hand and ended up staying 12 years.

"Brett's grandma and grandpa had a big ranch here," said Patty Johnson. "That's where his mom grew up. They had eight kids in their family. They came one summer to help with the cattle drive. Grandpa was thrown from a horse and hit his head on a rock and he never came out of it. So, Brett's parents moved up here to run the ranch."

Grandpa died six years later, but Lane and Connie Keisel waited until Kalli, their last child, graduated high school before moving back to Provo.

"Brett still considers this his home," said Steve Johnson.

It's a place that has a history of grabbing people. The Johnsons stayed. Brett plans to return after football. His buddies love the wide open spaces in between the mountains and say they'll stay as long as they can. The stoplight in town is one of only two in the county, and it regulates an intersection right out of the Old West. On one corner is the Cowboy Clothier, on the other corners are a saloon, a bank, and Homespun Gifts. There are more antelope out on the range than people in town, and those people like it that way.

"When I came here," said teacher Ted Menke, "I thought it would just be Redneck, Wyoming. I figured everybody with a cause would be hiding out in the hills here. But it hasn't been the case."

Menke moved to Greybull in 1982 to care for his parents. "We were going to stay a year, just like everyone else," he said. "But you get here and you fall in love with the mountains and the hunting and the other manly man things that all the men do here while our wives are driving an hour to get to a Wal-Mart."

Brett has read as much as he can about Native Americans, after finding an arrowhead on an early cattle drive. He's also an avid outdoorsman. His friend Jeff Hunt said fishing, hunting and football are 1a-1b-1c with Brett.

"The first time I ever went horseback riding was out at his parent's place," said Hunt. "Growing up in Wyoming, most people do have horses. They had them right outside their house. When I'd stay the night sometimes we'd go out and ride them. The first time I remember we went out Brett put me on one of their slower, older horses because I'd never been on a horse. I had no clue what I was doing and the horse ended up running through a plowed field and stepped on a big, old dirt clod and she rolled over the top of me and almost broke her leg. We thought they'd have to put her down. It took her a while, but she did get back up. The whole family was pretty upset. I was very upset over it because I thought they were going to have to put their horse down just because I didn't know what I was doing."

Was anyone concerned about Jeff Hunt?

"I was fine," he said. "I was shook up a little. It's one of those days I'll never forget, but I did get on their horses a few more times."

I COULDN'T get my Johnsons straight. Patty, after telling me her husband's a teacher in the district, introduced me to Ed Johnson, a teacher in the district. Midway through the interview, I asked him why his daughter married Brett Keisel.

"No, he married her daughter," Johnson said as he pointed to Johnson. "But I predicted it when they were in eighth grade. I had them in science class and Brett would just torment her something fierce. And I told them they were going to end up getting married some day, and both of them said the same thing: 'No way!'"

"My favorite memory," said teacher Ted Menke, "is this great big 6-foot-4 guy hauling down the hall after this little 5-foot-4 inch girl who was obviously running the show – always."

Sarah, according to her parents, actually wanted to marry Brad Pitt. But …

"She got Mr. Pittsburgh instead," said her father Steve Johnson.

Brett and Sarah had a son in the spring of 2008.

"We think a lot of Brett," said Steve. "He's not Mr. Big Head. He's always been a regular guy, always appreciative. You give him a shirt for Christmas and he's really appreciative. He's down to earth and has really good family values. He's the guy you'd want your daughter to marry."

Right on.

✦ ✦ ✦

MOST OF the 6,589 miles I'd racked up to this point had been a breeze. I love the road, but was beginning to lose my edge. I pulled out of Greybull anticipating a leisurely drive to Denver, where the Steelers – because of the bye week – wouldn't arrive for another week.

That gave me plenty of time to reach the off-season condo I'd rented in the mountains overlooking Denver. There I would meet my wife and daughter for a long weekend, and then take three or four days to explore one of my favorite cities. But the drive south to the Colorado border was excruciating. I'd always wanted to see Wyoming, and, baby, I was seeing it – the brown, the rock, the prairie dogs. When the sign told me I was 97 miles away from Casper, restlessness kicked in. When I reached Casper, and the sign told me I was 146 miles away from Cheyenne, restlessness turned to anxiety. And when my car stopped, with *at least* a sixteenth of a tank of gas still showing on my gauge, anxiety turned to panic. I called Triple-A and 25 minutes later I was back on I-25 with enough gas to reach one of the few exits in the hinterlands north of Cheyenne.

"This happens a lot," said Gregg, the erstwhile Triple-A serviceman. "The wind out here kills gas mileage."

As Gregg emptied his gas can, I told him I was on my way to cover the Steelers-Broncos game in Denver.

"And they're going to spank my Broncos, aren't they?" he said. "Gol-ly, last week was bad."

Last week the Broncos lost 41-3 to the San Diego Chargers. Gol-ly, indeed.

Chapter Thirteen
THE ROCKIES

CALL JIM RUSSELL the 'Burgh Diaspora guy, or the guy who'll do his best to explain, even intellectualize, the phenomenon that is Steelers Nation.

The 'Burgh Diaspora is the blog through which Russell links to Pittsburgh natives who've taken their education and moved elsewhere. Russell calls it Pittsburgh's lost investment. He estimates that as many as 1.5 million people left the Pittsburgh region since the late 1970s, when the steel mills began to close. That's the "Diaspora," which is defined as any scattering of people with a common origin. It was first used in association with the Jews.

Russell was born in Erie, moved to Schenectady, N.Y., at 6, and met his Pittsburgh-born wife while studying geography at the University of Vermont. He interned as a lobbyist for Amnesty International in Washington, D.C. and because of his grasp of geopolitics and globalization was hired by the University of Colorado to teach introductory courses in human geography. He's put his career on hold to stay home in suburban Denver and raise his newborn son, but Russell still roots for the Steelers on the weekend and the city of Pittsburgh during the week. I asked him if the Steelers' fan base really is unique.

"Sometimes I think it doesn't even matter because Pittsburghers and Steelers fans believe it," he said. "They believe they are unique. They believe they are special. It's a self-fulfilling prophesy."

But Russell agrees that there's more to the phenomenon than perception. He sees the numbers and they're difficult to ignore. Russell has researched migration statistics, made adjustments as he saw fit, and came up with his top 10 'Burgh Diaspora hot spots:

1. Washington, D.C.-Baltimore
2. New York
3. Tampa-St. Petersburg
4. Miami-Fort Lauderdale
5. Phoenix
6. Chicago
7. Atlanta
8. Los Angeles
9. Charlotte
10. Boston

But, he said, the numbers don't tell the complete story, either.

"Take Mexico for example," Russell said. "You would figure there'd be mostly Dallas Cowboys fans there. Well, there's some debate over who's number one in Mexico and arguably it's the Steelers. So the Steelers are at least number two, and there are clearly no proximity connections whatsoever. It's just that when Mexico started getting NFL games the Steelers were the dominant team. The Cowboys weren't too shabby, either, so you would think that given the success and proximity the Cowboys had, there wouldn't be anything substantial as competition. To me, that signals there's something special going on."

And that is?

"First and foremost it's the success," he said. "And by that I mean the style of play and the stability. When it comes to the people who cut their teeth on '70s football, they identify with the Steelers. And the Rooneys have cultivated such an amazing stability that it's a readily identifiable icon. We live in a time where there's a lot of cultural upheaval – people are living all over the place, five, six careers in a lifetime – and the Pittsburgh Steelers in a lot of ways are the same team I remember from my childhood. So there's a nostalgic element to it."

WHAT IS the Pittsburgh identity?

"Go to a road game where the Steelers are playing and you'll find out," Russell said. "On the road, people invent what they think Pittsburgh is. It's how they connect with home. Every away game I go to I have Parma on the strip ship me kielbasa. That's part of how we celebrate Pittsburgh."

Of the road games Russell's attended, he was most impressed by the turnout of Steelers fans at Dallas during Ben Roethlisberger's rookie season. Russell estimates that 30,000 Steelers fans showed up for the October game against the 2-2 Cowboys. The Steelers rallied from a 10-point deficit in the fourth quarter to give their QB a 4-0 start to his career.

"That fan club threw the most amazing tailgate I'd ever seen," Russell said. "There had to be 5,000 to 10,000 Steeler fans at their tailgate. It was packed. I could barely move. The next day I was driving back to Denver listening to sports talk radio. They didn't talk much about the game or Ben, the rookie phenom; it was all about 'They took over our stadium.' The Cowboys were decent, still in the hunt, and the game was competitive, so where was the great Cowboys fan base? That would never happen in Pittsburgh, even in a bad year."

What does Russell expect at Invesco Field on Sunday night? The Steelers are 4-1 and the Broncos – playing second fiddle in town to the World Series-bound Rockies – are 2-3 and coming off their worst home loss in 41 years.

"Denver's a bad sports town," he said. "The most rabid Broncos fans don't live in Denver. They're in Wyoming, in Montana. You could drive from Denver to the Canadian border and listen to the Broncos game unbroken. The whole interior west, even in eastern Washington, is pretty much Broncos country. In 2003, I was there at Invesco, an atrocious game to watch. It was really bad. We got there early, like you would if you were going to Pittsburgh for a tailgate, but the lots weren't open. We came at 8 in the morning and no one was there. Within 30 minutes there was a line of Steelers fans. That's it. Not a Broncos fan could be seen. All of us Steelers fans congregated in the same place, about 10,000 of us there partying, playing the Steelers polka next to a Steelers RV. It's like a jam-band following, the Grateful Dead, just a little bit different. Half are local Steelers fans and the rest come from all over the place. Steelers fans do travel well, but there is some regional aspect to it.

"This week, I don't know what to expect. I'm not hearing the kind of buzz that I heard around San Diego before that great game in '05. But Broncos fans are dumping their tickets like crazy. I'm going to guess 15,000 Steelers fans, which would be the smallest showing I've seen on the road. I'm just not sensing a buzz, even though it's so easy to find tickets these days."

✦ ✦ ✦

DALE DODRILL has a dual football identity. He played for the Steelers, and his son Garrett was born in Pittsburgh, but Dodrill — raised and educated in Colorado and living in the Denver suburb of Lakewood — was part of the first Broncos coaching staff. In 1960, there was head coach Frank Filchock and assistant coach Dodrill. That was it, until 1962, when Jack Faulkner became head coach and added Ed Hughes, Ray Malavasi, Red Miller and Mac Speedie to the staff.

Dodrill quit coaching after the 1966 season to open an insurance agency. He now has two in the Denver area that are run by his sons.

"They still allow me to come in because I flunked retirement," said the 81-year-old Dodrill.

The memorabilia on the office walls suggests his family remains fond of the Steelers. How fond?

"About $600 worth," Dodrill said. "That's how much we spent on Steelers gear when we went back a few weeks ago. And we're going to put it all on tomorrow and go up to the park here and get a picture taken of our whole family for our Christmas card."

And send it to your Denver friends?

"You bet."

DALE DODRILL was the Steelers' first middle linebacker. Like most teams back in 1953 and 1954, the Steelers moved from a five-man defensive front to a four-man front, and the 220-pound Dodrill flourished at his new position.

"I saw the old tapes," said son Garrett. "He was pretty quick; very quick."

As part of the 75th Anniversary celebration, the Steelers named a Legends Team comprised of those who played before 1970. Dodrill was named to the team and called it "a great honor, the greatest honor since playing for them."

Born in 1926 in Stockton, Kansas, Dodrill not only grew up during the Great Depression, he grew up in the thick of the Dust Bowl. His family fled Kansas for Loveland, Colorado, in 1936. "That's when your own dirt wasn't dirty," he said. "You couldn't describe it bad enough."

In 1944, after having been rejected by every other branch of the service for being flat-footed and color blind, Dodrill joined the Army's 30th Infantry Division, which served in France and Germany. He came home and enrolled at Colorado A&M to play football.

With flat feet?

"I am not flat-footed and I am not color blind," he said with a shrug.

The Steelers saw ability in Dodrill at his postseason college all-star game and drafted him in the sixth round in 1951. He moved into the starting lineup midway through the season.

"Back then you had to play at least two years, going on three, before they didn't consider you a rookie anymore," he said.

Dodrill returned to Colorado in the off-season, but there was no parade. His parents wanted to know when he was going to get "a decent job." In 1958 he captained the NFL's No. 1 defense. After the 1959 season he retired with five Pro Bowls to his credit, but no championships.

"It sometimes becomes drudgery when you can't win," he said. "Everyone should have the same set of mind in order to accomplish that, and it's hard to get that many people in the same boat."

Dodrill entered and also left the league with Pro Bowl defensive back Jack Butler. He also played behind Ernie Stautner, the only player to have his uniform number officially retired by the Steelers.

"Jack was a great player. He's a good man and I've enjoyed knowing him," Dodrill said. "Ernie Stautner was altogether different. I remember we were playing the Browns and he was offside three times in a row. That's when the center used to be able to flex his hand, and that's why they changed the rule. The Browns were also the first team to run the fullback fake trap, where they pull the guard and the fullback would come in and block the tackle. Then they just started giving the fullback the ball, so they ran that on Ernie for two big gains. The first time I said, 'Well, who blocked Ernie?' And he said 'They had two of the SOBs on me.' Then later they ran it and I said, 'Who blocked you?' He said, 'I had three guys on me.' But really nobody was blocking him. It was an influence play. But Ernie did enjoy going through people instead of around them. He punished a lot of people."

Dodrill tackled Jim Brown and Hugh McElhenny and Tank Younger, but he thought the toughest of them all was Steve Van Buren.

"Because of injuries he retired in '51, but I used to tell people if he comes back, I may not."

DODRILL NOT ONLY came back, he became a Legend. The day before the 2007 home opener, the Legends were given a tour of Heinz Field. Dodrill was impressed by the carpeted locker room – all 6,000 square feet of it.

"When I played, we had a wood pallet, a dirt floor and a nail on the wall," he said.

I asked him about the Chief.

"He cared about you. He cared about people. He did a lot more listening than he did talking. I remember my last year I got back from a game and at the airport, when we got off the plane, I told Mr. Rooney I'd like to talk to him sometime. He said, 'What is it?' And I told him I wanted to be traded. He said, 'Well, you'll have to talk to Buddy Parker. He has all the control.' And I was surprised Art Rooney would really relinquish all control. I asked Buddy and he came back two, three weeks later and said nobody's interested. I knew that couldn't be true, but he just said, 'No, Mr. Rooney has an investment in you,' and I said, 'He certainly got his money's worth by now.'"

Why did Dodrill want to be traded?

"I didn't fit into Buddy Parker's system, or Bobby Layne's," he said. "Bobby was a great guy. I had no problem getting along with Bobby. He was a colorful guy. Hanging with Bobby would probably help your position. And I drank my share of beer. We did it once in a while but not constantly. And I wasn't as big as some of the other guys. He liked bodyguards with him."

Did Dodrill remember John Unitas at the 1955 camp, before the Steelers cut him?

"Certainly," he said. "You didn't have a good scrimmage unless somebody got into a fight, and then it took the coaches a long time to go five yards and break it up. But Unitas used to upset them because he'd be back there not paying any attention to it. Nothing disturbed him. They liked to see people get excited, but he was cool as a cucumber. When he played for the Colts, it became evident that he had poise, so a lot of people wondered why the Steelers didn't see anything in him. But Weeb Ewbank had him on the bench. George Shaw rolled out one too many times and that opened the door for Unitas. So, Weeb couldn't even see the potential in him."

Dodrill also recounted the time he went to Omaha, Nebraska, to apply for an offseason banking job.

"They said they'd get back to me in a week. Two weeks went by and I called the guy. He said there was a problem with my employment history. He said they can't find a steel company in Pittsburgh by the name Pittsburgh Steelers."

Dodrill sat back in his chair and smiled. "I don't really think about the '50s too much," he said. "So it's rather enjoyable to reminisce."

"I think he'd have paid to play football. I really do," said Jan, his wife of 53 years.

"Good thing the Steelers paid me," said Dodrill, "because I didn't have any money to pay them."

✦ ✦ ✦

COLORADO A&M became Colorado State in 1957, just after giving the Steelers Gary Glick, the colossal bust who was the first pick — or bonus pick, as it was called back then — of the 1956 draft. The Steelers evened the scales in 1960 when they chose Brady Keys out of Colorado State, a steal in the 14th round.

In his biography, Keys wrote that he gained 22 yards on his first carry of his first game, but was yanked after the run and chewed out by coach Buddy Parker for reversing field. Keys spent the rest of his career at right cornerback. He retired to a lucrative entrepreneurial career that's still thriving.

The Steelers didn't have any more luck with Colorado State until they drafted two of the school's defensive ends who'd combined for 24 sacks in 1998. Joey Porter was drafted by the Steelers in 1999 and Clark Haggans in 2000 and both started at the outside linebacker positions in Super Bowl XL.

On a trip to gorgeous Fort Collins – 65 miles north of Denver (and the site of the college of my next lifetime) – I asked the Colorado State sports information director why there's a Joey Porter Locker Room and not a Clark Haggans Locker Room.

"Because Joey gave us $200,000," he said.

From Fort Collins, it's 33 miles southeast to Greeley, Colorado. There, I wanted to know why Ben Dreith is in the University of Northern Colorado's Hall of Fame and not Aaron Smith.

Dreith is known for his "giving him the business down there" call in the 1986 playoffs. He was a three-sport star at UNC from 1946-50, while Smith, the all-time UNC sacks leader (44), carried the school to NCAA II national titles in 1996 and 1997.

"I was just going through our stuff on Aaron," said UNC recruiting coordinator Kevin Grable. "He was 6-5, 210 pounds when he came here. Do you believe that?"

The skinny frame explains why Smith slipped through the cracks after an all-state career at big-school power Sierra High School in Colorado Springs. Smith was a two-sport star in high school, but only Joe Glenn – now the head coach at the University of Wyoming – took a chance on him and Smith ended up at Northern Colorado.

Grable was a wide receiver on both UNC title teams, and as the recruiting coordinator he's looking for another Aaron Smith. At 0-7 and riding a 15-game losing streak at the time of my visit, it was obvious that UNC and Grable hadn't had much luck.

"You like the long arms, big hands, speed, great length, good frames," Grable said. "I mention Aaron all the time. Every year since he left I say, 'Hey, he came in at 210 pounds.' So, yeah, I use Aaron's name a lot."

✦ ✦ ✦

SHELBY SMITH is a 17-year-old beauty in Fountain, Colorado, and she's enthusiastic and bright and she has a dream: She wants to attend college in Pittsburgh. "I went out there for a summer to visit my Uncle Aaron and I love the atmosphere, the people. I love the green," she said.

While waiting for her Rockies to sweep the Cardinals in the National League Championship Series that night, Shelby told a quick Uncle Aaron story that had been passed down to her.

"He was crying as a 3-year-old and his parents gave him the stuffed bear that he wanted," she said. "So what does that tell us? That he can get what he wants if he cries hard enough."

The gang at Dave Smith's house was amused. "Aaron was the spoiled one," said Uncle Steve.

To understand the irony, let's go back to the beginning. Aaron is the youngest of the four Smith brothers:

- Dave Smith, 40, is a 6-foot-2, 235-pound facilities mechanic for Intel Corporation. His favorite pastime is stockcar racing and he hosted this little gathering in Fountain Colorado. His wife Kathie helps him raise Shelby and 14-year-old Daniel.

- Steve Smith, 37, is the self-described "runt" of the family at 6-foot, 190 pounds. He was a Steelers fan as a kid and was the free safety at Sierra HS when Alex Molden was one of the school's cornerbacks. Steve's eagle eyes miss little and his memory and tongue are sharp and quick, so it's not a surprise that he played free safety. He's also the single father of Brandon, 14, and Kyler, 12. He's his own boss as an electrical contractor.

- Kevin Smith, 35, is 6-foot-4 and might be the strongest of the Smith boys, but he didn't love football. "If I had his size, I'd be playing some pro ball," Steve said of Kevin, who wasn't present because he works in Washington, D.C.

- Aaron Smith, 32, is the 6-foot-5, 300-pound defensive end with the Pittsburgh Steelers. Most savvy football fans realize he's the team's defensive MVP. TV announcers call him underrated so often that it should be part of his first name. "He's definitely blue collar," said Steve. "And I'd like to think our father instilled that in all of us."

Their father was a 6-foot-5, 320-pound disciplinarian who booted the three older boys out of the house at the age of 16. Aaron had to leave when he was 12.

Understand that the brothers view the results of their upbringing as a positive, but their story is far from that.

Let's start with Great Grandpa Smith. He was run over by a freight wagon and killed, so his son, Grandpa Smith, had it rough growing up 40 miles east of Colorado Springs in the town of Rush. "No matter what we tell you about my father," Steve said, "he was so much milder on us than his father was on him."

Mr. and Mrs. Smith lived with the four boys in a trailer in Colorado Springs, but Mr. Smith's construction partner cleaned out Smith's accounts and left town. So when Aaron was six months old the family moved to a small farmhouse near Rapid City, South Dakota. The town was booming, so Mr. Smith was hoping to pile up a stake large enough to re-start his business as a general contractor.

Times were tough on the Smiths in South Dakota. "We were collecting aluminum cans for gas and we would road-hunt at night for rabbits," said Dave. "I will not eat rabbit to this day."

"But some of my best childhood memories were in South Dakota," said Steve.

"Absolutely," agreed Dave. "That was the best time. We lived on a 40-acre alfalfa farm and around the farm went a creek in a horseshoe shape, so we had our own little island of alfalfa farm, fishing, pigs, cows, playhouses. We had running water in it. It was absolutely wonderful at times, but it was also the hardest times we lived through as a family."

Dad soon developed diabetes and was told he had only a year or two to live, so the family moved back to Colorado to be closer to the rest of the family. Aaron was three at the time, and the diabetes turned his father into a tyrant.

"That's something we need to clarify," said Steve. "My father, I still have really good memories of my father – a very big man. I remember him coming home and the two of us grabbed a finger and he was swinging us like a helicopter in the front yard. I remember wonderful, fun times with my father. I try to express that to my two younger brothers, because Aaron and Kevin don't remember those good times."

"They only remember the times after he got sick and he really did not take care of himself," said Dave. "That was the main thing. When he didn't take care of himself he felt horrible and took it out on us boys, unfortunately."

"It was pins and needles," said Steve, "and that is the reason I joined sports. I didn't want to be home. If I was involved in a sport, that meant I didn't have to be home until at least three hours after everybody else was home. So whatever the brunt of any anger, hopefully it was just about done by the time I got home. Kevin and Aaron also learned to follow that pattern."

Dave preferred hunting and hot rods, while Steve urged Kevin and Aaron to take up sports. Steve even raved about Aaron's karate skills and ability as a rifleman.

"Aaron's very driven no matter what he's doing," said Dave.

"Our competitive spirit was due in part to our father's mental abuse – to an extent," said Steve. "And I don't want to dwell on this too much because I think we're all good husbands, good fathers. We're all very active with our kids, which is a change we all decided to make as adults, to not be that way."

Mr. Smith apparently raised the boys with the idea that spankings were good for children.

"There were days when nobody did anything wrong," Steve said. "But he'd say, 'Okay, line up. You're getting a spanking.'"

"And we'd say, 'What for?'" said Dave.

"That's no lie," Steve said. "My father got to the point that if there were no spankings to be had, no punishments to be dealt that day, it wasn't unusual for him to say, 'Head to the room, get your pants down, it's time for your spanking.' The next thing you knew we were arguing about why we were getting a spanking. My father's rule was: 'Just for principle. I'm sure you did something. I just don't know about it.'"

"It was tough," said Dave.

All of the boys began working at young ages, and they paid their parents 25 percent of their take-home pay. Dave believes the fight that got him kicked out of the house was indirectly tied to money.

"I got kicked out because I wouldn't do the dishes," said Steve. "I was working and paying my 25 percent. I had to buy my own car, insurance. Aaron was the first one out of all four of us who got a car bought for him and my mom paid for the insurance. I think my mom to some extent thinks he got the shaft from my dad in a lot of ways. My dad hunted with us, but Kevin and Aaron, my dad had no connection with those two."

Aaron – "the spoiled one" – was so fearful of his father he began sleeping with a Bokuto – a long wooden sword used to train Samurai fighters – next to his bed.

"He even slept with it next to his bed the next couple years after my father passed away," said Steve. "It tells you a little bit about what type of childhood we had."

"There was a constant fear in our house," said Dave.

"Constant tension," said Steve.

It came to a head when 12-year-old Aaron spilled milk on the counter. Dad went after Aaron, but Kevin stepped in and threw his dad across the kitchen, denting the refrigerator door.

"The next morning," Steve said, "my mom pulled my brothers aside and said, 'We're leaving. When I tell you to go, you'd better grab what you can and we're out of here.'"

Mom didn't move too far away. The boys wanted to stay within the school district, so the three found a place a quarter of a mile from dad. It's why Aaron continued to keep his Bokuto bedside.

"Dad could still come over at any time and break into the house," said Dave.

"And he was really mad now because mom left him," said Steve.

Mr. Smith passed away during Aaron's freshman year at Sierra High. Both of the older brothers had made their peace with their father and try to look on the bright side.

"Because my father was the kind of person he was, I think all four of us boys learned to lean on each other, and we are very close," said Steve. "I think I talk to Aaron five times a week on the phone."

BOTH DAVE and Steve Smith said that Aaron struggled with his father's death. He quit football his sophomore season, but Steve pushed him back into the sport.

"For about a year," Steve said, "it was really tough between him and I because I took on a fatherly role – telling him what to do, how to do it, how to act – and one day he said, 'Why can't you just be my brother instead of my dad?' From that point on we started getting along a little bit better.

"Aaron had the drive. Nobody ever pushed him. I did push him when he quit, but he did that because his dream was to play basketball."

"He was actually a lot better at basketball than I thought he was at football in high school," said Dave. "He was a man among boys in football, don't get me wrong, but I thought he was just a great basketball player."

The brothers said that Aaron was far more animated in high school than he is with the Steelers. He'd throw the Hulk Hogan pose on the field. "Or he'd do this thing with his arms, a sort of body-building pose, 'Which way to the gun show?'" Dave said.

Aaron was the center on the Sierra basketball team and his rival was 6-foot-9 Lewis-Palmer High center Pat Garrity, who went to Notre Dame and was the Big East Player of the Year before moving to the NBA.

"Aaron had to play against him two or three times a season," Steve said. "They manhandled each other. That's how Aaron got his first broken nose – in basketball. Blood was everywhere on the court, and I remember Aaron throwing a fit because the ref didn't call a foul. The ref said 'No foul, no foul,' so my brother took a handful of blood and threw it in his face and said, 'Tell me it's no foul!'"

"Aaron's settled down a lot since then," Dave said.

Aaron settled on football as his sport by his senior year and was being recruited by Colorado State, UCLA, Wisconsin and Colorado. Steve thought those schools were scared off by Aaron's lack of bulk and his grades.

"He was in the honors classes for gifted kids," Steve said, "but in his junior year someone gave him a hard time about being a smart athlete and then he chose to let his grades drop."

He ended up at Northern Colorado where he filled out and blossomed into a maniacal pass-rusher. He was spurred on by his brothers. Dave bet Aaron in his sophomore year that he wouldn't get 15 sacks. Dave lost and had to change the number on his stock car.

"I'm number 91 to this day," he said.

Dave then bet him the next season that Aaron couldn't set the school record for sacks. Aaron got 21.5 and shaved his brother's head.

When the NFL draft rolled around, Aaron was considered by many as one of the nation's sleepers, and some experts believed he'd be drafted in the second round. Perhaps they got that info from the Broncos.

"The Broncos called our house and said they'd take him with the 61st pick," said Steve. "Instead they picked a guard."

The Broncos passed on Smith twice in the third round as well. He wasn't drafted until the Steelers took him in the fourth round with the 109th pick. He saw action in six games as a rookie in 1999 and started the 2000 opener. He became a Pro Bowler in the 2004 season, chased down Shaun Alexander from behind (and from the opposite side) in Super Bowl XL, and entered Sunday's game in Denver riding a streak of 121 consecutive games played. His line coach with the Steelers, John Mitchell, often says that he won't get out of coaching until Aaron's contract is up.

"Everybody on this team and everybody he plays against knows Aaron's one of the best," defensive captain James Farrior once said. "It's his work ethic. He comes out every day and works on his craft. He never takes a play off."

"I don't know if it's our childhood upbringing or not," said Steve. "Kevin ended up going to boot camp, and he said the drill sergeants made everybody in his basic training group cry at one time or another. They couldn't get Kevin to cry. They made him spend 16 hours in the dark, dressed in his boxers in the rain and mud, trying to make him break or cry, and they couldn't do it. Because we grew up with my dad as tough as he was, they couldn't say anything to make him cry. Aaron was the same way. He said we can thank our dad for giving us so much negative, that you rise above it, and you focus on what you need to.

"I'll ask Aaron about the new rookies and he'll say they have talent but that they have to have it in the head. He says the ability to deal with it mentally thins the herd pretty quick."

✦ ✦ ✦

"I HOPE WE obliterate the Broncos," said young Brandon Smith. And he wasn't the only Coloradoan who felt that way. The pre-game parking lot bubbled with Steelers fans for the Sunday night game, but Broncos fans were scarce. "This parking lot's an absolute joke," said Jim, in from Arizona. "If you walked through Pittsburgh two hours before game time you'd never see anything like this. Look at this!"

"I'm Crazy Doug from Cheyenne," said a Steelers fan wearing a large gold wig. "Twenty two of us came down for this. I see the Steelers every time I come here."

Anyone ever try to take your wig?

"A guy tried to take it at the 2005 AFC Championship game," Crazy Doug said, "but another guy I didn't even know tackled him for me."

Dave Brown, 30, didn't wear a wig, or face paint. The Mt. Lebanon native traveled from his home in North Carolina. "It cost about $500, $600 to come out here," he said. "Win or lose I've never regretted going on the road to see them."

His fondest road memory?

"The AFC Championship here in Denver," he said. "I think Steelers fans, younger Steelers fans, had been of the mindset similar to the Boston Red Sox mindset: 'We're very good, but when we get to the end something bad is going to happen. Neil O'Donnell's going to throw an interception; Kordell Stewart's going to do something bad; we're going to have a punt returned for a touchdown against us. We're a good team – a great team – but we can't get over the hump.' And that day was glorious. We got over the hump; exclamation point. That's why it was big."

✦ ✦ ✦

BRONCOS FANS made it to the stadium in time to see their team take a 21-7 halftime lead. This crippled the Steelers for two reasons:

1. The incomparable Aaron Smith injured his knee on a leg-whip by teammate Travis Kirschke during the first defensive series. This allowed the Broncos a critical 31-yard scramble by quarterback Jay Cutler after Smith's replacement was pushed from one side of the field to the other. More of that was expected in the second half without Underrated Aaron.

2. The Steelers passed on 10 of their first 13 offensive plays against the NFL's worst-ranked run defense. They did so to set up the running game, but that plan was out the window with a 14-point deficit.

The Steelers rallied in the second half. Linebacker Larry Foote's interception to start the third quarter led to a Ben Roethlisberger touchdown pass to Santonio Holmes. The Broncos scored for a 28-14 lead, but Roethlisberger threw touchdown passes to tight ends Matt Spaeth and Heath Miller to tie the game late. Cutler, playing the best game of his young career (22 for 29), then drove the Broncos 49 yards for a game-winning 49-yard field goal at the gun.

The injury to Smith was deemed minor, but he would miss the next two games, the first games he'd miss since his rookie season. The rest of the locker room couldn't understand the loss to mediocre opposition with an extra week to prepare.

"It was a game that means a lot to me," said Brett Keisel. "Everyone around my home is a Broncos fan, so, yeah, we fell short today and it sucks."

Chapter Fourteen
HIGH PLAINS DRIFTING

MARK GORSCAK scouts for the Steelers, but he's becoming better known for starting the 40-yard dash at the Indianapolis combine. I know Mark for his taste in obscure rock and roll. He's burned me hundreds of CDs over the years, but for this trip – particularly for the drive through Kansas – Mark burned me one of those book CDs. It's about a prospect Mark scouted at Emporia State University in this state. Here's Mark:

"There was a player in 1999, the 2000 draft season when Max McCartney was our scouting coordinator. The player's name was Brian Shay. He set the all-time rushing record for all-divisions. BLESTO had a free-agent grade on the kid, so I had to go out there. The first time I drove out I went the back way from Manhattan (Kansas). There's a back way you can cut across.

"I'd watched the tape on him. They had like 3-yard line splits, just like Texas Tech. It was kind of a gimmick offense because the splits were so wide and everyone was so spread out. It created natural running lanes. The kid was a powerful runner, but he had no elusiveness, nothing. He was a short, squatty, powerful guy. He looked like everyone's second strength coach. I watched the tape and he had no speed, no elusiveness, so I rejected him. Max said, 'You rejected him? He's the ALL-time leading rusher in ALL divisions.' I said, yeah, but he can't play in the National Football League. He said, 'No. Go back. Go watch more tape.'

"So I had to go back again. At the time, we were a drive-by team. I already went about two weeks ago and now I've got to go back there. They told me I could fly if I wanted to, and that's the only way I could do it. So I get on the plane to Kansas City and from there I got on a puddle-jumper to get there. Well, the puddle jumper is a lawn dart – 10 seats here, 10 seats there. There was a flight attendant and she was also the co-pilot. I was the only person from the team, so I sat in the middle. She gave me my Coke and then went to co-pilot the plane. We land at Emporia Airport. It's not international by any means. We pull up and we're about 200 yards from the gate and the pilot says, 'Hey, do you mind if I leave you off here?' He said he was in a hurry, so I said OK. I get my suitcase and take it about 200 yards and I get in the airport and there isn't a soul in the place. I needed a rental car, and I didn't have a cell phone at that time and there wasn't a pay phone anywhere. So I go outside to look for a pay phone. All of the sudden a truck barrels down and I thought he might know how I could get a rental car. It was a rickety old farm truck. This farmer had bales of hay in the back. The leather seats were all cracked up. Bottles were rattling in the front seat and all that good stuff. He pulls up and said, 'Hey, are you Mark Gorscak?' I nodded, and he said, 'Hop in. I'll take you to the rental car.' I threw my suitcase in the back on the hay and I sat up front in this dirty farm truck. He dropped me off at the rental car place in town about five, six miles from the airport. I had to bring it back there and they promised me they'd get me to the airport.

"So now I've got to go see Brian Shay again. He's the same guy. He hasn't changed. I watched practice, this short little sawed-off dude about this tall and all bound up running through those big, wide holes all spread out. All you had to do was shield block and he'd get six yards a crack. Can't catch a lick. They never throw to him. He never blocks. He runs back kickoffs and he's a straight-liner, that's it. So I had to put a grade on him or Max is going to send me back out. So I put a free-agent grade on him.

"I go back to the car rental, drop off the car, we chit-chat. I asked them how I was going to get back to the airport. They said, 'Oh, yeah, that's right. Hold on.' She calls up her daughter. Her daughter's going on a date, so the daughter and her date are going to pick me up and take me to the airport. A green Gremlin stops and picks me up. It's the kid and her daughter. And her daughter was smokin' hot, too. So I throw my suitcase in the hatch of the kid's Gremlin. I go in the back seat to sit and I'm all squashed up going back to the airport.

"I call Max up and Max is pissed again: 'You gave the most prolific runner in all divisions a free-agent grade?' I said yeah. He said, 'That's not good enough.' So Max gave him a grade and now Dick Hoak had to watch. Hoak was pissed he had to watch. He said to me, 'This Brian Shay, he can't play.'

"So in the all-star game, the East-West Shrine Game, he had a little bit of success running the ball. They ran a fake punt and he got about 50 yards on this fake punt. Well, number one, you're not allowed to run a fake in the all-star game and he ran it anyway. That's why he got the 50 yards. They weren't playing anything. So now that gets shoved back in my face. God rest Max's soul, but he says, 'Look at the punt return in the all-star game he had.' Now I've got to go back a third time to work the kid out. I'm thinking, you've got to be kidding me.

"So we go out there. There's this pack of scouts who go to every workout, no matter how big or how small. So this kid's supposed to work out at Kansas' workout. It wasn't in the contiguous neighborhood, but at that time I think it was a 75-mile radius and he wasn't in the radius and couldn't workout. So he had to go back to Emporia. Nobody wanted to go and work this kid out, but there were a couple bosses that made sure we worked out the No. 1 runner in NCAA history. So now there's a caravan going to work out Brian Shay. It was maybe 10 scouts. He ran the 40 and the refrigerator fell on his back around the 20-yard line and he started huffing and puffing. He ran like a 4.8, a 4.85 40. That ain't good enough to play when you're that short and you're all tight and bound up. He ran the second 40 and we thought he was going to die. Now we run him through all the drills and this kid's just sucking wind. So now most of the scouts are really pissed off. First of all they had to go to Emporia, Kansas, so we're going to work this kid out and get our money's worth. As soon as he gets done doing the shuttles and jumps and all that stuff, he's gassed. But this one guy, an old DB coach, he had an arm and he's going to make him run routes. He was running this kid on deep routes, posts, nothing short for a running back. It was like a punishment for the kid, and this kid couldn't catch a lick. It was like, why are we here? So I went to Emporia three times for a kid who was a reject. He ended up signing a free-agent contract with the Kansas City Chiefs – which was a political deal, I think – and he didn't last very long. He got cut in training camp."

✦ ✦ ✦

THE TOWN of Jenks, just southeast of Tulsa, Oklahoma, was revved up over an NFL Films documentary about their high school's glorious football tradition. The premiere at the local theater was two days away and rumor had it that Sean Mahan, in his black and gold jersey, had made the flick. Sean's best friend, former Jenks High and University of Tulsa defensive end Justin Dixon, says the black and gold would **make** the flick.

"I've always been a Steelers fan," said Dixon. "I loved Cowher. I would've loved for Sean to have played for Cowher because I'd liked to have known what he was really like."

Mahan and Dixon played on the first of six consecutive state championship teams at Jenks, a big-school power that's won eight of the last 11 state titles.

Dixon was the tight end and Mahan played left tackle. The left guard was a future four-year starter at Nebraska, Jason Lohr. The tailback was future NFL linebacker Rocky Calmus, who ran left as often as he could.

"We were playing against Midwest City in '96 and they were going for their third state championship in a row," said Jenks Coach Allan Trimble. "We were behind at halftime and Rocky's fired up and he said, 'If y'all just give me the ball we'll win the game.' And we ran the ball 21 or 22 straight times behind Sean and Lohr. We scored 21 unanswered points and won the championship in '96. You could pull that film out and see the dominance that Sean and those guys had."

It was a bittersweet year for Mahan, though. His father died of a heart attack early that school year, and then two years later, early in Sean's freshman year at Notre Dame, his mom died suddenly.

"Physically he's strong, but his internal strength is a whole lot more," said Sean's aunt, Mary McNamara. "He was very close to his parents, but if you saw Sean he stayed strong, he stayed steady, he never wavered, stayed on the football team and never slowed down for a minute. He never got off track for a minute; not for a minute. He had to work out a lot of grief, but football gave him a focus and he knew that was his key and his talent and gift."

Mary and her husband Steve, a lawyer in Tulsa, took Sean in after his parents died. Steve was proud to see his nephew land at his alma mater, Notre Dame.

"He got to play for Jenks, Notre Dame and Pittsburgh," Steve said. "Not a lot of guys can say that. All three of those programs are prestigious."

"We'd never been to Pittsburgh," said Mary. "But we had to go to Washington, D.C. last summer, so we drove through Pittsburgh and my God it was gorgeous. I had no idea Pittsburgh was so beautiful. People say that about Tulsa, too. My gosh, we had so much fun just looking at the beauty of the city itself. I think he's very, very, very happy."

✦ ✦ ✦

COMING OUT OF my 30th burger joint in 30 days, I may have been a tad delirious when I decided then and there that Wichita, Kansas, has the second-best rock station in the nation behind "The Moose" in Bozeman, Montana. But, really, at the time the only music I was hearing was coming from the station in my head. It was playing Bruce Springsteen and he was telling a story about how he and Wayne, on the Fourth of July, drove 800 miles without seeing a cop. That's exactly what my odometer was telling me because, on this trip, I've been pulled over only once. After interviewing the Smith brothers outside of Colorado Springs, I was blowing through the empty streets of Denver in the hope that I'd beat the large crowd certain to emerge soon from the Rockies' NLCS playoff game. There was only one other guy on the road, and he was a cop. He pulled me over, but, with the Rockies on their way to a sweep, let me off with a warning.

So here I was in the middle of Missouri, making a run for St. Louis, but I was wary. My karma-meter was telling me I was due, and I was too tired to argue with my karma-meter, because, after all, this is Lap 12.

Let me explain. In high school, before my mother let me quit the torture that had become known as the swim team, I swam the 500-yard freestyle. It's a gruesome 20-lap race, and the low point was always Lap 12. That's when you're out of gas, but you're still too far away from the finish line to have any hope. Well, here in the middle of Missouri it's Lap 12, baby, and my attention span is at an all-time low. So I made a very un-Springsteen-like decision and turned on the cruise control. It got me all the way to the Arch in downtown St. Louis, where I met with the parents of Steelers fullback Carey Davis. He had finally made an NFL roster after being a final cut the three previous seasons for three different teams.

"I was running an event down in Birmingham, Alabama. I wasn't in town," Carey Davis Sr. said. "When his mom called and told me that he not only made the team, but was going to start, I was around about 3,000 people and – honest to God's truth – I just fell to my knees and started crying for him."

Carey Davis Sr. and Annette Slack split up soon after Carey Jr. was born, but the parents remained friendly and raised their son "by two parents in different homes," said Carey Sr., a supervisor for DirecTV. "Like most dads I spent as much time with him and always enjoyed what he's done and lived vicariously through his accomplishments. He's always been a pretty good kid and stayed focused. He really proved that by making the Steelers this year after being in the league the last four years and really trying so hard and not giving up. A lot of young men would've given up by now. He's been cut numerous times but each time he'd come home, we'd talk about it, I'd ask him what he wants to do, and he said he's still going to work at it, he's still going forward with it."

It paid off. The younger Davis made the Steelers and was named starting full-back before the opener. He's a St. Louis kid who idolized Terry Pendleton growing up. He was raised by a smart, pretty mom in one house and a tall, strong dad in another. He lived with his mom, Annette, who, after working as a nurse for 18 years, passed her bar exam and for the last nine years has prac-ticed medical malpractice injury defense. She works in a high-rise office build-ing in downtown St. Louis with a window view of the arch. She's an intelligent lady with a core understanding of sports. Take a listen:

- "Carey's first two years of Pop Warner he couldn't play in the games. Now, I'm ex-military, so I'm running with him and we got the weight under control. We got all the weight off, but then I had to go away for a military tour and my girl-friend fed him everything there was, and in two weeks he put all the weight back on. So he didn't make the team and he said, 'Okay, I'm done.' I said, 'Oh no, you were perfectly fit and ready to make that team when I left here. If you have to carry the water every day you're going back.' So he went to practice every day. He learned all the plays. The very first game he went to down in Florida and they put him in and he got the game ball. That triggered him to check his discipline and get it done."

- "We grew up in Hazelwood (Mo.) out in North County. It wasn't bad. I brought him downtown to Mathews-Dickey Boys Club. It's right at Highway 70 so it gets kind of bad, but I wanted him to have different environments and be able to adjust to different environments. And quite frankly that's where they were play-ing the better football."

- "We brought him down to the city to play basketball and there was this church called Church On the Rock, and those kids were ferocious. So Carey was mov-ing, I told him, 'No, no, no. You are bigger than everybody here. This is your lane. Those people have to find a different way to go. You need to impress upon them they need to go the other direction.'"

Now, keep in mind, this is the **mother**, the sweet, slender, pretty mother. Two more:

- "We used to watch the draft a lot, and I remember one year Warren Sapp got caught the day before the draft and he started plummeting. I said, 'See, this is what happens. They have enough bad boys. They don't need any more.' I said, 'Not only are they looking at what you're doing on the field, they're looking at your character off the field so you have to be well-rounded.' I didn't have to tell him that because he'd always been a good kid. He's never even had a fight."

And, finally:

- "I still have fantasies about Franco Harris."

Franco should be so lucky.

THE BEST PURE baseball town in the country is St. Louis, and Carey Davis – both of them – loved the game. But Carey Jr. decided one day that it was just too hot to continue playing catcher, so he quit to play football. The decision got him a scholarship from Ron Turner at the University of Illinois.

"He was a one-back in college and caught the ball a lot out of the backfield," said Carey Sr. "When I saw him catch a few balls early this season with the Steelers, I was really excited for him because that's what he does real well."

The younger Davis had two nicknames. His childhood friends called him "Fats" and his high school teammates called him "Baby Bus." Jerome Bettis got his start in St. Louis, and Davis has a similar build. In fact, Carey's shoulders are so big that John Clayton turned him into the league commissioner last spring for wearing pads in minicamp.

Just kidding.

But Davis entered his senior season at Illinois as one of the top fullbacks in the country until he injured his knee before the 2003 season. He wasn't expected to play in the opener against rival Missouri.

"I was in Germany and nobody told me he got hurt," said Annette. "He had a scope and they didn't tell me. Then I saw on TV that he couldn't play in the Braggin' Rights game because of surgery. So the phone was a mile and a half away and I took off running for the phone, and he said, 'I'm fine, I'm fine.' But I was flying in for the game and I told him not to play. He said, 'No, I'll be fine. I can play.' I said, 'No, you cannot play.' He said 'OK' and that's how we ended the conversation. I get to the game and he's suited up right in front of me. I started hollering to him. I know he heard me, but he never turned around. He had the best game of his life, but the next week he ended up with a staph infection."

Annette didn't know whether the surgery caused the infection, or whether it was caused by the dirty uniform he put on so soon after surgery. So the situation worsened.

"When he was on his way to surgery he called me and I was right here at this intersection," Annette said. "He was screaming into the phone, 'You need to get here right now!' I told him I needed some time to get to Illinois. He said, 'You just need to get here now! They're cutting off my leg!' I think I got there in an hour and a half from right here. They were re-scoping him after the staph infection to find out what was wrong with him."

The infection cost Davis the rest of his senior season and he wasn't drafted. The Colts signed him after the draft and thus began a winding journey for not only the big, fast and talented player, who just seemed to miss by an inch everywhere he went, but for his family as well.

ONLY 26 YEARS OLD, Carey Davis had been cut by the Colts, Falcons, Buccaneers and Dolphins before the Steelers signed him to their practice squad late in the 2006 season.

He plays a position that's fading from most schemes, but was clearly one of the Steelers' best kick coverers at training camp.

"He had a great year last year at Tampa, where he was the leading rusher coming out of preseason," said Annette. "We thought that would do it, but it's not the numbers. It's a lot of different variables. It just wasn't his time."

"He got cut the last day every time," said Carey Sr. "I think if he'd have been cut on the first day he'd be somewhere else teaching right now, but I think because he was always so close he knew he was good enough and he just needed the right situation."

Did either parent advise their son to give up football?

"Nope," said Annette. "There were some long stretches and the nerves get frayed and the house gets a little smaller because he's walking around and he's not very pleasant. And then when it can't get any worse, the phone rings."

Which cut was the toughest?

"Tampa Bay," dad said. "He was so close. My brother lives there and he called me every day: 'They're writing him up. They think he's fantastic. He's going to play.' It was the year Mike Alstott had the neck problem, so we thought he had a chance to play. That was the toughest one because it was just like this year."

"It made the hype this year harder to accept," said Annette. "He was being written up, but we were like, 'Okay.' And they'd be like, 'You're not excited?' Well, I'd been excited before. I'm just so happy it worked out in Pittsburgh."

Chapter Fifteen
LONELY OL' NIGHT

IN THE road-trip book *Road Swing*, author Steve Rushin rolled into Indiana in search of the remnants of his hero Larry Bird, who, of course, is an icon at Indiana State. So it got me thinking about my hero, another icon at Indiana State, Tunch Ilkin.

You *are* an icon at Indiana State, aren't you Tunch?

"You *are* kidding me, aren't you?" said Tunch.

But Tunch warmed to the idea. The Steelers' color analyst and former Pro Bowl tackle gave me the addresses of his old haunts in Terre Haute, but with this disclaimer: "When you reference this part of my life, remember it was B.C. I was wild as a billy goat back then."

B.C., of course, stands for Before Christ. Tunch is a devout Christian, but that couldn't possibly be as interesting – in a secular way – as Tunch B.C.

THE BALLYHOO Tavern looks like one of those old corner sports taverns from a bygone era.

"The Ballyhoo is called the University's country club," John Sharman said. John's the "Voice of the Sycamores" and was more than glad to help the cause.

"If you're a student here," he said, "you've been to the Ballyhoo at least two times. And if you've only been there two times, you'd better be a straight-A student."

It's the first stop for ISU students on the Homecoming Day pub crawl/parade. The Sycamores lost that game last week, 56-7, to fall to 0-8. I experienced a similar result.

The bar sits in the middle of campus and warehouses the photos and jerseys of the ISU legends. There's the jersey of Larry Bird, and there's Bob Ross (I don't know, either). Here's an autographed photo of the 2000 NCAA tournament basketball team, and a pair of photos of ISU's volleyball powerhouses. Rick Murphy, who once played in the World Football League, has his No. 45 up behind the bar. And there's the legendary No. 22 worn by Melanie Boeglin (did I spell that right?). Oh, geez, John Wooden coached here from 1946-48. I've heard of him. Who are the rest of these people?

"A lot of them paid to have their jerseys put up here," said Derek, the night-time manager.

Derek played free safety at ISU about 15 years ago. I asked him if he could answer a few questions about Tunch Ilkin.

"No problem," he said, so I turned on my camcorder.

Me: You have jerseys of Larry Bird and Bob Ross and photos of Kurt Thomas and the 1997 cross country team. Why no Tunch Ilkin?

Derek: I couldn't tell you that.

Me: What can you tell me about Tunch?

Derek: I don't know anything about him.

Me: Thanks for your time, Derek.

Derek: No problem.

And that makes the score 56-7.

Let's try the off-campus bar that Tunch warned me about: Simrells.

Whoa, he was right. This is a dump in the classic sense. Wrecked cars fill the parking lot and inside the place smells of death. If someone would dust a bit I'd be able to see the crusty old memorabilia behind the glass cases near the pool table.

The bartender with the long black hair and lip ring told me that, no, I could not interview him. In fact, I was told to take my camcorder back outside.

On to the new Applebees. This restaurant opened in Tunch A.D., but it's stuffed with old ISU memorabilia. The manager didn't recognize Tunch's name, but he was young. So I looked, and I looked, and I weeded out the Larry Bird shrines, the Kurt Thomas smile, and the famous photo of Bruce Baumgartner carrying the flag at the front of the Olympic parade. Then I found what I was looking for: At the very top, an inch from the ceiling, was a group photo called "1978-79 Sycamore Stars." Well, Tunch had to be up there. So I pardoned myself and climbed on a chair to take a closer look – at 13 basketball players. No Tunch Ilkin anywhere.

MY FRIENDS and I once went to the old Stanley Theater in Pittsburgh to watch The Kinks. This was circa 1979, when the Stanley was a place to not only see the best bands, but also your friends from school. The time to stroll through the lobby was during the warm-up act, but my friend Kenny wasn't interested and stayed in his seat. When I returned, Kenny was stoked. "That was the best warm-up band I've ever seen," he said.

Yeah, right. I asked Kenny the band's name.

"Johnny Cougar," he said. "I think you're going to hear a lot from that guy down the road."

Down the road came in January 1996. I was in the Three Rivers Stadium press box before the AFC Championship game. My buddies and I crammed into the press lounge to smoke cigarettes and eat sausage and gawk at the bodacious chick in the Colts jacket. But who's the stringy-haired beanpole with her? Well, the beanpole walked over and asked for a light. It was John Cougar Mellencamp.

"You have to sing a song for us first," said another reporter.

"For a fucking light?" Mellencamp said.

I gave him the lighter, and he thanked me and moved on.

So that brings us to the front doors of the Hulman Center on this late-October day on the Indiana State campus. I was on my way – by virtue of a solid lead – to the school's Wall of Fame. Rumor had it that Tunch Ilkin has been remembered at Larry Bird U, but there was a problem: The doors were locked.

"It's John Mellencamp," the voice of the Sycamores told me. "He's practicing right now. I think we have to know somebody to get in here."

Mellencamp would perform the next night, with Los Lobos, at the Hulman Center. It was being celebrated as a rare visit by the state's favorite son. I was told that Mellencamp ordered a four-day lockdown of the facility, that even the basketball team had to find another place to practice. But I was with a guy who knew the secret handshake. John Sharman flashed his gang sign and we were ushered in, but only to the outer wall of plaques. There, as we both stood open-mouthed, was a plaque of the great Tunch Ali Ilkin. I know I'll never forget the moment. And thanks to John Mellencamp, we had a soundtrack.

FINALLY, SOMEONE HERE is older than me and John Mellencamp. He's Dennis Raetz, Indiana State's all-time winningest football coach. He'd been summoned at mid-season to replace a deposed coach and bring a modicum of respect back to the program. Raetz was the school's defensive coordinator when Tunch played, and Raetz remembered him.

"I remember that I asked the head coach if he could move over to defense," Raetz said. "In all candor, when we came here, we had only 43 players, so you remember the kids who were here and certainly Tunch, in all probability, was the best player on our team at that time. The only kid close was a kid from McKeesport, Pennsylvania, named Gerald Gluscic. Both Tunch and Gerald are in the Indiana State Hall of Fame, so there were some really good players here, just not many of them."

Raetz said that Tunch was one of the top two offensive linemen he ever coached. The other was Mike Simmons, who went on to play for the Tampa Bay Bucs. I asked Raetz about Tunch B.C. and hit the jackpot.

"I think the same thing that makes you a good football player sometimes gets you in trouble," Raetz said. "I think in order to be a good football player you have to have a certain amount of orneriness in you. Tunch never did anything to really cause problems for us as a coaching staff, or himself, within the framework of the university, and that can't be said for – heh heh – everyone we've ever had here. But his orneriness revolved around the fact Tunch liked to fight. He liked to do some things that caused problems due to immaturity, not due to any malicious-ness or having anything to do with character flaw. It was just immaturity."

Coach, you may have blown this scandal wide open. Please, continue.

"Well, I'll just say that when you're 18 or 19 years old, and away from home for the first time, and discover the merits of drinking beer, and get around a certain type, you at times express yourself in ways you probably wished you wouldn't later."

ON THE field, Tunch played center, then tackle, then some center again. He, of course, played right tackle for the Steelers under Chuck Noll and is now a media superstar in Pittsburgh. He's the rare reporter who'll criticize an athlete for his performance and then face him the next day in the locker room.

"If you play football as long as he did and sit through as many film sessions as he has," Raetz said, "and are as intelligent as Tunch is, I think there's a way to criticize what you're seeing instead of criticizing the human being, and I think that's part of coaching. You've got to be able to make players realize the criticism is not personal. I think that's a skill that certain people have."

Tunch has it. Raetz has it, too, and that's why he's been asked back. ISU once was a proud athletic program that went to the final four, the college world series, led an Olympic parade, won a national gymnastics title, and was ranked No. 1 in Division I-AA football for nine weeks of a season. That was under athletic director Bob King.

"The bad thing about Coach King is he had the audacity to have a heart attack and a brain aneurysm six months apart and he had to retire," Raetz said. "But he's the one. He saw potential in Indiana State and was able to get it."

The school just hired a new athletic director who gives Raetz hope for the ISU future. It's the reason he decided to stand in on an interim basis. I asked him how Tunch could help.

"Tunch can help in many ways," he said. "Financial resources, or his capacity as a broadcaster, reconnecting with the university and offering in that capacity. But part of that is our responsibility to reconnect with him."

And part of that should require the building of a new statue, or at least a jersey behind the bar, for a school icon.

✦ ✦ ✦

TOUGH DECISIONS: Do I leave Terre Haute for the game in Cincinnati today? Do I spend another night in Terre Haute to watch Mellencamp (and the warm-up band)? Or do I drive to the University of Louisville and check on former Steelers? Well, the funds are low and it's raining, and those aren't my only problems. My muffler broke and my car is making horrific sounds. I called the SID at Louisville, but the timing was all wrong. Pitt would be in town later that night (for Saturday's game) and it was too late in the week for interviews.

Ah, heck with it. I drove to Louisville and sat in my car as the rain poured down. Oh, woe is me.

And then I reminded myself about William Gay.

"William Gay's just trying to SURVIVE," Mike Tomlin bellowed one day in training camp.

It was a planned reaction meant to dissuade us in the media from overplaying the rookie's great game in Canton to start the preseason. But the line stayed with me after I heard the William Gay story.

Gay attended Louisville where he became a first-team All-Big East cornerback. He was drafted in the fifth round by the Steelers to complete his amazing story. Anything he might accomplish in the NFL will be gravy, considering Gay's childhood in Tallahassee, Florida.

"My mom was killed when I was eight," he said. "She was murdered by her husband. He was my little brother's dad but she wanted a divorce. I don't know what was going through his head, but he knew she was about to leave because we were moving to my grandmother's. Then he came where she was chillin' and shot her."

What kind of effect did this have?

"It was tough because I was going down the wrong path," Gay said. "It got to the point where I was at school and anybody that said something about my mother, I was ready to fight. I'd just get outraged at school or out-of-school programs to where I had to go home. It was just crazy. My uncle sat me down and said, 'Hey, do you want to go to jail? Or do you want to go to school and have a better life?' It really hit me when I was young. I didn't want to go to jail, so I just switched it over and became a whole new person. It worked out for the best."

Have you talked to your stepfather since?

"No, he killed himself right after that," Gay said. "She was still alive, but he thought he had killed her, so he went back to his car and shot himself. She was still alive, but she couldn't make it because they couldn't get the bullet out."

Where did this happen?

"In the neighborhood we were at, my grandmother's. We stayed at the projects. We were a couple houses down. Her friend stayed a couple houses up and that's where she was. Luckily, she dropped us off at my grandmother's house first, then went to her friends, or you never know what he would've done to me and my little brother."

What happened to your real father?

"My dad died when I was 12. It hurt losing a father but I never really got the chance to get close to him. I'd see him like every Christmas, but my mother separated from him early in my life so I never got to know him. I guess he got tied up into drugs and stuff. You know how that goes."

Who gave you the most help?

"It was a collective group. First of all, my grandmother got us out of that situation of being in the projects. She got together all the money that my mother left behind and she put it into a house to get us into a better situation. And then all my uncles and aunts, we stayed together. I had a close-knit family around."

Did it help to go off to Louisville?

"That was the best thing for me, to get away from Tallahassee. I knew so much from being in the projects. I knew where trouble was and all that. I knew I needed to get away and learn something new because my whole family stayed in Tallahassee their whole life. They never got to see any of the United States. I was like, 'Hey, let me go see things.' I jumped out on my own. It was rough at first, but I'm going to take it for all it's worth."

Chapter Sixteen
O-H-I-O

A PETITE blonde from Boardman named P.J. was talking about her Steelers and the games she's watched them play in her home state of Ohio. In Cleveland, for instance, she was pregnant with her second child and a Browns fan pushed her down from behind. She said she was just minding her own business at the time.

"She was running her mouth," corrected her husband.

"I was *not* running my mouth," said P.J. "We were leaving and he saw my Steelers shirt and pushed me. I said something after, but my husband here didn't do anything.

"It was bad," she continued, "but not as bad as Cincinnati."

Cincinnati?

"Cincinnati was horrible. I had a Kimo von Oelhoffen shirt on and that was the playoff game when Kimo took Carson Palmer out in the first quarter. As we were leaving, some woman behind me said, 'We should take Ben out the way Kimo took Carson out.' And I turned around and very calmly said, 'Shove it up your ass.' And she said, 'You've got to be kidding me,' and she started screaming at me and then she said something about my Kimo shirt. And I said, 'I don't care what you said because I've got to go home and make my plane reservations for Indianapolis next week.'

Now, P.J. is 5-foot-2, 115 pounds.

"I was a parole officer so nobody scares me," she said. "I was OK, but HE didn't have my back."

He, of course, is Joe, her mid-sized husband.

"Every time the stories come up it's pretty much me not helping," said Joe. "It is what it is. I can only hope that you write the truth."

A few minutes later, after P.J. left for the restroom, Joe told his version of the truth.

"My wife," he said, "was the only person in the whole stadium, besides Kimo von Oelhoffen, with a Kimo von Oelhoffen jersey. As we were leaving the stadium, happy to leave with our victory and go right up on I-71 and go home, somebody started yelling at her because they saw the Kimo jersey. So my wife, of course, being herself, was running her mouth back at the person. I was like, 'Please, honey, just take our victory and go home.' But they kept going back and forth, back and forth. There were 65,000 other people that hated Kimo. Me and my wife and Kimo were the only people that loved Kimo at that time. Honestly, that was the only time I've ever been scared. I was hoping my wife would run, but she was too busy turning around and running her mouth."

✦ ✦ ✦

"AND HERE he is right there, Kimo von Oelhoffen," said young Marty Angiulli. "After all the garbage we went through, we put him up behind the bar, a signed picture."

Marty Angiulli and his father with the same name run Martino's On Vine, one of the nation's great Steelers bars. It's on Vine Street in Cincinnati and the Angiullis were preparing to host Greg Lloyd for that night's pep rally. The Steelers were in town to play the Bengals on Sunday and plenty of bad feelings remain from the von Oelhoffen tackle that knocked Carson Palmer out of the 2005 playoffs. It's the reason that after Thursday night's college game, Bengals fans are banned from Martino's during Steelers Week.

"If we don't, there'll be fights," said young Angiulli. "It's still their Super Bowl in their eyes. Most of these kids are in their early to mid 20s, so they don't remember the Bengals ever winning. The one good season they had the Steelers hurt their stud quarterback, knocked them out of the playoffs, and went on to win the Super Bowl."

The Angiullis moved to Cincinnati from Vandergrift, Pa., when young Marty earned a scholarship to play football at the University of Cincinnati. The rest of the family came along when his son was born.

The Angiullis kept their original restaurant – Night Courts – open in Ford City, Pa., and opened Martino's a block and a half away from the UC football stadium. That was 13 years ago.

"On Sundays we wanted to watch the Steeler games so we got the NFL Package," Mr. Angiulli said. "We didn't advertise it, but we had the Steelers on every TV, and then week after week the crowd kept growing and growing, and then the Super Bowl season came along. The Steelers had to play here in the playoffs and every TV station in Cincinnati and in Pittsburgh carried us. I mean, you come in here and look at the place, there's nothing but Steelers stuff up. That made us. We took off after that."

Even though the place has room – legally – for 366 people, close to 600 jammed in for the playoff game in Cincinnati. Angiulli talked to the Cincinnati fire department and they told him not to worry. The next largest crowd was 400 for the Super Bowl.

"We used to always go to the game," dad said. "But now it's become so over-whelming; so many people come in here. Tomorrow both floors will be packed. We have people coming from all over the city, every week. Tomorrow, I don't know what's going to happen. I don't know how bad it's going to be."

Mike Tomlin and two of his assistants – Larry Zierlein and Amos Jones – frequented Martino's when they coached at UC. Marty said the parents of scout Phil Kreidler used to show up every week. "They were one of our first customers. They'd sit in one of those booths and they'd kiss after every score," he said.

"Last week Chris Henry was in here watching the second half of the Steelers-Broncos game," said young Marty. "They went upstairs – Chad Johnson and Chris Henry – and signed one of our 'We Dey!' shirts. Odell Thurman wouldn't sign it."

Former UC basketball coach Bob Huggins got his DUI after a visit to Martino's. "He said on TV that he came from here," dad said. "We had the press sitting in here trying to find out what he drank, how he drank."

Mr. Angiulli calls Cincinnati "a big bandwagon city" and says he'd never be able to open a Bengals bar, or any other bar, in Pittsburgh.

Not even a Cowboys bar?

"Don't get me started," he said before getting started. "In the '70s we won the Super Bowls and Dallas was America's Team. I hate Dallas because of that and I resented the media for it. Maybe that's made us Steelers fans closer. We should've been America's Team, so I think that pissed all of us off."

I FINALLY found Kurt Emmert. He's the fan from Indianapolis who keeps all of the fans clubs updated on Steelers events.

"I've got to keep Steeler Nation in touch," he said.

Emmert calls Indianapolis another fair-weather city. He chides Colts fans who didn't attend their sparse – by comparison to Pittsburgh's – championship parade after Super Bowl XLI.

"They tell me it was too cold," Emmert said. "I said it was just as cold in Pittsburgh when 300,000 of us showed up for that parade."

Next to Emmert at the bar were three Steelers fans in for the game from Alabama. They don't know anything about fair-weather fans because where they come from there are consequences for rooting the wrong way.

"I used to sell at doctor's offices," said Glenn Campbell, a Western Pennsylvanian living in Birmingham. "And in Alabama, when I'd go into a doctor's office, I'd see either a picture of Bear Bryant or Pat Dye. They'd ask you: 'Alabama or Auburn?' I'd say Penn State and they'd say, 'No, no, Alabama or Auburn?' And you look at the wall and you see Pat Dye – 'Oh, I'm an Auburn fan' – because you're selling to them, so you got to be on their side and you've got to play both sides. It's very passionate; very passionate."

Glenn wore his Polamalu jersey to Martino's. His buddy, "The Captain," wore his Lambert jersey. The third Alabaman, in the tank top at the end of the bar, had a Steelers logo and a woman's name tattooed next to each other on his back. He's both an Alabama fan and a Steelers fan. Do they come more passionate?

"I'm the guy who runs around the bar cheering and giving everyone a high five," said John.

Whose name is tattooed on your back, John?

"Ignore that name. That's my ex-wife," he said. "But there'll never be an ex-team."

✦ ✦ ✦

EVEN AFTER the Broncos game, the Steelers led the league in fewest points allowed after seven weeks. This reflected well on "Coach Dad" LeBeau, who was returning once again to his old stomping grounds in Cincinnati as the Steelers' defensive coordinator.

"Coach Dad, that's a new one," said Brandon LeBeau.

Brandon is Dick's 29-year-old son. He's an accountant who'd just received work acting in commercials. He has dreams of a bigger stage some day, but on this Saturday night in the hotel lobby, as his dad watched the Penn State-Ohio State game in his room, Brandon was talking football.

"I think the game in Denver will make them more focused coming into this week," he said. "They won't come out and not look sharp."

The defensive performance against the Broncos was a letdown for the Steelers after shutting out the Seahawks. That game, Brandon said, had made his dad very happy.

"He was tickled. To shut out a team like that when you're dealing with injuries, going into a bye, that was the happiest I've seen him after a football game for awhile."

Since the last time he beat Seattle?

"Maybe," said Brandon.

What was the Super Bowl celebration like?

"Wow," he said. "At that post-game party everyone had a smile on his face. The smile never left dad's face. He'd been in football 47 years at that point and basically he was celebrating the one thing he'd never achieved. The vibe at the party itself obviously was outstanding, but so was getting to see him enjoy that night. My friends left at 5:30 in the morning. He had gone to his room but he was still up. We went up and just stopped by and he was in there watching the golf channel with the smile still on his face."

LeBeau had given his VIP Party bracelet to Brandon's girlfriend, and the couple partied late into the night with the likes of Hank Williams Jr. Brandon had a picture taken with the famed country singer/Steelers fan and told Williams that his dad is also a big fan.

"You tell your dad he's the MVP," Hank told Brandon.

"He said that about four times," Brandon said. "I relayed the message to dad and he chuckled."

Dick LeBeau was born in London, Ohio, about 80 miles northeast of Cincinnati near Columbus. He played at Ohio State and then spent 14 years as a cornerback with the Detroit Lions. He got into coaching in 1973 with the Philadelphia Eagles and became an assistant with the Bengals in 1980. He was promoted to defensive coordinator in 1984 and there devised the zone-blitz schemes the Steelers use today.

LeBeau joined the Steelers in 1992, became Bill Cowher's coordinator in 1995, moved back to Cincinnati for the same job with the Bengals in 1997, and took his first and only head-coaching job with the Bengals in the middle of the 2000 season. He was fired after a disastrous 2-14 season in 2002 and became a special assistant with the Buffalo Bills in 2003. He rejoined the Steelers in 2004 and is perhaps the most beloved assistant coach in team history.

Brandon videotaped practices and edited film for his dad during his stint as head coach with the Bengals. It gave Brandon a unique perspective of his father: He saw him kick tail when necessary, but he also saw another side.

"There was a guy that had a sports talk show down here, and you know how sports talk is," Brandon said. "It was during the 2-14 season and this guy was all over dad. He's all over the team. He's all over everyone. He started coming to press conferences and asking 'the real questions.' If you can imagine a guy taking a talk-show personality to press conferences, well, that was this guy. But this guy's son has an ailment and he sent out all these invitations to this fundraiser. Dad got one. I'm sure he didn't mean to send it to dad; they just sent them all out. But what this sports-talk guy's son has, dad had lost a child to in his first marriage. Dad wrote him a letter and he made a donation to the fund. I do believe the guy quit coming to the press conferences, but I'm sure he didn't change what he did on air."

Brandon said the Cincinnati press was tougher on his dad 11 years earlier, in 1991, when the defense allowed an average of 27 points per game. Only four starters remained from the Super Bowl defense of 1988, and two of those starters would be replaced in 1992.

"When Sam Wyche was here, the end of his tenure," Brandon said, "they had a real bad season and the defense took all the blame, right or wrong. I was in junior high at the time and they were all over dad, all over the defense. It was bad. But when he was the head coach here, even though the record was a lot worse, the media wasn't too bad. A lot of fans here still say a lot of positive things about dad. It was completely different than his first time. The losing was tough, and no one liked it, but it could've been a lot worse."

Brandon was 10 when Joe Montana broke the city's heart with a last-minute game-winning drive in January, 1989. The Bengals led Super Bowl XXIII by three points until Montana threw a touchdown pass to John Taylor with 34 seconds left.

"That's the last time I cried after a football game," Brandon said. "I remember it vividly. I remember exactly just watching that game end the way it did, with San Francisco celebrating on the field, and just being amazed. I remember getting loaded up on the buses and I just laid down on my mom and started bawling. It was business as usual when we got home. I'm sure dad was disappointed but he wasn't down. It was just like Super Bowl XXX."

One year after the Steelers' loss to the Cowboys in Super Bowl XXX, LeBeau made a lateral move to Cincinnati to return to his family.

"There were rumblings that he and Coach Cowher didn't get along," Brandon said. "They had a lot of success together. When you're winning football games it makes it a lot easier to work together. But family definitely motivated him into that move."

In the Cincinnati area, LeBeau has his wife and son, his 95-year-old mother, and his brother Bob and his family. A son from Dick's first marriage lives in Pittsburgh.

"I'm one of dad's biggest fans, but grandma has me beat," Brandon said. "She's proud of her boy. When we get those close games I start worrying about grandma a little bit. But that move back to Cincinnati was very much motivated by family, his family and his family in London. He gives a lot of credit to his mother for the kind of person he is. They have a wonderful relationship. It's neat to see them interact. She's still sharp and she still wants to fuss over him when he goes up there. She's always getting up to make him something. She loves to fuss over dad."

Brandon wasn't surprised when LeBeau returned to the Steelers in 2004.

"In Pittsburgh, people love to meet anyone remotely associated with the Steelers. You could hold the (coach's headset) wire and people would be excited to meet you," Brandon said as five or six autograph seekers hovered nearby. "So it's different in Pittsburgh, because of the way he's received up there. That's part of the reason he came back. He came in for the interview, then he went to a Pitt basketball game. He hadn't been in Pittsburgh in six, seven years but several people walked up and said, 'Coach, you have to come back.' That just blew him away.

"They love him up there and it's neat. For as bad as things went when he was here, most football fans I meet have positive things to say about dad, but it's on another level up there. In Pittsburgh, it's adoration. That's why Pittsburgh's a special place for him."

How long will he stick around?

"Well, 2008 will be his 50th year in the league," Brandon said. "Maybe that's what he's waiting for. Honestly, I don't think he knows."

✦ ✦ ✦

THE DEFENSIVE game plan was obvious from the start: Hit the receivers and get in their heads. It worked on Chad Johnson; not so much with T.J. Houshmandzadeh.

Johnson took a couple of blows from Deshea Townsend on the first drive and the Steelers' defensive backs didn't stop until Johnson slammed his face into the turf in the third quarter and lost his set of gold teeth. Troy Polamalu picked it up and handed it to Johnson, who was effectively finished for the day. Polamalu wouldn't talk about it after the game – "I don't want to be a part of a big story," he said – but his hard-hitting, big-talking sidekick did. Anthony Smith stepped in for an ill Ryan Clark and delighted in blasting the Bengals' receivers both physically and verbally.

"Chad told me he don't wear a mouthpiece," Smith said. "I told him he'd better start."

Perhaps the biggest defensive play occurred late in the first half. The Steelers led 14-3 and the Bengals faced 3rd-and-6 from the Pittsburgh 7. A pass over the middle to Reggie Kelly was met quickly by Townsend, Polamalu and William Gay. They held Kelly short of the first down by a good yard and a half, almost two yards. The Bengals kicked a field goal and the Steelers drove 67 yards for a touchdown to put them up by 21-6 at halftime. The Steelers won, 24-13.

Offensively, the star of the game was Ben Roethlisberger. In the first half he and Hines Ward took advantage of a young Bengals secondary for two easy touchdown passes. Roethlisberger set up one of the touchdowns by changing plays at the line of scrimmage and heaving a 42-yard bomb to Santonio Holmes. The play revealed Roethlisberger's growth as a fourth-year quarterback, but the big guy out of nearby Miami University put the rest of his skills on display as well: He blindly threw a ball out of the end zone to save a sack; he ran for first downs; he rolled left and threw back right. He was in total command. His one mistake – an interception in the red zone – led to the Bengals' only touchdown.

"Ben was awesome today," said coach Mike Tomlin.

His passer rating for the season improved to 102.2, a distinct improvement on the 75.4 rating Roethlisberger posted in 2006.

Obviously, he was back – literally and figuratively.

"It's nice to win here, especially being so close to Miami, you know, school, and seeing a lot of Miami jerseys around," he said. "It feels good to beat a team like this. It really does."

Roethlisberger's career won-loss record improved to 39-14. His won-loss record in his native Ohio improved to 9-0.

Was he aware of the latter stat?

"A little bit," he said. "They tried to bring it up yesterday in the TV production meeting and I wouldn't let them talk about it. I don't even want to talk about it now."

✦ ✦ ✦

THE REST of southwestern Ohio was talking about it. Not only did the Steelers win a pivotal game in their division, but Ben Roethlisberger outplayed Bengals quarterback Carson Palmer and moved into the Pro Bowl-level echelon of AFC quarterbacks with Tom Brady and Peyton Manning.

This notion was supported by Cincinnati talk-show host Mo Egger. Another self-described madman in what's become a tiresome ilk, Egger polled callers (and Internet voters) on whether Roethlisberger had indeed surpassed Palmer as an NFL quarterback. The early vote was 57 percent for Roethlisberger and 43 percent for Palmer. I listened to Egger's show as I drove out of Cincinnati on my way to visit a group of Roethlisberger's friends in Findlay, Ohio. The town is 154 miles north of Cincinnati, or far enough away so that the Queen City could cannibalize its former college star. The respect from Egger was begrudging.

"Carson versus Ben – your life depends on winning one game – who do you pick?" Egger asked. This was his opinion: "Carson's arm? Far better than Ben's. Physically? Carson's far better than Ben. I looked at Carson Palmer yesterday and he had a golden opportunity to take this team, take this game, and win it by himself, and he couldn't do it. … Say what you want about Ben. I know we're not supposed to like him and he plays with Barbie dolls, but the guy wins. The guy wins. Carson Palmer doesn't win."

Egger expounded on his "Barbie doll" comment to include that ratings grabber: homosexuality. Apparently, someone had called the station Friday night to "report" this and Egger – as the basic jackass talk-show host will do – ran with it as a news item. Egger, though, praised Roethlisberger for his work on the field.

"Ben does more to help his team win than Carson does," he said. "I even watched them on the sideline, and yesterday I paid pretty close attention. Ben's over there on the sideline banging people on the shoulders, pumping guys up, attending to injured players. Carson's just kind of standing there going, 'Dude. Dude.'

"If my life depends on me winning one game, and I've got to pick a quarterback, I'm going with Ben Roethlisberger. It pains me to say that. It kills me to say that. Roethlisberger is slimy. He weirds me out. His beard sucks. But the guy wins."

✦ ✦ ✦

TIM TAGLIAPIETRA, known as "Tags" in Findlay, was outraged. OUTRAGED, I say.

"You've got to be kidding me," was how Tags responded when told of Mo Egger's incendiary comments. "Don't these guys have to worry about the truth anymore?"

Um, no.

"You know, we see stuff like this all the time when we go places," Tags said. "Ben's a guy that people love to hate. Maybe it's the success, but if you know him I don't see how you can be like that. To me he's very sincere, a very caring person. He's involved in a lot of things. He helped locally with funding a canine dog unit in Findlay, and I know he's doing it across the country. He's helping the local midget football program through his foundation. But the big success has a tendency to do that to people. They get jealous of you."

Tags, 48, is a manager at Cooper Tires. He got to know Ben through the Hatfield family. Rick Hatfield, 50, was an assistant coach at Findlay when Ben played, and Chaz Hatfield, 26, was one of Ben's receivers in high school. All three men talked about their friend over lunch Monday at Tony's Restaurant in Findlay. They talked about Ben's competitiveness, and even revealed that his No. 7 is not an homage to John Elway, but to James Bond.

"What I remember most about Ben," said Chaz, "is the confidence even more than the competitiveness. When you're in the huddle with him, on the field with him, you just put all your trust in him. Everyone did. Everyone believed in him."

Chaz talked about the most-discussed high school game in Findlay history. Napoleon led by 28-24, but Findlay had the ball at its own 33 with 24 seconds left.

"Everybody thought it was over," Chaz said. "For me looking at the scoreboard, seeing we were down and presumably it was over, I still knew we had him."

Mike Iriti, who later played with Ben at Miami, caught a 50-yard bomb from Roethlisberger, who then had Iriti switch sides ("No one could tell us apart," said Chaz, the other receiver) and Roethlisberger hit him in the end zone with a 17-yard pass to win the game.

"There's another one," said Chaz. "I went to Ohio University and he went to Miami University, but I made it to just about every home game in Miami. One game, against Akron, they were down by three with three seconds left and were at their own 30-yard line. I was sitting with a friend of mine, who was also a good friend of Ben's. We were tailgating and cheering on Ben, so at the end of the game we agreed to rush the field if they came back. The stands were empty. Everybody thought it was over. Seventy yards to go and there's one throw. He throws it to the 5 and a defensive back tips it into the end zone and someone catches it and scores. We jumped the fence and we were on the field. I jumped on Ben's back while he was being interviewed. It was his redshirt freshman year and I was screaming about the Heisman and one of the TV producers rips me off his back and throws me on the field.

"You just sort of always knew. That's why I thought about rushing the field in the first place, even when I wasn't playing with him."

MIKE IRITI'S father Tony is the mayor of Findlay. Or, he was. He lost the Republican primary in the spring of 2007 and the last months of his term were spent dealing with the clean-up efforts of a "100-year flood" that devastated the city in September. Mayor Tony joined us as we were finishing lunch.

"People think of Findlay as having small business," he said, "but we have a small business at the end of Main Street called Marathon Petroleum Company, a $60 billion company that employs 1,600 people and just pumped 7.5 million gallons of water out of its basement. So there's really a diverse approach to the flooding problem. It's made the community very resolved."

Whether Super Ben could help or not was not an issue with the mayor, but it was the chatter on the local paper's web blog that morning. The mayor shook his head in disbelief.

"Did you read that?" Tony asked his friends. "We wouldn't even consider asking Ben for help, but you have some Browns fans around here, who won't give it up. Obviously, me being from Pittsburgh, an admitted diehard Steeler fan, doesn't help."

Tony grew up in the Pittsburgh suburb of Etna and moved to Lima, Ohio, in the mid 1970s. He was part of a touring rock band called Road Apple before meeting a girl in Lima. Tony moved to Findlay in 1970 to set up a computer system for Hancock County. He resurrected the local youth football program in 1992 and coached his son.

"Ben had just moved into town," Tony said. "He came from Elida (38 miles southwest of Findlay). He moved into town in fifth grade. We had just started the youth football season and it just so happened that he got on my team. I'm not sure how that happened (laughs). So I asked Ben what position he'd like to play. He said, 'I'd like to be a running back.' I said fine. My son Mike was the quarterback and Ben was the running back. We're about three games into the season and of course you've always got to have that trick play, and so I asked Ben if he could throw the ball, and Ben said, 'I think so.' And so I told Mike to pitch it to Ben and for Ben to take about three steps, stop, and throw it back to Mike going down the sideline. And so of course he hits him right in stride going down the sideline. I said, 'Ben, you are now the quarterback. Mike, you are now the receiver.'"

BEN AND Mike Iriti attended different middle schools in Findlay. The third star athlete in town, Chad Baxter, went to the third Findlay middle school. All three played quarterback, so the freshman coaches were understandably excited about the group. Of course, the head coach of that freshman team, being no common idiot, chose Ben, and Ben remained the quarterback on the JV team as a sophomore.

As a junior, he moved up to the varsity and was moved to wide receiver because the coach, Cliff Hite, played his son at quarterback. Ben returned to quarterback as a senior and threw for 4,100 yards and 54 touchdowns.

Of course, the guy who made Ben a quarterback in the first place was upset about Hite's decision well before Ben's junior year.

"Even in his junior year, Ben threw two touchdown passes off a double pass with gloves on," Tony said. "I got in trouble with Cliff's wife, the coach's wife, because I was being honest. I won't say that Cliff made a mistake his junior year; I think he made a mistake his sophomore year. There's no way in the world Ben should've been playing JVs. He was a man among boys on the JV team then."

But, wouldn't Ben have ended up at Ohio State had his varsity coach had any sense?

"Exactly," Tony said.

And, wouldn't Ben have then ended up being drafted by the Cleveland Browns?

"Exactly," Tony said. "He'd have never played for the Steelers, so it all worked out."

CHAZ HATFIELD described a typical day growing up with Ben Roethlisberger: "We'd watch SportsCenter for an hour and then we'd go play basketball for four, five hours. It's always been about playing sports."

"He dunked once on my daughter," said Rick Hatfield.

Tags remembered Ben refereeing his son's basketball game and figured he yelled at him a time or two over calls. "I saw him play in high school and followed him in his sports," Tags said. "He's very visible. And like Rick said, he's super, super competitive. That's what drove them. The group that played with him, they all were that way.

"I played ping pong against him," Tags continued, "and he's beating me left-handed laughing and I'm playing my ass off right-handed. Things like that made you realize, hey, maybe this guy's got it."

Roethlisberger was a three-sport captain at Findlay. He was a rangy, power-hitting shortstop, a sharp-shooting point guard and the quarterback who led the team to a 10-2 record before losing in the second round of the playoffs. He was named Ohio's Division One Offensive Player of the Year in 1999 and finished second in the Mr. Football voting to WR Bam Childress, now with the Philadelphia Eagles.

"When you look at that senior year," said Mayor Tony, "Ben had more control over the offense than he does with the Steelers offense. For those of us who know him and know what he can do, you want to shout, 'Just let him go. Just let him play.'"

For the most part, the Steelers' offense has deteriorated into a dropback-and-scramble scheme with an offensive line more suited to run-blocking. It's resulted in Roethlisberger taking a consistent pounding.

"I watched the Denver game," Tony said, "and I listened to John Madden rattle on about how good the offensive line was as Ben was scrambling for his life. The only thing that saved him in the second half was that he ran faster. And some day we're going to have receivers that can beat linebackers. I know he doesn't have a lot of time to throw, but he doesn't have any receivers open, either."

During Roethlisberger's rise to the top of the football world that Super Bowl season, his home region didn't exactly ride with him. There's the story that Ben's parents attended daughter Carlee's away basketball game the day of the AFC Championship game. All fans wearing a jersey, other than that of the Steelers, were allowed in free. The next week, prior to the Super Bowl in Detroit, Mayor Tony asked the Findlay natives to wear black and gold to support Ben. It's one of the reasons Tony gave when he joked about his political downfall.

"The Browns fans were upset," he said. "That's the way this town is, too. Most people around here want to see Ben throw five touchdowns a game for 300 yards and the Steelers lose."

"I think he's learned. We've all learned," said Tags. "We've been out, having dinner, and Cleveland Browns fans are very boisterous. Every city he goes to he runs into that. I think some people hate the Steelers because their following is so huge in every city they go to. It's like every game's practically a home game for them."

✦ ✦ ✦

THE SETTING sun later that day cast long shadows over Jack Lambert Stadium as I pulled into the parking lot on the last night of the road trip. The small, unpretentious stadium looks like Russ Grimm Stadium in Scottdale, Pa. You expect something bigger, grander, until you remember that it's just part of a small-town high school.

Lambert grew up in the farming town of Mantua (MAN-uh-way), population 1,046. It's located a few miles north of the Ohio Turnpike in northeastern Ohio. He played football for Crestwood High School from 1967 to 1969 and was a tall quarterback who might've weighed as little as 145 pounds as a sophomore. He played catcher on the baseball team and forward on the basketball team. He lost his front teeth in basketball practice while banging inside for a rebound. A famous Lambert quote came to mind as I walked around his old stomping grounds:

"Quarterbacks should wear dresses."

He made the comment after being reprimanded by the league for a hit on Cleveland quarterback Brian Sipe. I thought of the line as my camcorder focused on a group of Crestwood football players on the track beside the field. The players were dressed in cheerleading outfits for the school's powderpuff girls game being played that night. They put their arms around each other and mugged for my camera, but only one of them laughed when I guessed that they all played quarterback.

The stadium was dedicated to Lambert in 1980, but fell into a state of disrepair in the 1990s. "It was a shambles," said Gary Huber, a former coach at nearby Rootstown High. "The stands were condemned. They finally renovated the stadium a few years ago."

Huber had agreed to meet me for coffee in downtown Ravenna. "I'm 65," he said. "My brother played with Dick LeBeau at Ohio State. When I was 9 or 10 he took me to the Ohio State-Stanford game and Jim Parker played for Ohio State with LeBeau and (Howard) "Hopalong" Cassady. Dave Leggett was the quarterback. Ohio State won, 34-20. John Brodie was the quarterback at Stanford."

Huber started on another story, this one involving Ohio State and Indiana basketball and how his brother took a big, dead fish to the game under his trench coat and threw it on the court after a bad call. Then he began talking about Lambert.

"I was the head coach at Rootstown back then," he said. "When Lambert was a sophomore I had a pretty good quarterback, an up-and-coming quarterback, and we ran the old run-and-shoot. Tiger Ellison at Ohio State had made it famous. He wrote a book called "Run and Shoot Football: Offense of the Future." We thought we had a pretty good quarterback so we tried it against Lambert.

"We were playing at Crestwood and at that time a lot of teams played during the day. The people in Mantua, they have a little bit of a town and they didn't like the idea of playing on Friday nights. They said they'd pay for the lights at the stadium if the high school would agree to play their home games on Saturday night. So we played against Crestwood on a Saturday night when Lambert was a sophomore. The final score of the game was something like 56-48, a run-and-shoot score, and I remember Lambert was running quarterback sneaks at the end of the game to kill the clock and hold onto the lead. That's what stands out: This 6-foot-5-inch sophomore quarterback, who later became known for his defense, was running quarterback sneaks to run out the clock. He was just so gangly as a young quarterback. He was always tall and thin. By the time he was a senior he might've weighed 175. He was not that great of a quarterback. He was known more for his defense even in high school.

"The next year we played them at Rootstown, my quarterback was a junior. We had a good end who caught 27 passes the first three-and-a-half games, but after Lambert injured my quarterback he only caught four more passes the rest of the year."

What about the injury?

"In the third quarter we ran a play we called 'wagon train throwback,' where we'd hand the halfback the ball, he'd throw back to the quarterback, and the quarterback would hopefully get the first down. Well what happened is the quarterback caught the ball, started to run upfield, and just as he got to the sideline there was Lambert. I don't know if you ever heard of Erich Barnes for the Lions and the Browns. He was famous for a clothesline tackle. And so as my quarterback gets to the sideline, Lambert comes in to make the high tackle and my quarterback – I can still see him on the film – he kind of winced a little bit to accept the blow and Lambert ended up hitting him high, but his body went into him and tore up his knee and the quarterback never played again. Somebody had written a book and in the book Jack mentions hurting this kid and that it always stuck in his mind."

Huber gave me the player's phone number and I tucked it away. If Jack wants to know, then I would find out. Coach Huber proceeded.

"Lambert was known for being just a mean – even in those days – he was just a tough, mean player. They played a 5-2 monster and every play as a coach you had to know where he was. You tried to get that across to your players, to make sure you knew where he was. He was just awesome in high school football. He was one of the best players in the league at the time. I know he had a heck of a coach. The guy had been the last linebacker cut by the Broncos at the time, so he had a guy that knew defensive football, knew how to get the most out of Lambert and utilized him as a good player.

"He was just a tough athlete. I saw him play high school basketball. A friend of mine was his high school coach and I remember him playing basketball with a broken toe and I think they cut part of his shoe out to have room for his toe and he played with a broken toe.

"I don't recall how the other kids felt about him. They probably didn't like him because he was mean, tough. I'm sure they respected him. Everyone wanted to know where he was every play. You wanted to make sure you at least saw him coming because he was a killer."

✦ ✦ ✦

JOHN ESKRIDGE doesn't hold a grudge, but he never went so far as to root for Jack Lambert.

"Are you kidding me?" Eskridge said. "I always rooted against him."

Eskridge "was a good quarterback, on his way to being a great quarterback," according to his high school coach Gary Huber. But his career was sidelined by the vicious hit from Lambert. Eskridge tore ligaments in his knee and has since undergone four operations with a replacement surgery expected in 2008.

"I couldn't say it was a cheap shot," Eskridge said. "He hit me as my spikes caught. I don't think a flag was thrown. Hit me in the neck with his forearm and I didn't know which hurt worse, my head or my knee. I never was hit like that before. The pain was indescribable."

Eskridge was a junior in high school at the time. He didn't play football again – " back then, when you hurt your knee it was a catastrophe" – but he came back to average 29 points per game his senior year in basketball. He earned a scholarship to Kent State, but re-injured the knee the first week of his freshman season. He played only one basketball game in college.

"Who knows where I would've ended up?" he said.

His three older brothers were either all-district or all-state athletes. His brother Jim played basketball at Pitt.

"I saw a replay of the hit and the whole sideline was jumping up and down because he knocked me out," Eskridge said. "When you go back and look at films, he was raw, unorthodox. They had better athletes. He was almost kind of dorky. I shouldn't use that word, but I never thought he'd have made it like that. But then he was always super-aggressive. He wasn't a cheap-shot artist. There was a part of me that rooted for him because he was local, but I never really was a Steeler fan. I've always been a Browns fan, and when it's in the blood it's hard to root for someone else. But, yeah, he was a wild one."

✦ ✦ ✦

HOMER SMITH was down at the Hogan's Heroes Restaurant over in West Middlesex having lunch with one of his pals the other day when someone asked Homer why his great nephew Anthony has to "yap, yap, yap the whole time."

Homer told him that "if Tomlin has a problem with it, he'd stop it right now."

Homer lives in Hubbard, Ohio, two miles from the Pennsylvania border and four miles from his hometown of West Middlesex, Pa. He raised Anthony Smith, the Steelers' physical and chatty free safety, and today Homer was worried that Mike Tomlin would reprimand Anthony publicly at his Tuesday press conference.

Anthony was coming off a terrific ball game against Cincinnati as a replacement for Ryan Clark, who would eventually have his spleen and gall bladder removed, so Homer Smith had reason to tune into the press conference. Tomlin was asked about Anthony Smith midway through it.

"Anthony played really well," Tomlin said. "He did. He tackled well. He was great in deep defense. He covered grass that he needed to cover, made some plays, separated a few people from some balls. I like how he played this weekend."

And then came the follow-up Homer was expecting. Tomlin was asked if Smth's post-play chatter should be tempered.

"Guys play football," Tomlin said. "It's an emotional game played by emotional men. Guys get excited. They do. I require that guys be themselves and pour all they have into their performance. He does that."

Homer took it in without reaction. It appeared that his great nephew had passed the first test of his second season.

"Remember when Hines was complaining about Anthony hitting the guys too hard in training camp?" Homer asked. "Well, his agent told me that every time Hines complained about it, Tomlin would tell Anthony, 'Hit him again.' That's what the agent told me, 'Hit him again.'"

Nobody need tell Anthony Smith to hit anyone again. The safety is one of the most aggressive players on the team. In fact, Homer believes that by plucking Anthony out of the inner city of Youngstown, he saved his life.

"His grandmother and his great grandmother never quit thanking us enough," Homer said. "Oh, I'm telling you, if we hadn't taken Anthony when we did, Anthony – as aggressive as he is – he'd probably be the leader of a gang."

Is that an exaggeration?

"No," Homer said. "When we got him he was a fifth grader and guys on the South Side of Youngstown were telling him to pick red or blue, Crip or Blood. That's when we got him."

THE BIG, expansive, green backyard ends with the flag "way back there, can you see it?" Homer said, as he pointed to the golf flag that marks the hole. "Anthony cut this grass every Saturday."

Homer Smith, a Youngstown State graduate and former supervisor at Delphi Packer Electric, and his wife Charlotte adopted two children – Brad and Chad. Twelve years later they adopted two more – Donny and Matthew – and then took in Anthony. The latter three boys are the same age.

"Anthony's dad is my nephew," Homer said. "Before we took legal custody of Anthony, he would come and stay with us every holiday, every summer. He lived in the inner city of Youngstown. His parents were both in bad situations. His mother came to us. I don't even want to talk about his dad."

Before moving in with Homer, Anthony Smith IV played midget football in Youngstown with Maurice Clarett and Louis Irizarry and "they just beat on people," Homer said.

Clarett and Irizarry accepted scholarships to play at Ohio State, but both ended up in jail. Anthony, meanwhile, moved out to Hubbard and worked his way up into the NFL.

Anthony's father's side of the family attempted to step back into his life at Homer's draft-day party. After Anthony was picked in the third round by the Steelers, one member of the Youngstown crew said, "Now we've got to get a lawyer."

"Get a lawyer for what?" Homer asked.

"We've got to go get that money," was the response.

"I said, 'Awww, man.'"

WAS ANTHONY Smith always such a hard hitter?

"All the time," said his brother Donny. "I remember one time in high school he crushed this kid who caught a pass in the flat. The guy didn't get up for some time. That's the hardest hit I remember, and Anthony had the flu that day."

Anthony, Donny and Matthew played high school ball together at Hubbard. Up until ninth grade the Smith clan represented three-fifths of the basketball team. In football, Matthew played quarterback, Donny played defensive line, and Anthony was a running back and safety.

"They played Ravenna in the playoffs," said Homer, "and someone came across the middle and caught a pass and he hit the guy so hard the announcer said we have to wait till he gets up. He went to Syracuse and one of his friends, Jimmy Riley, went to Louisville. Jimmy had to wait till his fifth year to catch a pass, so he didn't play much. But one time a Louisville receiver caught a ball over the middle and Anthony hit him so hard people went crazy. Jimmy called his dad and said, 'Anthony hit this guy so hard I was getting ready to go in.' But he's always done that. He's always been real strong, but then after he started getting big he really started hitting everybody. He never had any fear. Ever."

Chapter Seventeen
NORTHEAST EXTENSION

ALL OF THIS for me?

The Monday night game against Baltimore was my homecoming in Pittsburgh, but of course it had nothing to do with the festivities. The Steelers brought together their greatest players to unveil their All-Time Team. It was a celebration of the franchise's 75th anniversary, but the current team stole the show. The Steelers bombed the hated Ravens, 38-7, in their best performance of the season. Ben Roethlisberger threw five touchdown passes in the first half; Hines Ward threw blocks that laid waste to two different Ravens; James Harrison, well, he just went off; and then there was the affection from the Monday Night Football crew. Folks in Pittsburgh need love and Tony Kornheiser gave it to them at halftime:

"People around the country like the Pittsburgh Steelers. They like the fact that they play tough football in a tough city. This is not a New York team, not a Los Angeles team, a Chicago team, a Boston team, no Red Sox Nation situation. This is family owned, tough and durable. They have tradition, stability and continuity. Everywhere you go you find Steeler fans. They travel well. People like them and they believe that this is the kind of city where the right kind of football's played. I think they're the one organization in the NFL that just about everybody likes, except maybe people from Cleveland."

THE 38-7 WIN over the Ravens was the peak of the Steelers' season, and it served as a microcosm for its two key players: Ben Roethlisberger had a perfect passer rating and came within an inside-the-5 tackle of throwing six touchdown passes, yet all anyone wanted to talk about after the game was James Harrison.

In a town that reveres defense, the Silverback made 10 tackles, had 3.5 sacks, hit the quarterback six times, intercepted a pass, knocked away another pass, forced three fumbles, recovered one, and did it all with panache. He squared up and delivered kill shots with the proverbial rising blow as balls bounced all over the field. He chased, tackled, yanked, stole, recovered, and ran – sometimes in sequence. He nearly had a safety, but the referee ruled forward progress had been halted at the one. Harrison that night became a cult hero, at least that's the way Mike Archer, his former position coach with the Steelers, put it.

✦ ✦ ✦

ONE NIGHT during James Harrison's rookie camp in Latrobe, Mike Archer went out for a drink at nearby Sharky's Bar. The rookie's unnatural strength was obvious even to reporters in those first couple of weeks of camp, so we asked Archer about him.

Archer was pounding a drink at the time, and when Harrison's name came up he turned sharply and glared – as if Harrison was the reason he was pounding the drink in the first place.

"I can't wait till we cut him," Archer said.

More than five years later, Archer was asked if he remembered the conversation.

"I remember," Archer said. "I'm happy for him. He's an interesting young man and I'm happy for him because it's a great example of never giving up."

The defensive coordinator at North Carolina State, Archer said the Steelers signed Harrison after the 2002 draft as part of a free-agent package deal to get the guy they really wanted – a forgotten cornerback from Miami. The cornerback never signed.

"But we got James," Archer said, "and he was late for his first minicamp. He was late for the rookie camp and Bill (Cowher) got all over me about that. I remember calling him in Akron, wanting to know where he was, but he, you know, he was surly at times. And that's an understatement."

Archer's questions to Harrison about his assignments were often answered with a terse and challenging, "I don't know." But Harrison fell in line as he gained confidence. Because of injuries to Jason Gildon and Clark Haggans in the 2002 camp, Harrison played most of the Steelers' third preseason game, the one that opened Ford Field in Detroit. Harrison played in the base and the dime and impressed Cowher.

"Bill said after the game, 'This guy's got a chance,'" Archer said. "We both wondered if cutting him would be a mistake. We weren't sure if someone would pick him up.

"The other thing about that game is James played with a broken thumb. Nobody knows that, because when practice started the next week for the regular season, after he cleared waivers, he was on the practice squad and he practiced every snap."

Harrison wasn't activated until December that season but he played special teams in the regular-season finale and played well, according to Archer.

"I left the team after the playoff game down in Tennessee," Archer said. "I know he went to camp the next summer and then they cut him. I don't know all the particulars. I've been back a couple times. Somebody told me that he thinks I was the reason he got cut. I don't really care, but that's not true."

Harrison let go of any grudge he'd held against Cowher that Monday night with a hug before the Ravens game. Harrison said later that he only disliked Cowher's decisions, not the man. Still …

"I don't think there was any love lost there," Archer said. "You know how Bill is. When James was late for his first minicamp, Bill jumped my ass and said, 'If he doesn't want to be here, tell him not to come,' or something like that. You know how Bill is. So I explained it, but I worked with him every day. He was a different cat. He was a surly street kid. He reminded me a little bit of Greg Lloyd. He didn't trust anybody. Then some of those guys – Joey and Jason and Clark – they did a good job with him that year. Those guys kind of took him under their wing and said, 'Hey, you can play in this league. You've got the strength, but you've got to learn and they're trying to help you learn.' And then once he accepted that, then he really began to make progress where I could tell he cared about football because he would ask questions. He was playing inside backer and outside backer on the practice squad – with a broken thumb – and never missed a beat. I think he's got a tremendous amount of pride. Greg Lloyd had a tremendous amount of pride and this kid reminds me of that. I had some discussions with him a couple times because of some incidents. I'd say, 'If you don't want to play, then go on and we'll bring somebody else in here.' And I could see his eyes. His eyes pierce right through you like, 'Don't you tell me I can't play. I'm going to prove you wrong.'

"Our players here, when they watched that game, they said, 'Coach, did you know that No. 92?' I told them I did, and they said, 'God, dog, he's pretty good.' I told them he was a free agent, that nobody wanted him, and that he's a cult hero now. I'm sure in Western PA they're wearing No. 92 jerseys and they're not for Jason Gildon anymore."

✦ ✦ ✦

HARRISON FORCED two more fumbles the following week against the Cleveland Browns. The second was the pivotal defensive play of the game, and perhaps the season.

The 5-3 Browns had won four of their last five to creep within a game of the Steelers at the midway point of the season. And in Pittsburgh, the Browns pulled out to a 21-9 lead and had the ball midway through the third quarter when Harrison yanked it loose from Jamal Lewis. It set up a Ben Roethlisberger touchdown pass to Hines Ward and the Steelers' rally was underway. Still dragging emotionally from the Monday night game, the Steelers summoned one more drive, an 8-minute, 78-yarder, to wrest the lead from the Browns in a game that would be looked back upon as the AFC North Division title game.

The Steelers held onto the lead, in spite of a 3rd-and-7 QB draw for no gain on the their final third down of the game. The Browns missed a long field goal at the gun and the Steelers held a two-game division lead, and the tiebreaker edge, as they traveled to New York to play the 1-8 Jets.

✦ ✦ ✦

WILLIE COLON grew up in South Bronx and was excited early in the week to talk about his first homecoming as a pro.

"Everybody's pumped up," the 6-3, 315-pound Steelers right tackle said of his family. "But my goal is to get the job done. I'll shake hands and kiss babies after."

Colon might make a great politician some day. He's bright and verbal and business-like. He's also street wise. Colon grew up in the projects with a younger brother and older sister. They were raised by a mother, who was diagnosed with lupus in the late 1980s, and her twin sister – as well as the 10 or so drug dealers and gangbangers who greet visitors daily at the entrance of their building.

"A lot of my friends are Bloods," said Colon. "In my neighborhood, if you didn't join the clique, they'd turn against you. But I had my brother with me and I had a couple of my boys, so we never really got messed with too much. We were the only kids in my neighborhood who went to an all-boys Catholic school. We were tough. We stuck together and we didn't take a lot of shit."

Colon and his brother Antonio went to Cardinal Hayes High School, a few blocks away, and neither came close to veering off the straight and narrow.

"I just couldn't do that to my mother," Colon said. "I was just able to stick by that, and sports kept me off the street a little bit."

Was it that easy?

"Listen man, I've seen guys die in front me. I've seen shootouts. I've seen it all, things a kid at a young age should never see. You just realize that if you don't want that lifestyle, you don't go where those people go. Football and basketball kept me out of a lot of those situations. Instead of going home and sitting on the couch, I had practice, I was in the weight room, I was doing stuff. That was my escape from a lot of things that were really going on. The only bad thing, my building in the project center was really drug-infested, so going home sometimes was annoying because you had all those drug dealers in the front of your building. But that's just motivation, man. God blessed me and kept me safe."

Colon went to Hofstra University in Long Island to play football. He was the Steelers' fourth-round draft pick in 2006 and became a starter the final two games of his rookie season. He hasn't come out of the lineup since. Even the drug dealers who told him all the way up that he'd never make it, that it was a hopeless situation, are proud of him.

"They respect that you're trying to do good," Colon said. "They're older now, in their 30s and 40s, and they say, 'Wow, man, I remember when you were just walking home with your jersey,' and they laugh, because they watched it. In their eyes, they see there is some good in this world, that there is one guy that made it out. My cousin was a big-time basketball player, but he turned to the drug life. He was ranked higher than Shaq coming out of high school, so it's kind of like, 'He didn't turn out like that guy; he actually made it.' So a lot of them are proud. It's funny that you feel pride from a neighborhood drug dealer, but it's the human side of a lot of folks. They're just happy because you're representing the Bronx, and I do respect the Bronx."

✦ ✦ ✦

KATE MARA spends the NFL season on the other side of New York City, the posh side, but she was called back to Los Angeles this week for superstar stuff.

Kate, or Katy, as we in the superstar business call her, is one of the hot young actresses in Hollywood, and her role as Annie Cantrell, a cheerleader and the love interest of one of the star players in *We Are Marshall*, spawned another round of stories about her ties to both the Pittsburgh Steelers and New York Giants.

Kate, or Kathleen Rooney Mara, as we in the sportswriting business call her, is the great-granddaughter of both Art Rooney and Tim Mara, founders of two of the oldest and most storied franchises in NFL history. Her dad Chris Mara is the vice-president of player evaluation for the Giants. Still, Steeler Nation considers Kate royalty. "If I am I'm honored," she said over the phone. "I just love going to Pittsburgh because there's nowhere on earth that has fans like the Pittsburgh fans." What has she seen?

"It's shocking," she said. "I was in London with the Giants for the Dolphins game two weeks ago and there were Steeler fans at that game. I don't know if they were British or not but it's extremely moving given the fact that my great grandpa is Art Rooney. Steelers fans really know the history of the team, and that's different than any old fan."

Kate is the daughter of Kathleen Rooney and the granddaughter of Tim Rooney, who, as a 15-year-old, wrote the panicked letter to the Chief that the team was about to cut the best quarterback in camp, a kid named John Unitas.

"Let the coach coach," the Chief wrote back.

"I love it. That's a great story," said Kate.

I told her I had many, many more nuggets of useless information, like this one: The only NFL team that draws more Google hits than the Steelers is the Giants.

"I LOVE that," she said. "That's the coolest thing I've ever heard.

"The reason I'm so proud," she continued, "besides the fact I'm just proud of my family, but the reason I'm so proud to be a Giants/Steelers fan is the teams have been around forever and there's so much incredible history, and I really feel like both sides of my family make an effort to preserve that history and the way we thought of football and played football for so long. They try to keep it alive, which I think is really rare and really special."

Kate, 24, has sung the national anthem at games since she was 15. She sang before the last Steelers-Giants game, at the Meadowlands, in 2004. She sang before a couple of Steelers games at Heinz Field, and does the Giants' home opener every year. She grew up in Bedford, New York, and attended the Tisch School of Arts at NYU. She moved to Manhattan and now lives in Los Angeles, and when pressed admits the Giants are her absolute favorite.

"I grew up in New York and my dad's worked for them forever," she said apologetically. "When you actually get to know Parcells and Lawrence Taylor and guys like that, it makes the bond and the attachments that much deeper. And my dad, my God, he has to go to work there every day, so if we lost it wasn't a good week. He was never insane about it, but we knew the week wouldn't be great if we lost.

"The Steelers are different for me. When I think of the Steelers I think of Art Rooney. I picture his face. Whenever someone mentions the Steelers, that's what I think of automatically. And, really, there's a different feeling when your mom's involved. The Steelers are my mom's side and women tend to be more emotional in a way, and so the stories I always hear about the Steelers are the early, emotional stories about him and about how he affected Pittsburgh and how everybody knew his name and how he always had that cigar in his mouth. I just remember how deeply connected my mom felt to him as her grandfather. It's a very personal sort of thing and that's where the love of the Steelers comes from; it all comes solely from Art Rooney."

Kate was only 6 years old when the Chief passed.

"I do remember the cigar smell," she said. "Now, I hate smoke, but to this day the smell of cigars completely reminds me of my family — my grandpa and my great grandpa. Timothy Rooney also smoked cigars, just like his dad did, and it really reminds me of that. It's really bad. People are like, 'Oooh, how can you like that smell?' But it makes me think of home. It's not a normal smell in my house, but it's definitely a grandfather thing."

The last time she was in Pittsburgh for a game?

"I think I was there last year. It's so awful that I missed — and I'm still upset about it today — but I missed the Super Bowl. I was in tears. It's a funny story now because people make jokes about it, but I have in my contract that if a movie is shooting during the Super Bowl, I get time off. I am incredibly adamant that if the Giants or Steelers are in the Super Bowl I have to be off for that Sunday because I missed it two years ago. I was so devastated that I had to work."

Kate's intention on this mid-November day was to attend a game at Heinz Field before the weather turned too cold.

"I do sit in a box, but I like to go for the day, for the weekend. I love Pittsburgh," she said. "I love the people there. My mom grew up there and since she's from Pittsburgh. I really know the vibe, and the sound. They have a very, very specific accent. There's nobody else like it. And there's a feeling there that you don't get anywhere else. I just really love it. People are really warm there."

✦ ✦ ✦

THAT WEEKEND in New York, the odds were with the Steelers, but against me. My plan included a visit to the projects in the South Bronx to visit Willie Colon's mother, Jean Davis. Willie told me to go during the day, but I worried about my safety even then.

"Just act like you belong," he said. "They'll think you're a cop. You dress like one anyway."

Shirt tucked in, lightweight blue jacket, a camera giving the appearance of heat in the shirt pocket. Yep, I was there to bust some ass.

I rolled in about 10 a.m. and was surprised by the grass fields surrounding the project buildings. There was a church across the street and parents were ushering a long line of children to and fro. Colon's building was clean and tidy outside, and I headed to the front door as if I knew exactly what I was doing. The pavement in front of the door was clear ... until I got there. Three men materialized and fist-bumped each other. One opened the door for me and I walked in, forgetting to buzz Ms. Davis. So I stepped back out, got the return buzz, and walked back in.

So far, so good. I approached the elevator and asked two would-be riders whether the elevator worked. I turned around for the answer, but neither would look at me. They just shook their heads nervously and said they didn't know.

OK, this cop thing's working. But instead of waiting for the elevator I bounded up a stairwell that reeked of urine. I reached Jean's room and she introduced her twin sister Joan. It was a small apartment. It's where the twins raised three children, and if all three were as big as Willie Colon it had to have been cramped. Yet, these sisters got it done. Both Willie and his brother Antonio graduated from Hofstra and both are working in Pittsburgh. Older sister Joy earned a masters degree from Buffalo State and is the assistant principal at Junior High 45 in the Bronx.

"Even though she was diagnosed with the lupus when William was young," Aunt Joan said of her sister, "I think it made her stronger because, no matter what, her goal was that her boys and her daughter all went to college and become successful. Her goal was to keep them so busy they wouldn't have time to think of something else. She put them in everything: football, baseball, basketball, sea cadets."

Of course, it cost money to send kids to Catholic school, and probably sea cadets, too.

"You sacrifice when you want the best for your kids," Joan said.

The apartment was dark. Jean struggled a bit, but made her way around. She gets in and out of the building as well. She said there used to be even more drug dealers down below.

"When the kids were growing up you thought they were giving away cheese because there used to be lines," she said. "But you couldn't keep the kids inside. They had to go out and play with their friends and have a life. You just hoped that they used what you put into them. One day William and his brother and my godson and another friend went to the store. It was an ordinary day. Coming back they saw this guy get killed right before them. I looked out the window and they jumped in the bushes to hide from the bullets. These are things that they were faced with."

"That's what William means when he says he fought to get out," said Joan. "We stressed to him to be his own person. That and family were the big reasons he got out, and also the fact that my sister got sick made him not want to disappoint her. It was like, 'She can fight lupus; I can fight this.'"

Colon is a chairperson for the Pittsburgh chapter of the Lupus Foundation. Lupus is a condition in which the immune system attacks the body's own cells and tissue. Jean receives dialysis treatment three times a week, and says she's thankful because her health could be worse.

"When William got drafted he told me he did it for me because he was tired of seeing me struggle," Jean said. "I told him it's his dream. He doesn't owe me anything. I'm the parent. Everything I did, all parents should do. I'm your mother and I love you, but people came to me right away: 'When you moving?'"

That, in fact, was my next question.

"Pry her out of here?" Joan said with a laugh. "She feels comfortable. She knows everybody."

"It just amazes me that people think I'm supposed to be coming out the building in minks and diamonds," Jean said. "Why? That's his money. If I call him and need money, I'll get it."

"When he signs his next contract," Joan said, "I'm going to kidnap her and take her on a trip."

THE POLICE CAN'T make the drug dealers go away. Does that upset these women?

"First of all, you've got to get the police to come here," said Jean.

"Now THAT bugs me," Joan said. "The cops' attitude has changed. When I was growing up, if you got in trouble the officers in the area wanted to know why you're doing something stupid. But it's different now. It was hot one day this past summer and the kids were playing with the water. The kids threw water at a cab so the cab pulls off and the next thing you know I thought they had shot the president. Cops came from everywhere. So this guy is walking past us and the cops right away went after him. We were sitting there telling the police he didn't have anything to do with it. They were like 'Who did it? Who did it?' I told them it was kids playing with water. So if you throw water, they're everywhere. If you hear shots, you could sit there for a half hour, 45 minutes before they show up."

How often do you hear shots?

"It's gotten a little better," Joan said. "We used to hear shots every night, like two, three o'clock in the morning. But that has gotten better."

"THE KEY WITH KIDS," Aunt Joan was saying, "is you have to support them. They don't have to be sports stars, either. You just get on the bus or the train and you go see them. It wasn't about winning or losing. It was about being there. They used to have those little plays that were just awful. You couldn't wait for it to be over. But they saw you there. They saw the support. That's so important."

"Their basketball team was so horrible," said Jean. "Eight o'clock in the morning I was sitting there, 'Why am I here?' And it was the same parents every time."

Willie Colon played basketball for three years at Cardinal Hayes, but was more of a physical presence than a skilled player. Now, his cousin, Carlton Hines, he was a player.

Carlton Hines played for The Gauchos, an AAU Team out of the Bronx that's been graced by the likes of Pearl Washington, Chris Mullin, Sidney Green and Mark Jackson. The list goes on. Hines played on a 1988 team with Conrad McRae, Eric Mobley, Kenny Anderson and Jamal Mashburn. On May, 14, 1987 *The New York Times* previewed The Gauchos' game against the Soviet junior national team. This paragraph was written midway through the story:

Naming the fifth player, Mr. Britton's voice became an awed hush. "Carlton Hines – sophomore," he practically whispered. "He has the potential to be one of the best players in the city. He's 6 foot 4. He's something else. We call him Rambo."

The Gauchos beat the Russians that night and Hines was one of the stars. He was on his way to basketball stardom, but couldn't stay away from drugs and was murdered a few years later during a deal in the Bronx.

"It's all about family," Joan repeated. "You could have all the money in the world, but it don't matter if you don't have that love and support.

"My mother always told me it doesn't matter if you're 15 or 50, you can make it. It depends on how hard you work at it and how much love and support you have from your family."

PITTSBURGH NATIVE Curtis Martin was to be honored by the New York Jets at halftime Sunday for his outstanding career. Martin told reporters he was "bringing 50 people and they're all Steeler fans."

"It amazes me," Joan said. "Wherever we go, we see it."

While Willie Colon grew up a diehard Giants fan, his mom and aunt were diehard Steelers fans. When asked for a reason, they gave a familiar response:

"Franco Harris," said Joan. "I saw them honor him last week and I wanted to jump through the TV."

"My son Antonio is in Pittsburgh with William," Jean said. "He called me from the stadium to tell me what it was like, and I said, 'Shut up. I don't care.' I told him I just wanted him to jump over the railing and get me Franco's autograph."

"I was in church when I got the call that William was going to the Steelers," Joan said of draft day 2006. "I forgot I was in church. I really did. I was so excited I started screaming and hollering. I lost it. I stepped out to answer my phone and got the word. I went back in church and said, 'We're going to Pittsburgh!' And everybody turned around and I thought, 'Oh my God I'm in church.' after the service was over I said to the pastor, 'Gee, I interrupted the service.' He said, 'Oh, that's OK. God understands.'"

✦ ✦ ✦

THE STEELERS lost to the Jets the next day in overtime, 16-13. The breakdowns came late from the defense and special teams, and all day by the Steelers' pass protection. The Jets entered the game with nine sacks in nine games, but sacked Ben Roethlisberger seven times.

While the fans and media in Pittsburgh debated the specific problems in pass protection, the fans and media in New York concerned themselves with another topic: Why was half the crowd rooting for the Steelers?

In other cities, the phenomenon has become routine, but in sports-crazed and heavily populated New York, it came as a shock. "At least half of this crowd is Steelers fans," an awed Phil Simms told the TV audience. WFAN Radio in New York reported the Steelers fans to Jets fans ratio was 70-30. After the game, Ian O'Connor led his column in the *North Jersey Record* this way:

> *The visiting towels indicted the winning coach. Thousands and thousands of gold-colored towels spinning frantically in the marshy wind, claiming Giants Stadium as decisively as a flag planted on the moon.*

> *It took Eric Mangini only 14 regular-season home games over two seasons to completely surrender his turf. Heinz Field moved some 375 miles to the east Sunday, so in a stunning victory Mangini managed to find a large measure of defeat.*

After the game, Mangini told reporters that "Whenever there's a situation like that, you try to minimize the things they're able to cheer for, and the amount of things they are able to wave their towels for." Wrote O'Connor:

> *"What a remarkable, telling statement. The head coach of a winning home team was hoping to take the crowd out of the game."*

O'Connor wrote that he couldn't recall "a takeover of a home Jets game any more hostile and humiliating." Ben Roethlisberger summed up the Steelers' point of view when he said, "We're used to it."

✦ ✦ ✦

EIGHT DAYS later, the Steelers eked out a 3-0 win over the winless Miami Dolphins in "The Muck Bowl." Neither that nor a 24-10 win over the listless Cincinnati Bengals the following week lessened the sting from the loss to the Jets.

The Steelers were 7-0 at home but 2-3 on the road with a trip to New England looming. Their chances that game had diminished due to comments made by free safety Anthony Smith. He guaranteed a win over the Patriots to a Pittsburgh radio reporter in the morning. The station leaked the news in order to establish a buzz for that afternoon's show, but all it did was establish a horde of reporters around Smith's locker after practice. Here's how it went:

Reporter: Did you make a prediction earlier today?

Smith: Yeah, why not? We've got the No. 1 defense. We don't expect that to change, so why not? We think we're going to win every game anyway, so yeah.

Reporter: What's the prediction?

Smith: We're going to win.

Reporter: Are you going to pull a Joe Namath and guarantee it?

Smith: (Laughs) Yeah, I can guarantee a win as long as we come out and do what we've got to do. If both sides of the ball are rolling and our special teams come through for us, we've got a good chance of winning.

Someone told Mike Tomlin what was said and he walked into the media room with a smile on his face. It was only subterfuge. The smile turned to rage as he demanded to know which reporter pushed "the guarantee" portion of the text. No one budged and Tomlin walked away without his answer. He'd be hearing the quote in his sleep the next four nights, and then had it chanted back to him Sunday in Foxboro.

✦ ✦ ✦

DURING A CONVERSATION about fan violence in Cleveland, Dan Rooney said, "I've seen worse up in New England and in Oakland, where the fans are really tough."

My close encounter with New England fans occurred at the end of the 1997 game in Foxboro. The media were herded down to the field before the end of the game, the game in which Steelers defensive end Kevin Henry intercepted Drew Bledsoe in the last minute on a surprise pass play. The Steelers then tied the game and won in overtime.

We stood behind the end zone and in front of the low bleachers when the Henry interception inspired a barrage of bottles toward the field. The cops brought out attack dogs and lined them up in front of us to face the stands, so we were between the hostile fans and the salivating dogs. Looking at a Jack Daniels bottle on the ground, I pondered being konked by the bottle and falling forward into the one particular dog that was eyeing me up. I looked to my left where KDKA radio's Goose Goslin stood with a grin.

"He'll rip your lungs out, Jim," said the Goose.

The Steelers won that game and then beat the Patriots 7-6 in the playoffs that year. That only intensified the hatred within Patriots fans.

"I went to a game at Foxboro the next year," said Tim Murphy, a Steelers fan and Rhode Island native. "It was a non-Steeler game, but I had my Steelers jacket on. They were playing the Bills. It was in '98, but I figured I was fine. I got an 'F-you, F-you, F-you' and I thought, typical Boston fans. Then I'm at a urinal and some asshole's trying to instigate a fight with me. I'm ignoring him, and all of the sudden I feel warm on my leg. The dickhead's pissing on me. I turned around and said, 'What's wrong with you?' He had three buddies. One guy pushed me. I said, 'This isn't even a Steelers game.' And they said, 'Aw, they suck.' I pushed one and then someone broke it up.

"Later I went to a game at Fenway with a Steelers shirt and guys are still busting my chops. One guy threw a beer at us and hit my wife. I said, 'What the fuck's wrong with you guys?' I'm a Celtics fan and I go to games and watch how they treat opposing fans. I'm like, 'What's wrong with you guys?' This is a sporting event. It's amusement."

Doesn't Murphy see similar behavior from Steelers fans?

"They're rowdy and passionate and if they're intoxicated, yeah, you'll see that," he said. "But at a Pittsburgh event you might get that in half the games; whereas in Boston you'll get that every single game and you'll get it two or three times a game. What you get in Pittsburgh is what you expect in every city: the barbs, the instigation. But in New England, particularly in New England, they want to push you to the brink because – and maybe this has changed with the recent success – but they've had a major inferiority complex."

✦ ✦ ✦

IF YOU THINK you're tough, someone around the bend is tougher. By the same token, if you think you're a weary traveler, watch out because Bill Hillgrove lies asleep in the back of the bus.

Hillgrove, the play-by-play man for the Steelers, and Pitt football and basketball, was hanging on by a thread this afternoon in New England. He'd just touched down after another whirlwind week that began with the Pitt-WVU football game eight days back. The next day he did the Bengals-Steelers game. On Monday, he flew to New York to receive the Chris Schenkel Award. Hillgrove returned to Pittsburgh on Wednesday to do the Pitt-Duquesne basketball game. He did the Pitt-Washington basketball game in Seattle and flew back to Pittsburgh on Saturday. He got home at midnight, stayed up till 2 a.m. Sunday to do his prep work, got three hours of sleep and left his house for New England at 5:30 a.m. It helped that the Steelers-Patriots game wouldn't kick off until 4 p.m.

"One of the reporters said I was just snoring on the bus," Hillgrove said. "I think I fell asleep while I was talking to him."

Hillgrove said the closest he ever came to missing a kickoff was the 2005 Steelers game in Houston when he arrived 15 minutes before kickoff.

"The only way I made that one," Hillgrove said, "was because of Manny, my limo driver. We get six blocks away from the stadium and it's gridlock, and Manny says in his broken English, 'Excuse me sir. I stop the car.' And he stopped the car, got out, opened his trunk and pulled out a red and blue light that he put on top of the car, and now we're official. We're going down one-way streets and cops are waving us through. That's the only way I made it."

Hillgrove has done Pitt games for 38 years and Steelers games since 1994. He'd heard about the vast Steelers fan base, but was still surprised when he saw it up close.

"The hotels on the road are unbelievable," he said. "But there's a downside to that. The downside is a socioeconomic factor, and that's the fact we chase these young people to other cities to get jobs. That's the sad part. The good news is they remain very loyal Steelers fans."

✦ ✦ ✦

THE STEELERS opened with a field goal, but the undefeated Patriots responded with a touchdown, and then a play-action fake caused Anthony Smith to bite and Randy Moss was open for a 63-yard touchdown.

The Steelers managed to stay close through the first half. They trailed by only 17-13 at halftime, but Smith was fooled again on a double pass and the 56-yarder from Tom Brady to Jabar Gaffney had the stadium rocking. On the Patriots' next possession, cornerback Deshea Townsend was injured, putting him on the sideline next to injured safeties Troy Polamalu and Ryan Clark. The Steelers were forced to use linebackers to cover the Patriots' slot receivers, so Bill Belichick called 14 consecutive passes. When the smoke cleared, the Patriots led 34-13 and the crowd was chanting "Guar-an-tee! Guar-an-tee!"

After the game, the same New England reporters who'd ripped Anthony Smith all week long were now crowding around his locker pretending to be his friends. They all put on their sad faces and used their most earnest voices:

Anthony's New Friend: How surprising was it to see your face on the scoreboard with the fans chanting guarantee?

Anthony: I wasn't worried about that. When we come back, we'll have our opportunity again.

Anthony's New Friend: Is that a guarantee for the playoffs?

Anthony: Are you trying to make me make another guarantee?

Anthony's New Friend: I'm asking if it is?

Anthony: If we do what we're supposed to do, we're going to be back here.

Chapter Eighteen
CHECKERED FLAG

ANTHONY SMITH'S new friends couldn't squeeze another guarantee out of him, and maybe Smith knew something deep inside because the Steelers fizzled down the stretch. Aaron Smith's torn biceps in New England cost the team one of its most valuable defensive players, and on offense Willie Parker – the running game – broke his leg against the St. Louis Rams.

Those weren't the only injuries, nor were those the only reasons the Steelers lost three of their last four regular-season games and then lost their playoff game to Jacksonville. The Steelers couldn't protect their quarterback and by the same token couldn't generate enough heat on opposing quarterbacks. It was a deadly one-two punch that rivaled the loss of Smith and Parker in terms of impact.

More was won off the field. The Steelers were named the No. 1 sports team brand in North America by a New Jersey-based market research and executive search and recruiting firm. The firm surveyed 12,000 fans in 47 markets and the Steelers finished first in fan loyalty and team popularity and third in ownership. In naming the Steelers the winner of the Turnkey Team Brand Index, chief executive Len Perna said, "Down through history, ownership, players, coaches, stadium, and style match the hard-nosed work ethic of their city."

The Steelers also finished first in the NFL's local TV ratings with an average of a 48 share. The team was fourth in merchandising. An NFL executive said, "In my 15 years on the job the Steelers have always been in the top five."

In another poll, the Steelers ranked first among women, and in a survey held by FoxSports.com, the Steelers' uniforms were voted No. 1.

Down the road a bit, the *Washington City Paper* reported on an autograph show in the D.C. area in which attendees had to first buy coupons online to better serve the 60 athletes in attendance. Among the athletes were current and former Redskins stars LaRon Landry, Chris Conley, Earnest Byner and Joe Theismann, but the only Redskin listed among the 15 most sought-after athletes was former Steeler Antwaan Randle El. The rest of the top 15 consisted of former and current Steelers. Former quarterback Terry Bradshaw was No. 1 and former *backup* quarterback Terry Hanratty was No. 10.

Members of the Steelers' extended family fared pretty well in 2007. LSU won the national championship, even though WVU did bounce back to make a late, second run. Kate Mara, the benevolent queen of Steeler Nation, watched her other team, the New York Giants, knock off the New England Patriots in the Super Bowl. This affected Steelers fans because now the ugly Patriots fans and their arrogant quarterback and genius head coach could never match the Steelers' feat of four titles in six years in the '70s. Along those lines, the Dallas Cowboys couldn't win their sixth Super Bowl after Kate's Giants took care of them as well.

On the high school level, Brett Keisel's buddy, Mike McGuire, coached his team to the Wyoming state championship at the end of his second season on the job, and the high school Deshea Townsend set off on its dynasty – "South Panola University" – went undefeated for a fifth consecutive year in Mississippi. The team Sean Mahan set off on its dynasty – Jenks High School – won its ninth big-school Oklahoma title in 12 years. Even Lawrence Timmons' Wilson High in South Carolina won a state title.

Steelers fans could also take a victory lap for the return of Ben Roethlisberger from his wrecked 2006 season. In his fourth season, Roethlisberger responded with a franchise record passer rating of 104.1. He threw 32 touchdown passes to break Terry Bradshaw's record of 28 set in 1978. Yet, for all of Roethlisberger's heroics the players voted James Harrison the team MVP.

"He threatened to blow us all away," explained Keisel.

That might be an exaggeration, but only a slight one.

✦ ✦ ✦

MY FRIEND Bob smacked me upside the head when he entered the media room for the final Mike Tomlin press conference of the 2007 season.

Now, when Bob gets upset – like the time he told me "Roy Blount never used a damn camcorder!" – I pay attention. And when he cracks me across the head, I ask him what the hell he did that for.

"What the hell'd you do that for?"

"You have a tendency," he told me, "to leave things unexplained."

He read the puzzled look on my face.

"People need things explained," he said. "Don't just tell a story and expect them to understand the point you're trying to make. Spell it out."

But, really, I thought I'd find a tidy summation somewhere along the journey. I traveled 9,928 miles by land, flew to the Florida Keys, the tip of the Baja Peninsula, and the westernmost point on our nation's map – Polihale Beach in Kauai, Hawaii, from where souls, according to legend, depart for the underworld – and really I can't explain the phenomenon of Steelers Nation any better than I could before the trip. I told Bob that.

"I understand," he said. "Steelers Nation is like Stonehenge. It's just there. You probably shouldn't explain it or define what makes it great, you just *know* that it's great."

The Professor of Diaspora, Jim Russell, challenged me similarly in Colorado, so I asked him what he expected out of this book. He said he'd like answers to these questions:

Is there a tie that binds these Steelers fans?

I'd say no. That's what makes this phenomenon unique and interesting. The lady tending bar under a stuffed moose head and arguing about the Steelers in northern Idaho had nothing more in common with the guy sitting in the New Orleans bar than the team. One adores the Steelers because of their colors and the other appreciated the fact the Steelers didn't pummel his favorite expansion team back in the day.

Is there a commonality?

Other than the team, no, I don't think so.

Is there something we can identify as the essence of this community?

Uh, boy. There probably is, but my mission statement was to simply explore and report. If there's an essence, hopefully it can be found between the lines.

I just hope the journey itself will carry the day. As for what I learned, well, I hope to be able to teach my daughter that she can achieve her dreams from anywhere, from the projects of the South Bronx to the lush hinterlands of South Oregon, from environments of either love or tyranny, and that anyone can accomplish his or her goals, whether the community's with you or agin you, that it's all up to – ouch!

"Listen up," said Bob. "Tomlin's writing the end of your book for you."

"… It's a challenging gig but I love it," Tomlin was telling the gathered media. "I couldn't have a nine-to-five. I'm not wired that way. My wife would not love me. At the same time what makes me tick is I think what makes a lot of these guys tick: the challenges, the urgency, the finality of it all, the fact that people care. Steeler Nation is a big source of energy and motivation for me. From the outside looking in, you respect it. I talked about it when I got here. Being a part of it is different. It is. You want to deliver for Steeler Nation. It's a driving force. It's one of the reasons I'm energized. It's awesome. It's an awesome place. I'm looking forward to fighting the fight again."

✦ ✦ ✦

A COUPLE of us reporters were enjoying the roomy atmosphere in the cafeteria at the Steelers' South Side facility during the early May weekend of the 2008 minicamp. The rookies were in town and the first breath of the upcoming season was being taken, yet there were few of us covering it. We knew why, and the two of us joked to Ed Kiely that we hoped the Penguins would remain in the Stanley Cup playoffs throughout the rest of the spring and even the summer because the locker room was now a place to get some thinking done, as opposed to elbowing for room around Hines Ward and all.

Kiely had been the Chief's friend and PR man from the 1950s on, and, just like the Chief, he enjoys the company of those who work for the team and the newsmen who cover them.

"There was a time," he said, "when baseball ruled this town. I know, because people always told me, told us, that we were crazy to bang our heads against the wall here. We were the team that had the small crowds, the team the smart sports people in town laughed at. But look what happened. It's not a baseball town anymore is it? Hasn't been for a long, long time. We learned something from that. We learned that you can't take any of this for granted. Look at that hockey team. This town is going crazy over the Penguins. In 20 years you may be wondering what happened. You may be wondering how this became a hockey town."

People such as Kiely are the reason the Steelers' nation rose in the first place. The Chief surrounded himself with men who weren't just football men, but were people men. Guys like Kiely and the Chief and the Chief's son, Dan Rooney, took it one good man at a time. It's why the Chief attended so many wakes and funerals in his day. It's the reason he walked to the games, walked around the locker room to congratulate or console even the lowliest player, talked to newsmen, asked about their families. His son Dan does the same.

"There's an old story that sums it all up pretty well," Art Rooney Jr. was saying as the word of an impending sale of the team swirled throughout the early summer of '08.

"A man visiting the city got a cab at the airport and told the driver to take him to a place that would give him the best understanding of the essence of Pittsburgh. So the driver took him to Heinz Field and stopped in front of the statue of my father, and said, 'This is what it's all about.'

"Now, I don't know whether that story's true or not," Rooney Jr. said, "But in my mind, it is."

Acknowledgments

My eight-year-old daughter Samantha made a little sign for my desk that reads: "pursurverence." It really was a great help, so I want to thank her first. My wife Lydia doesn't need to go first, so I thank her next.

Most importantly, I thank Jan and Bonnie Jones. Without them, this project never would've gotten off the ground.

I also want to thank my poor editors. Al Silverman had first crack when this was a long-winded 420-page tome. He was kind as he ripped my guts out. Then the follow-up editors, Bob Labriola and Mike Ciarochi, had the courage to not tell me what I wanted to hear. Because of these three, I was able to re-read with motivation until I shaved this puppy down to where I like it. Mike, thanks for the title as well.

I'd also like to thank Don Faulkner for his suggestions along the way. He also gave me the encouragement I needed to "pursurvere." Movie producer Thomas Tull also kept me pumped, and introduced me to another great help, Brooke Borneman. Thank you both.

I also want to thank Dave Lockett and his assistant Burt Lauten of the Steelers' PR staff. They never even winced when they saw me coming. Omar Khan was also a terrific help.

While the book *Neil Young Nation* by Kevin Chong provided the impetus, my muse throughout was The Drive-By Truckers. I put the first CD of *Southern Rock Opera* into my player outside of Bozeman, Montana, and it's been there ever since. Maybe next year I'll get around to listening to the second disc of the record.

Of course, I thank the players for trusting me in their inner circles, and I thank all of those I interviewed. Those who didn't make print provided insight, but much had to be cut. I hope to post the outtakes at PittsburghSportsPublishing.com.

QUICK ORDER FORM

- Telephone orders: Call 724-861-3554.
  Have your credit card ready.

- E-mail orders: orders@PittsburghSportsPublishing.com.

- Postal orders: Pittsburgh Sports Publishing, 709 Short Street,
  Irwin, PA, 15642.

Name: _____

Address: _____

City: _____ State: _____ Zip: _____

Telephone: _____

E-mail address: _____

$24.95 per copy

Please add $3.00 shipping charge for every three copies ordered.

Pa. residents add 6% sales tax.